W. V. Quine

Philosophy Now

Series Editor: John Shand

This is a fresh and vital series of new introductions to today's most read, discussed and important philosophers. Combining rigorous analysis with authoritative exposition, each book gives clear and comprehensive access to the ideas of those philosophers who have made a truly fundamental and original contribution to the subject. Together the volumes comprise a remarkable gallery of the thinkers who have been at the forefront of philosophical ideas.

Published

John Searle
Nick Fotion

Charles Taylor
Ruth Abbey

Thomas Kuhn
Alexander Bird

Robert Nozick
A. R. Lacey

W. V. Quine
Alex Orenstein

W. V. Quine

Alex Orenstein

PRINCETON UNIVERSITY PRESS
PRINCETON AND OXFORD

Published in North and South America by
Princeton University Press, 41 William Street,
Princeton, New Jersey 08540.

First published in 2002 by Acumen
Acumen Publishing Limited
15a Lewins Yard
East Street
Chesham
Bucks HP5 1HQ, UK

Library of Congress Control Number 2001097703

ISBN 0-691-09605-8 (hardcover)
ISBN 0-691-09606-6 (paperback)

Designed and typeset in Century Schoolbook
by Kate Williams, Abergavenny.
Printed and bound by Biddles Ltd., Guildford and King's Lynn.

www.pup.princeton.edu

10 9 8 7 6 5 4 3 2 1

Dedicated to the memory of

Paul Scatena,

student and friend

Contents

Preface

I would like to express my gratitude to several graduate students for their assistance in preparing the manuscript, especially Edward Kopiecki, William Seeley and Paul Eckstein. I benefited too from the comments of students in a class on Quine and those in a logic section. I am indebted to Anthony Grayling, Dagfinn Føllesdal and Ruth Millikan for carefully reading the manuscript and for their suggestions, Gilbert Harman and Dan Isaacson for their support, and Kit Fine, Mel Fitting, Roger Gibson, Elliot Mendelson and Gary Ostertag who were consulted on sections of the work. However, I reserve full credit to myself for any remaining errors. I also wish to thank Wolfson, Exeter and Saint Anne's Colleges, Oxford for affording me the use of their facilities, and the City University of New York for a PSC-BHE research grant.

Most personal and most important of all is my debt to Professor Quine (I could never bring myself to say "Van") for his works, correspondence, conversation and kindness to me.

Chapter 1

Introduction

Arguably, Willard Van Orman Quine is the most influential philosopher of the second half of the twentieth century. In many ways, his position and role in the second half of the century are comparable to Bertrand Russell's in the first half. Quine is the leading advocate of a thoroughgoing form of naturalism whose central theme is the unity of philosophy and natural science. Philosophy so construed is an activity within nature wherein nature examines itself. This contrasts with views that distinguish philosophy from science and place philosophy in a special transcendent position for gaining special knowledge. The methods of science are empirical; so Quine, who operates within a scientific perspective, is an empiricist, but with a difference. Traditional empiricism, as in Locke, Berkeley, Hume, Mill and some twentieth-century forms, takes impressions, ideas or sense data as the basic unit of empirical thought. Quine's empiricism, by contrast, takes account of the theoretical as well as the observational facets of science. The unit of empirical significance is not simple impressions (ideas) or even isolated individual observation sentences, but whole systems of beliefs. The broad theoretical constraints for choice between theories/systems such as explanatory power, parsimony, precision and so on are foremost in this empiricism. He is a fallibilist, and no belief is held as certain since each individual belief in a system is, in principle, revisable. Quine proposes a new conception of observation sentences, a naturalized account of our knowledge of the external world including a rejection of a priori knowledge, and he extends the same empiricist and fallibilist account to our knowledge of logic and mathematics.

Logic is confined to first order logic and is clearly demarcated from set theory and mathematics. These are all empirical subjects when empiricism is understood in its Quinian form. They are internal to our system of beliefs that make up the natural sciences. The language of first order logic – truth functional connectives, quantifiers, identity, schematic predicate letters and singular terms in the form of individual variables (names are dispensed with) – serves as a "canonical notation" in which to express our ontological commitments. The slogan "To be is to be the value of a variable" encapsulates this project. Deciding which ontology to accept is also carried out within the naturalistic constraints of empirical science; one's ontological commitments should be to those objects that are indispensable to the best scientific theories. On this basis, Quine's own commitments are to physical objects and to sets. Quine is a physicalist and a Platonist, since the best evidenced sciences require physical objects and the mathematics involved in these sciences requires abstract objects, viz. sets.

The theory of reference (which includes notions such as reference, truth and logical truth) is sharply demarcated from the theory of meaning (which includes notions such as meaning as opposed to reference, synonymy, the analytic–synthetic distinction and necessity). Quine is the leading critic of notions from the theory of meaning, arguing that attempts to make the distinction between merely linguistic (analytic) truths and more substantive (synthetic) truths has failed. They do not meet the standards of precision to which scientific and philosophical theories ought to adhere, and which he maintains are adhered to in the theory of reference. He explores the limits of an empirical theory of language and offers as further criticism of the theory of meaning a conjecture of the indeterminacy of translation. His naturalist empiricism is also brought to bear on the theory of reference, where it yields a thesis of the inscrutability of reference (known also as ontological relativity and as global structuralism), and then to the theory of knowledge, where it gives rise to a naturalized epistemology.

Quine was born on 25 June 1908 and grew up in Akron, Ohio.[1] He attended the local high school, where he pursued the scientific as opposed to the classical, technical or commercial courses. The choice was a natural one, as he exhibited a talent for mathematics. He also tried his hand at writing, contributing to the school newspaper and even winning a poetry contest. His extracurricular activities included an interest in geography and, during several summers, he drew and sold maps of nearby places. His pleasure in maps, along with a passion for travel, lasted a lifetime (years later he wrote reviews of atlases for the *New York Review of Books*). In his autobiography, *The Time of My Life* (1985), Quine mentions so many of the locations he visited that his friend Burton Dreben quipped that the autobiography should have been entitled "A Moving Van".

Among his earliest philosophical reflections was a scepticism about religious matters. His reading of Edgar Allen Poe's *Eureka*, which conveyed the excitement of coming to understand the universe, was another occasion of early philosophical thought. Poe's other writings furnished a rather mannered model for Quine's early literary ventures. Quine is one of the most enjoyable philosophers to read (as quotations later in this work will reveal) and perhaps Poe's use of alliteration was a factor influencing Quine's colourful style. In his last year of high school, Quine developed a serious interest in language, particularly in questions of grammar and etymology.

When Quine entered Oberlin College in 1926, he was of a divided mind about whether to major in mathematics, philosophy or, for its linguistic interest, classics. A poker companion informed him that a certain Bertrand Russell had a mathematical philosophy. His friend's knowledge was probably limited to the title of Russell's book *An Introduction to Mathematical Philosophy*. Quine saw a way to combine two of his main interests and chose mathematics as a field of concentration and supplemented it with honours reading in mathematical philosophy. He started this reading in 1928. No one at Oberlin was versed in the recent revolutionary developments in logic – the works of Frege, Russell, Whitehead and so on. However, with outside help, Quine's adviser, the chairman of the Department of Mathematics, came up with the list: Venn's *Symbolic Logic*; Peano's *Formulaire de Mathématique*; Couturat's *Algebra of Logic*; Keyser's *The Human Worth of Rigorous Thinking*; Russell's *Principles of Mathematics* and *Introduction to Mathematical Philosophy*; Whitehead's *Introduction to Mathematics*; and Whitehead and Russell's *Principia Mathematica*. Quine would study these and report to his adviser on what he read. He pursued Russell into other domains on his own, reading *Our Knowledge of the External World*, *The ABC of Relativity*, various volumes of essays, and even, eventually, *Marriage and Morals*.

In the autumn of 1929, in his senior year, Quine began working on his honours thesis. He generalized a formula from Couturat and proved the generalization within the strict formalism of *Principia*

Mathematica. If we form all intersections of n classes taken m at a time, and all unions $n - m + 1$ at a time, then the theorem says that the union of those intersections is the intersection of those unions. In order to do the proof, Quine had to master a significant portion of *Principia Mathematica*, one of the classics of the new logic. (He published a revised and much more elegant version of this proof a few years later in the journal of the London Mathematical Society.) His first scholarly publication, a review of Nicod's *Foundations of Geometry and Induction*, was written for the *American Mathematical Monthly* at the close of his senior year.

Quine applied to Harvard to do graduate work because its philosophy department was then the strongest in logic in the country. Its faculty included Alfred North Whitehead, the co-author of *Principia Mathematica*. Quine was awarded a scholarship and embarked on what was to result in a two-year PhD, studying with Clarence Irving Lewis, Henry Maurice Sheffer, David Wight Prall and, of course, Whitehead. Having completed his MA in the spring of 1931, Quine began his doctoral dissertation, "The Logic of Sequences: A Generalization of *Principia Mathematica*", that summer. In the dissertation there already appears a prominent theme of Quine's philosophy: a concern with matters of ontology, that is, with questions of what there is. On such questions the classic *Principia Mathematica*, for all its greatness, embodies a number of excesses and confusions. In his dissertation and later works, Quine distinguishes and clarifies (1) the levels at which language is used, for example, to talk about non-linguistic objects or about linguistic ones, (2) the concepts of classes, properties, their names and the expressions used to describe them, and (3) he clarifies the status of and then rejects some aspects of *Principia Mathematica*, such as Russell's ramified types and his axiom of reducibility. Wherever possible, Quine likes to get by with the fewest and clearest assumptions which will suffice to do the job at hand. Whereas *Principia Mathematica* is constructed on the basis of an ontology that comprises propositional functions, which are properties of a sort, and hence intensional entities, Quine's revision tries to accomplish the same goals with extensional objects such as classes.

In the same year, 1931, Quine had what he later described as his "most dazzling exposure to greatness", when Russell came to lecture at Harvard.[2] Russell was one of the most influential figures in Quine's life, mainly through such works as *Principia Mathematica*, *Introduction to Mathematical Philosophy*, *Our Knowledge of the*

External World and essays like the famous "On Denoting". Both men shared a preoccupation with questions as to what there is. For example, Quine adopted and improved upon Russell's view of how we express ontological claims. More significantly, as the dissertation already shows, Russell's influence is that of a rival whose theories spurred Quine to criticize and to generate more acceptable alternatives. In ontology, Quine favours concrete individuals and, where necessary, classes, whereas Russell argued for properties as opposed to classes. In addition, some of Quine's most famous systems of logic and set theory (theory of classes) are designed to achieve the same effects as *Principia Mathematica* while avoiding Russell's theory of types.

As important as Quine's two years of graduate work was his exposure to the European intellectual scene. Despite the strength of Harvard's philosophy department in logic, it was out of touch with the much more advanced work then being done in Europe. Quine's contact with this new material was to provide an intellectual awakening of the first order. During the first year (1932–33) of his four years of postdoctoral fellowships, Quine held Harvard's Sheldon Travelling Fellowship and has written of this period as a personal renaissance in middle Europe.[3] The reference is not so much to the time he spent in Vienna, as it is to the periods in Prague and Warsaw. In Vienna, Quine attended meetings of the Vienna Circle and became acquainted with Neurath, Schlick, Gödel, Hahn and Menger. (He had already met Herbert Feigl at Harvard the year before; indeed, it was Feigl and John Cooley who had suggested the trip.) Quine describes his six weeks in Prague and six weeks in Warsaw as "the intellectually most rewarding months I have known".[4] In Prague, he met Rudolf Carnap and attended his lectures. He read, in German typescript, Carnap's *Logical Syntax of Language*. Carnap was to become as strong an influence as Russell. The clash between Carnap and Quine, like that between Russell and Quine, has produced some of the most important philosophy of the twentieth century. Carnap was one of the more careful expositors of a number of ideas associated with contemporary analytic philosophy, and especially with the central theses of the logical positivism of the Vienna Circle: (1) the verifiability criterion for the empirical meaningfulness of sentences; (2) the linguistic (analytic) character of a priori knowledge such as mathematics and logic; and (3) the triviality or meaninglessness of ontology as a species of metaphysics. Over the years, Quine subjected each of these theses to severe criticism and the debate on these issues can hardly be considered to be over.

In Warsaw, Quine attended the lectures of Lesniewski, Lukasiewicz and Tarski. His exposure in Warsaw, Vienna and Prague to the developments in logic of that period brought Quine up to date in this area. In the next few years he would modify Tarski's and Gödel's "classic" formulations of modern logic to state some of his unique and most famous works in logic. Most immediately, he revised his dissertation into *A System of Logistic* (1934). Quine was very sympathetic to the Warsaw school of logicians and philosophers, particularly to those who took an extensionalist (i.e. abiding by certain replacement principles [see Chapter 7]), and at times even nominalistic (i.e. avoiding reference to abstract objects [see Chapter 3]), view.

Returning to Harvard in 1933, Quine was made a Junior Fellow of Harvard's Society of Fellows. This freed him from teaching responsibilities for the next three years. (B. F. Skinner was another Junior Fellow. However, Quine's behaviourism did not date from this acquaintance; it has its origin in his reading of Watson during his college days.) In this period prior to the Second World War, Quine worked out three of his distinctive positions: his conception of ontological commitment mentioned above; his most well-known systems of logic; and the first phase of his critique of the notion of analytic or linguistic truth. At this time, Quine also refined the ideas about existence and ontology which are by-products of the new logic. These ideas appeared implicitly at first in his dissertation and explicitly in such early works as "Ontological Remarks on the Propositional Calculus" (1934); "A Logistical Approach to the Ontological Problem" (1939); and, in 1948, in one of his best-known essays, "On What There Is".[5]

Throughout his life, Quine experimented with formulating different systems of logic and set theory. Most of these reforms were motivated by philosophical concerns. In the late 1930s and in 1940, he formulated his two most distinctive systems of logic and set theory, that of "New Foundations for Mathematical Logic" (1937) and that of *Mathematical Logic* (1940). Both systems are motivated by philosophical and in particular ontological concerns. They attempt to achieve the effects of *Principia Mathematica* – that is, a foundation for mathematics in terms of logic and set theory – while at the same time avoiding its excesses (especially the ontological ones). In addition, it is the formulation of these systems which provides the "canonic notation" of Quine's philosophy.

The 1930s also saw Quine develop his criticism of the position that a priori knowledge as it purportedly exists in logic and mathematics is merely linguistic. This view that all a priori knowledge is analytic was a cornerstone of much analytic philosophy and an essential component of logical positivism. In 1934, Quine gave a series of lectures on Carnap's work. Some of this material was eventually incorporated in his paper "Truth by Convention" (1936), in which he began to elaborate on his criticism of the view (to be found in Carnap among others) that at bottom, logic and mathematics are based solely on linguistic conventions. In 1940, Rudolf Carnap, Alfred Tarski and Quine were together at Harvard and the three (joined at times by Nelson Goodman and John Cooley) would meet at Carnap's flat and talk about philosophy. Carnap's manuscript *Introduction to Semantics* provided the topic. Midway through Carnap's reading of his first page, he distinguished between analytic and synthetic sentences (those based on language alone, e.g. "triangles have three sides" and those based on extra-linguistic facts, e.g. "the figure on the blackboard has three sides"). Tarski and Quine "took issue with Carnap on analyticity. The controversy continued through subsequent sessions, without resolution and without progress in the reading of Carnap's manuscript."[5] Over the next few decades the controversy was to grow until the entire philosophical community became involved. In 1951 Quine would publish his most famous paper, "Two Dogmas of Empiricism", where some of his criticisms of the analytic–synthetic distinction are crystallized.

During the Second World War, Quine served in the United States Navy for more than three years and rose to the rank of Lieutenant Commander. After the war, Quine returned to Harvard and in 1948 was made a full professor in the Department of Philosophy. He remained there, except for numerous trips to all parts of the globe and leaves spent at other institutions, until his retirement in 1978 at the age of 70.

In this period, Quine continued to work on the subjects discussed above. Much of that work is available in his collection of essays *From a Logical Point of View* (1953). At the risk of oversimplifying, his most original research at that time concerned the formulation of a new brand of empiricism – the view that knowledge is ultimately grounded in observation – and the exploration of its consequences. I will arbitrarily divide this work into three topics: (1) Duhemian–holistic empiricism; (2) holistic empiricism and the theory of meaning; and (3) holistic empiricism and the theory of reference.

Quine's holistic or Duhemian empiricism first appeared in print in "Two Dogmas of Empiricism". Here Quine extends the thesis of Pierre Duhem (a turn-of-the-century physicist, historian and philosopher of science) that in science one cannot empirically test isolated hypotheses. One ramification Quine developed from this is holism. The vehicles of empirical content are whole systems of sentences and not isolated individual sentences. The positivist theory of the empirical meaningfulness of individual sentences is thus called into question. Furthermore, this new empiricism also challenges the concept that some sentences, such as those of logic and mathematics, are linguistically and not empirically grounded. According to Quine, the test of a system of sentences as a whole yields a certain leeway as to which individual sentence ought to be revised, and this leeway extends to revising even the sentences of logic or mathematics that are part of the system.

Beginning with "Two Dogmas", in "The Problem of Meaning in Linguistics" (1951), and eventually in *Word and Object* (1960), this new empiricism was brought to bear on the concepts of meaning, synonymy and analyticity. Quine began by doubting that these, or indeed any of the concepts from the theory of meaning, could be made clear in an empirical sense. In *Word and Object*, by emphasizing the public nature of how we understand language, he provides his celebrated conjecture of the indeterminacy of translation. This conjecture plays a role in showing the bankruptcy of philosophical notions associated with certain themes from the theory of meaning. In "Ontological Relativity" (1968), Quine applied empirical constraints to concepts from the theory of reference. This yields the thesis of the inscrutability of reference (also referred to by Quine as "ontological relativity" and, later, as "global structuralism").

In 1971, the paper "Epistemology Naturalized" appeared. Its theme was that epistemology be pursued along naturalistic lines. It prompted reactions of at least two sorts: criticism from those pursuing traditional epistemology, and programmes for taking a naturalist stance in epistemology and in philosophy in general.

Quine's retirement from Harvard in 1978 had no effect on his productivity or influence. He remained actively engaged in writing and lecturing, and involved in discussions concerning his work. Among the books published during this time are *Quiddities, An Intermittently Philosophical Dictionary* (1987), *Pursuit of Truth* (1992), *From Stimulus to Science* (1995); a collection of essays,

Theories and Things (1981); and his autobiography, *The Time of My Life* (1985). Several conferences have been held on his views, and volumes of the proceedings published. These include his replies to the papers given at the conferences: for example, Davidson and Hintikka's *Words and Objections*, Barrett and Gibson's *Perspectives on Quine*, Leonardi and Santambrogia's *On Quine* and Orenstein and Kotatko's *Knowledge, Language and Logic: Questions for Quine*. Paul Gochet edited an issue of *Revue Internationale de Philosophie* devoted to Quine and Dagfinn Føllesdal edited one for *Inquiry*.

Taking certain liberties, the present work is ordered to reflect some of the main themes in Quine's intellectual development. In Quine's earlier writings other than those in logic, he dealt first with ontological commitment, then the justification of logic and mathematics, developing a sceptical position on the then dominant appeal to an analytic–synthetic distinction. After that, Quine developed his holistic version of empiricism and then, finally, his naturalism, especially as applied to empiricism itself. Thus Chapters 2 and 3 deal with Quine's thoughts on how we express our views as to what exists and what Quine believes exists. Chapter 4 serves as an introduction to Quine's Duhemian–holistic empiricism by way of his critique of purportedly non-empirical knowledge. Chapter 5 presents Quine's views on the nature of logic and his criticisms of justifications of it in terms of analyticity as a different linguistic or convention based type of truth. Chapter 6 explores this critique of other candidates for the status of analytic truth – truths in virtue of meaning. At that juncture, Quine's conjecture of the indeterminacy of meaning is discussed. Chapter 7 takes up controversies concerning modal and belief contexts. The final chapter covers Quine's work on naturalized epistemology.

In each chapter I try to explain Quine's views as accurately and sympathetically as I can. In order to give a sense of their place in twentieth-century philosophy, I involve Quine in a dialectic with others such as Russell, Carnap, Field, Kripke and Chomsky. However, there is also a need to indicate criticisms of Quine's views. To ensure that the reader can determine where Quine is being explicated and where criticized I employ the phrase "Challenging Quine" to indicate the latter. I cannot do justice to all the important criticisms offered of Quine, and the challenges that are presented may not satisfy some readers.

In his autobiography, *The Time of My Life*, Quine spoke of the recognition he received from others who wrote about his work:

Chapter 2

Expressing an ontology

The new way of construing existence claims

Philosophers from earliest times have shown an interest in the nature of existence. However, in the latter half of the nineteenth century there arose a new way of thinking about this subject. Quine was to give it one of its most consistent and thoroughgoing expressions. The basic insight of this new view consisted in seeing the special relation between the word 'exists' and the word 'some' or any of its paraphrases. In 1874, the Austrian philosopher Franz Brentano claimed that all sentences are merely varieties of existential sentences. He began by equating particular sentences, that is, sentences usually beginning with the word 'some', with existence sentences.[1] So the particular affirmative sentence 'Some man is sick' was said to be equivalent to the existential claim 'A sick man exists' or its paraphrase 'There is a sick man'. The word 'some' is called the particular or existential quantifier and, similarly, the word 'all' is referred to as the universal quantifier. Brentano was one of the first to point out that existence claims have a special connection with quantification. To say that a cow exists is the same as to say that something is a cow. Existence claims are really particular/existential quantifications and the phrases 'some', 'there are' and 'there exists' are systematically intertranslatable.

This treatment of existence gives a special significance to the slogan that existence is not a predicate. It might help us get a clearer view of the matter if we examine exactly what is meant here by saying that existence is not a predicate, that is, that 'exists' differs from ordinary predicates. In 1931, Gilbert Ryle very nicely summed up the difference in his essay "Systematically Misleading Expressions".[2] Existence sentences such as

'Brown cows exist.'

and

'Purple cows don't exist.'

systematically mislead us into treating them as analogous to sentences like

'Brown cows flourish.'

and

'Purple cows don't flourish.'

This is due to a superficial grammatical resemblance, that is, 'exists' occurs in the predicate position. There is, however, a major difference between existence claims and flourish claims. The former are translatable into quantificational sentences like

'Some cows are brown.'

and

'It is false that some cows are purple'.

In these translations the word 'exists' disappears from the predicate position and its function is accomplished by the quantifier. Words like 'flourish' in the above example, or 'red' and 'mammals' in 'Roses are red' or 'Men are mammals', are genuine predicates. They cannot be translated into other sentences in which they no longer take a predicate position. Every existence claim is a covert quantificational claim and hence 'exists' is a bogus predicate. In other words, existence sentences of the form '--- exists' are disguised quantificational sentences of the form 'Something is a ---.' The proper role of existence is portrayed by the use of a quantifier and not by any other part of speech.

Although Brentano was one of the first to view existence in this way, two other influential factors should also be considered:

(1) a new doctrine of the existential import of sentences and
(2) the development of modern logic.

It is with the latter – the development of a full logic of quantification by Gottlob Frege, Bertrand Russell and others, eventually leading up to the work of Willard Van Orman Quine – that this new view of existence and quantification becomes most explicit and influential.

For one to gain perspective on these developments it would be helpful to consider an alternative account of existence which was supplanted by the quantificational one. The best-known representative of this account, Immanuel Kant, said, as did Ryle, that being is manifestly not a predicate. By this remark, Kant had at least two things in mind.[3] The first is that from the standpoint of traditional formal logic existence is explicated in terms of the copula, that is, 'is a' or 'are'. Consider the following examples.

> 'Socrates is a man.'
>
> 'Men are mortal.'

If these statements are true, then Kant would say that men exist and that Socrates exists. That is, affirmative subject–predicate sentences have existential import. When these affirmative sentences are true, the objects referred to by the subject term exist. However, the statements

> 'Unicorns are a special breed of horses.'

and

> 'Pegasus is a flying horse.'

are false because the subject terms do not refer to anything existing. For Kant, existence is connected with a true affirmative "subject-copula-predicate" judgement. '--- is a ---' implies that '--- exists' and existence is not a real predicate but is merely derivatively implied by the copula. The second thing Kant had in mind when he said that being is not a real predicate was part of his epistemological theory which he called transcendental logic. Here 'exists' or 'being' are not real predicates, in the sense that they are not determining predicates. 'Exists', unlike 'brown', adds nothing to our concept of an object.

To imagine or conceive of a cow as brown is to add something to our image or concept of the cow. However, to imagine a cow as existing does not add anything to our image of the cow: the images of an existing and of a non-existing cow are the same, whereas the images of a brown and of a non-brown cow differ. Empiricists like Berkeley and Hume had previously made similar remarks claiming that we have no ideas or impressions of an object's existence as such.

Although Kant's influence was a major factor leading to the prominence of the view that existence is not a predicate, for him this slogan did not mean that quantification provides the proper analysis of existence. Neither "existence is a matter of the logic (a mode) of the copula" nor "existence is not a determining property" is the same as the view that existence is a matter of quantification. Nonetheless, the widespread acceptance of the slogan "existence is not a predicate" was a factor in the acceptance of the view that existence is a matter not of predication but of quantification.

To see how the traditional Kantian conception and the current Frege–Russell–Quine conception differ, as well as why the latter came to be accepted, we must briefly examine the history of the doctrine of existential import. Logicians customarily distinguish singular and general sentences.

Singular sentences and their denials

Socrates is human.
Socrates is not Roman.

General sentences

A	Universal affirmative	All men are mortal.
I	Particular affirmative	Some cows are brown.
E	Universal negative	No cows are purple.
O	Particular negative	Some cows are not brown.

Singular sentences have as their subjects singular terms, for example, 'Socrates' or 'John', which purport to refer to single individuals. General sentences usually start with some variant of a quantifier followed by a general term, for example, 'men' or 'cows', which purport to refer to more than one individual. The problem of existential import concerns the existential assumptions made in connection with the above sentences, which are known in traditional logic as A, I, E and O form sentences. For example, if these A, I, E and O form sentences are true, then what does this say about the existence of the objects referred to by the subject? And if the objects referred to by the subject do not exist, are the sentences still true?

For Kant and a number of traditional logicians going as far back as Aristotle, affirmative sentences have existential import.[4] If an A or I form sentence is true, then the subject's referent exists. If the subject's referent does not exist, then the A or I form sentence is false. In the mid-nineteenth century, a different conception of existential import evolved. According to this new tradition (propounded by Brentano and Boole, among others), the above universal sentences have no existential import. They do not imply existence claims, but particular sentences do. 'All men are mortal' or 'All twenty-foot men are mortal' are construed as universal conditionals, merely stating that

> For anything, if it is a man, then it is mortal.

and

> For anything, if it is a twenty-foot man, then it is mortal.

The 'if it is a ---' clause does not imply an existence sentence. Conditional sentences like 'If it is a unicorn, then it is an animal' are true even though there are no unicorns. For this new tradition, the only general sentences with existential import are the particular ones of the I and O form variety. 'Some cows are brown' or 'Some cows are not brown', if true, imply that cows exist. With the adoption of this new view, existence is directly tied to the particular quantifier.

We turn now to the development of modern logic, into which Boole's and Brentano's views of existential import are incorporated and in which the new view of existence gains its fullest expression as part of a science of the quantifiers.

The new logic: a canonical notation

Over the years, Quine has developed one of the most consistent and thoroughgoing accounts of the new view of existence. One of the ways in which he has taken seriously the claim that existence is expressed in terms of quantification is by adhering to a language where the use of quantification is made explicit. He calls the language in which our existential commitments are overtly present for inspection a 'canonical notation'; this is the language of modern logic as developed by Frege, Peirce, Russell and others. One of the most important dates in the history of logic, 1879, saw the publication of Gottlob Frege's *Begriffsschrift, a Formula Language, Modeled Upon that of Arithmetic for Pure Thought*. What is this new logic with its new notation, and exactly how does it differ from the older logic? We shall concentrate on three points: (1) its treatment of the logic of sentences (this is often also referred to as the logic of truth functional sentences or as propositional logic); (2) its treatment of relations; and (3) its clearer conception of the quantifiers 'all' and 'some'.

The new logic of sentences

Deductive logic is, to a large extent, the study of implication. For instance, we say that 'If it is cloudy, then it will rain' and 'It is cloudy' jointly imply 'It will rain'. To say that the premises of an argument imply the conclusion is to say that, given premises and conclusion of the logical form in question, whenever the premises are true the conclusion will be true. The above case of valid implication is of the following logical form:

> If antecedent, then consequent.
> Antecedent.
> ___
> Therefore, consequent.

The system of logic in which we investigate the logical properties of conditional ('if, then') sentences is called the logic of sentences, or truth functional logic. 'If, then' is a connecting phrase which, appropriately applied to two sentences, forms a more complex sentence. Thus, from 'It is cloudy' and 'It will rain' we form the conditional sentence in the above argument. Because it is convenient to introduce special symbols to represent the principles of deductive inference, we will let the arrow, '→', represent the 'if, then' phrase and will use lower case letters, '*p*', '*q*', '*r*', '*s*' and so on to indicate sentence positions. Hence the pattern of a conditional sentence can be expressed in the schematic form '$p \rightarrow q$', and the pattern of the above argument by

$$\begin{array}{l} p \rightarrow q \\ \underline{p \qquad\qquad} \\ \text{therefore } q \end{array}$$

In the logic of sentences, in addition to studying the properties of '$\rightarrow$', we also examine, among others, such connectives as 'and' (conjunction, symbolized by an ampersand, '&'), 'or' (alternation/disjunction, symbolized by a wedge, '$\vee$'), 'if and only if' (the biconditional, symbolized by '$\equiv$') and 'it is not the case that' (denial-negation, symbolized by '$\sim$'). This subject is called truth functional logic because each of the different complex sentences has a truth value that depends on, or is a function solely of, its component sentences. So a conjunction 'p & q' is true only when both conjuncts (p and q) are true; an alternation is true when at least one alternant is true; a conditional is false only when the antecedent is true and the consequent is false; a biconditional is true when both of its components have the same truth value; and the negation of a sentence has the opposite value of the sentence it negates. All of this is summarized in the table below.

	(and)	(or)	(if, then)	(if and only if)	(negation)
$p\ q$	p & q	$p \vee q$	$p \rightarrow q$	$p \equiv q$	$\sim p$
T T	T	T	T	T	F
T F	F	T	F	F	F
F T	F	T	T	F	T
F F	F	F	T	T	T

In addition to studying implication, or how some sentences imply others, logicians also study logical truths, that is, sentences whose truth is closely associated with their logical form. For example,

	Schematically
If it's cloudy, then it's cloudy.	$p \rightarrow p$
Either it is cloudy or it isn't.	$p \vee \sim p$
It is not both cloudy and not cloudy.	$\sim(p\ \&\ \sim p)$

These exemplify respectively the principles of identity, excluded middle and non-contradiction for sentential logic. In traditional logic, they were spoken of as the three basic laws of thought. In Frege's *Begriffsschrift*, there appeared axioms and rules of inference for a complete system of sentential logic, complete in the sense that these axioms and rules would enable one to prove all the logical truths for this branch of logic. Now, various principles of this sort were known in both the ancient world and in the middle ages. For example, that '$p \rightarrow q$' and 'p' implies 'q', as well as the so-called basic laws of thought, were incorporated in the logic of the Stoics and in what medieval logicians called the theory of consequences. However, what is somewhat new in Frege's treatment of this branch of logic is his particular axiomatization of this science, that is, his way of starting with some principles and then systematically proving the remainder from them.

The new treatment of relations and the new conception of the quantifiers

The older Aristotelian logic was concerned only with sentences of the following types:

	Schematically
All men are mortal.	All *F* are *G*
No cats are dogs.	No *F* are *G*
Some men are tall.	Some *F* are *G*
Some men are not tall.	Some *F* are not *G*
Socrates is human.	*a* is an *F*

As such, the old logic was unable to deal formally with more sophisticated implications and logical truths involving relational sentences or multiple quantifications. For example, a famous argument which is often cited as having eluded formal treatment in the old logic was the following:

All horses are animals.
___
Every head of a horse is a head of some animal.

In the nineteenth century it became more and more apparent that the traditional Aristotelian logic taught was not capable of expressing the more complex logical structure of the sentences of modern science, especially those of mathematics. The old logic was inadequate in at least two ways: its inability to deal with relational notions such as '--- is the head of ---'; and its inability to deal with more complex types of quantifications, for example, the two quantifiers in the conclusion of the above argument. The need to solve these problems prompted both Frege and the American philosopher–logician Charles Sanders Peirce to arrive at a solution. They did so independently of each other, Frege in 1879 (in the *Begriffsschrift*) and Peirce in 1881. The result is known as quantification theory and it consists of a new approach to relational expressions as well as a truly general treatment of the quantifiers.

According to the older tradition, a sentence such as 'Socrates is human' is analysed as having three parts.

Subject	Copula	Predicate
'Socrates'	'is a'	'human'

And a relational sentence like 'John is taller than Mary' is treated similarly:

Subject	Copula	Predicate
'John'	'is'	'taller than Mary'

Frege and Peirce suggested a new conception of a predicate whereby the difference in logical structure between dissimilar relational sentences as well as between relational and merely attributional sentences can be clearly exhibited. For example, if we analyse 'Socrates is human' as having two parts, a predicate (in the modern sense) and an argument for subject,

Argument	Modern Fregean Predicate
'Socrates'	'is human',

then 'John is taller than Mary' is taken as having three parts, a two-placed relational predicate and two arguments:

1st Argument	Predicate	2nd Argument
'John'	'is taller than'	'Mary',

Three-placed predicates, as in 'John is between Mary and Bob', can similarly be analysed as '--- is between --- and ---', taking 'John', 'Mary' and 'Bob' as its arguments. To symbolize and schematize these sentences, we use capital letters such as '*F*', '*G*' and '*H*' to represent predicate positions, lower case letters '*a*', '*b*', '*c*' and so on for the subject arguments, and we put the predicate schema first, followed by the appropriate number of argument schemata. Thus, 'Socrates is human' has as its schematic form '*Fa*', 'John is taller than Mary' has '*Ga,b*', and the schema for 'John is between Mary and Bob' is '*Ha,b,c*'. In general, singular sentences are symbolized as predicate expressions followed by an appropriate number of subject expressions. This disposes of the problem of relations.

In traditional logic, the words 'all' and 'some' occurred only in connection with simple subject–predicate sentences (the A, E, I and O form sentences mentioned earlier). In the nineteenth century, more complex forms of quantification began to be studied. For instance, instead of merely saying 'All men are mortal', one could quantify with respect to the predicate and say either that all men are all the mortals or that all men are some of the mortals. Perhaps more important, though, are the cases in philosophy and science in which iterated quantifiers must be taken account of, as in 'Something is such that everything was caused by it' and 'For every number there is some number that is higher than it'. Both Frege and Peirce recognized that quantifiers serve to indicate whether we wish to talk about every or only at least one of the objects satisfying the predicate. Take, for example, the predicate 'is in space'. One could say of an individual such as John that he is in space by simply writing 'John is in space'. If, however, we wish to say (as some materialist might) that every individual is in space, we would repeat the predicate and do two additional things. First we would add a pronoun like 'it' to get 'it is in space', and then – in order to indicate which objects that can be referred to by 'it' we want to talk about (here we want to talk about everything) – we would supply a quantifier to operate on the 'it' position. The result would be the universal quantification 'For every "it", "it" is in space.' In logical notation, pronouns like 'it' are expressed by the use of variables, which are represented by the lower case letters beginning with

'x', 'y', 'z' and so on; 'x is in space', then, would correspond to the first of the two steps taken towards saying that everything is in space. But 'x is in space' does not tell us the extent to which the objects satisfy the predicate. We need a way of noting just this, and quantifiers provide the means to do so. The quantifying expressions 'For every x' or 'All x' operate on the variable, informing us of the quantity of objects referred to. A phrase such as 'x is in space', which has a variable without a quantifier operating on it, that is, binding it, is called a propositional function or open sentence. 'For every x', the universal quantifier will be symbolized as '(x)' and will precede the propositional function 'x is in space'. Thus 'Everything is in space' is rendered as '$(x)(x$ is in space$)$', and exemplifies the schema '$(x)(Fx)$'.

By extension, it is quite clear how other universal sentences are dealt with. For example, the universal affirmative A form sentence of traditional logic, 'All humans are mortal', is treated as a universal generalization of a conditional, 'For every x, if x is human, then x is mortal'. In symbols it appears as

'$(x)(x$ is human $\rightarrow x$ is mortal$)$',

and it has the schema

'$(x)(Fx \rightarrow Gx)$'.

To render a particular generalization such as 'Something is yellow', we first provide the propositional function 'x is yellow' and then the quantifying phrase 'For some x' or 'There is an x', which yields 'For some x, x is yellow.' The particular existential quantifier is symbolized as '$(\exists x)$'. In symbols, the sentence appears as

'$(\exists x)(x$ is yellow$)$'

and falls under the schema

'$(\exists x)(Fx)$'.

More complex sentences like 'Some cows are brown', that is, 'There is an x, such that x is a cow and brown', are represented as

'$(\exists x)(x$ is a cow & x is brown$)$',

and have the schema

'$(\exists x)(Fx \& Gx)$'.

With this clear conception of the role of a quantifier operating upon the variables in a sentence, we can now deal with iterated quantification. 'Something is such that everything is caused by it', that is, 'There is an *x*, such that for every *y*, *x* causes *y*', becomes

'$(\exists x)(y)(x$ causes $y)$',

the schema of which is

'$(\exists x)(y)(Fxy)$'.

'For every number there is a higher number' is rendered as

'$(x)(x$ is a number $\rightarrow (\exists y)(y$ is a number & y is higher than $x))$',

and its schema is

'$(x)(Fx \rightarrow (\exists y)(Gy \& Hyx))$'.

Philosophers have been well aware of the expressive power of this new notation. Frege likened it to Leibniz's quest for a *lingua characterica*, a universal language, universal in the sense that it would be comprehensive enough to do justice to the varied truths of all the sciences.[5] Peirce proposed that it would be "adequate to the treatment of all problems of deductive logic".[6] Both the early Wittgenstein and Russell were to construct philosophical systems based on this new logic.[7] Quine, likewise, singles out the new logic as of especial philosophical significance, maintaining that it provides us with a "canonical notation":

> Taking the canonical notation thus austerely . . . we have just these basic constructions: predication . . . quantification . . . , and the truth functions. . . . What thus confronts us as a scheme for systems of the world is that structure so well understood by present-day logicians, the logic of quantification or calculus of predicates.
>
> Not that the idioms thus renounced are supposed to be unneeded in the market place or in the laboratory. . . . The

> doctrine is only that such a canonical idiom can be abstracted and then adhered to in the statement of one's scientific theory. The doctrine is that all traits of reality worthy of the name can be set down in an idiom of this austere form if in any idiom.
>
> It is in spirit a philosophical doctrine of categories . . . philosophical in its breadth, however continuous with science in its motivation.[8]

A salient reason why Quine regards this language as being "canonical" is that it is here that our use of the existential quantifier '$(\exists x)$' is most explicit. To discover the existence assumptions, the ontological commitments, of a theory, we first state it in the language of truth functional connectives and quantification, and then look to the existential quantifications we have made. On Quine's view, "Quantification is an ontic idiom *par excellence*."[9] The logic of '$(\exists x)$' is the logic of existence, and a notation that makes '$(\exists x)$' explicit accordingly makes our existence assumptions/ontology explicit. Some of the most important philosophical differences concern competing ontologies. Physicalists, for instance, have an ontology comprising physical objects, while others, like phenomenalists, deny that there are physical objects and argue that only appearances exist. The traditional problem of universals is to a large extent a dispute over the relative merits of a nominalist's ontology, according to which only concrete individuals exist, and realist ontologies, such as that of the Platonists, which involve the existence of abstract objects as well as the concrete objects of the nominalists. Now, while many philosophers followed Frege and Russell in thinking of existence in terms of '$(\exists x)$', often they merely paid lip service to the connection, asserting the equivalent of '$(\exists x)(Fx)$' and then going on as though they were not committed to the existence of Fs. As Quine says,

> Applied to universals, this maneuver consists in talking expressly of . . . universals and then appending a caveat to the effect that such talk is not to be taken as attributing existence to . . . universals. Church cites examples from Ayer and Ryle. I shall limit myself to one, which is Ayer's: ". . . it makes sense to say, in a case where someone is believing or doubting, that there is something that he doubts or believes. But it does not follow that something must exist to be doubted or believed."[10]

One of Quine's contributions to philosophy is his insistence upon being scrupulously clear and consistent about one's ontological commitments. By systematically adhering to the notation of modern logic and to the interpretation of the particular quantifier in terms of existence he arrives at a precise criterion of ontic commitment.

The semantic side of ontological commitment

We will explain Quine's criterion by tracing the development of the idea from his earliest writings on the subject. In his earliest pieces, Quine relied on the notion of designation, that is, naming, to explicate the basis of the ontic significance of discourse. Later he shifted his emphasis to the notions of predication and truth.

In a 1939 paper entitled "A Logistical Approach to the Ontological Problem", Quine addressed himself to ontological questions such as 'Is there such an entity as roundness?'[11] That is to say, what are we doing when we make an existence claim, as in the above question about the universal roundness? Quine's answer involves making a distinction between parts of speech, names and syncategorematic expressions (roughly speaking, non-names). For example, the paradigmatic names 'Socrates' and 'Rover' name, that is, designate, the objects Socrates and Rover respectively, while the paradigmatic syncategorematic expressions 'or', 'is human' and 'is taller than' perform other functions than that of designating entities. The latter are simply not names. The ontological question 'Is there such an entity as roundness?' can be taken as inquiring whether 'roundness' is a name or a syncategorematic expression. Does 'roundness' designate some entity or has it some other non-designating function? But this question merely raises the further question of how to distinguish names from non-names. Quine's solution in this paper is to link names with variables and variable binding operations like quantification. The ability to quantify over an expression in a sentence evidences both (1) namehood for the expression and (2) ontological commitment to the object named. In 'Socrates is human', 'Socrates' functions as a name because we are prepared to apply relevant principles of the logic of quantification. One of these is the rule of inference commonly referred to as "existential generalization". According to this rule, when we have a sentence with a name in it (as in the above), we can replace the name with a variable such as '*x*' to obtain '*x* is human', and then bind the variable with an existential quantifier to obtain '$(\exists x)(x$ is human$)$'. It is certainly a valid principle of implication. Intuitively, it says that when a predicate truly applies to a given individual, this predication implies that there is something or there exists at least one thing to which the predicate applies. To say that $(\exists x)(x$ is human$)$ is to be committed to the existence of at least one concrete individual, for example, Socrates. Analogously, to be willing to infer from 'Roundness is a property of circles' that $(\exists x)(x$ is a property of circles$)$ – that is, to treat 'roundness' as a name designating an entity and then to existentially generalize on it – is to be committed to the existence of at least one abstract entity, namely, a universal such as roundness. Quine declares:

> Under the usual formulation of logic there are two basic forms of inference which interchange names with variables. One is existential generalization, whereby a name is replaced by a variable 'x' and an existential prefix '$(\exists x)$' is attached:
>
> . . . Paris . . .
> $(\exists x)(\ ..x\ ...)$
>
> [The second form of inference Quine mentions has here been deleted. It is universal instantiation.]
>
> . . . Hence, instead of describing names as expressions with respect to which existential generalization is valid, we might equivalently omit express mention of existential generalization and describe names simply as those constant expressions which replace variables and are replaced by variables according to the usual laws of quantification. . . . A variable is usually thought of as associated with a realm of entities, the so-called *range of values* of the variables. The range of values is not to be confused with the range of *substituends*. The names are substituends; the named entities are values. Numerals, names of numbers, are substituends for the variables of arithmetic; the values of these variables, on the other hand, are numbers. Variables can be thought of roughly as ambiguous names of their values. This notion of ambiguous names is not as mysterious as it at first appears, for it is essentially the notion of a pronoun; the variable 'x' is a relative pronoun used in connection with a quantifier '(x)' or '$(\exists x)$'.
>
> Here, then, are five ways of saying the same thing: 'There is such a thing as appendicitis'; 'The word 'appendicitis'

> designates'; 'The word 'appendicitis' is a name'; 'The word 'appendicitis' is a substituend for a variable'; 'The disease appendicitis is a value of a variable'. The universe of entities is the range of values of variables. To be is to be the value of a variable.[12]

In the slogan "To be is to be the value of a variable", we have the essence of Quine's criterion of ontological commitment. In the earlier essays, being a value of a variable – a matter of existential quantification – is associated with the semantic relation of naming/designating. But Quine subsequently came to believe that naming is not essential in order to refer to the world or to make ontological claims. More basic than the semantic relation of naming is that of predicating. A predicate such as 'is human' applies to (or is true of, or denotes severally) certain entities such as Socrates, Plato and so on. Quine expresses this well in his 1966 paper "Existence and Quantification":

> Another way of saying what objects a theory requires is to say that they are the objects that some of the predicates of the theory have to be true of, in order for the theory to be true. But this is the same as saying that they are the objects that have to be values of the variables in order for the theory to be true. It is the same, anyway, if the notation of the theory includes for each predicate a complementary predicate, its negation. For then, given any value of the variable, some predicate is true of it; viz. any predicate or its complement. And conversely, of course, whatever a predicate is true of is a value of variables. Predication and quantification, indeed, are intimately linked; for a predicate is simply an expression that yields a sentence, an open sentence *i.e., a propositional function*, when adjoined to one or more quantifiable variables. When we schematize a sentence in the predicative way '*Fa*' or '*a* is an *F*', our recognition of an '*a*' part and an '*F*' part turns strictly on our use of variables of quantification; the '*a*' represents a part of the sentence that stands where a quantifiable variable could stand, and the '*F*' represents the rest.
>
> Our question was what objects does a theory require? Our answer is: those objects that have to be values of variables in order for the theory to be true.[13]

There are at least two reasons why Quine thinks designation is not as essential as predication. In the first place, there are cases where we know that certain objects exist, that is, that $(\exists x)(Fx)$, but we cannot name all of these objects. Real numbers are a case in point. The natural numbers are the whole numbers 1, 2, 3 and so on, and the rational numbers consist of natural numbers plus the fractions, for example, 0, 1, 1½, 1¾, . . ., 2, 2½ and so on. The real numbers, though, include all of the above numbers plus numbers like √2, which cannot be expressed as fractions. Georg Cantor, the father of modern set theory, in effect proved in 1874 that if, as is customarily assumed, there are only as many names as there are natural numbers, then there is no way of naming all the real numbers. Since one wants to say that real numbers exist and yet one cannot name each of them, it is not unreasonable to relinquish the connection between naming an object and making an existence claim about it. However, we can still use the predicate 'is a real number' embedded in a quantified sentence to talk of real numbers, for example, '$(\exists x)$(x is a real number)' or '(x)(If x is a real number then ----)'. The reference and the ontological commitment are accomplished by the semantic relation of predication. In other words, we can apply 'is a real number' to each of the real numbers without naming each one of them individually. Variables stand in the same position as names and, in cases like the above, the reference cannot be made by names but only by variables. Variables and predication therefore can be used to register our ontological commitments where names cannot.

The second reason for Quine's de-emphasis of the role of names is found in one of his most famous essays, "On What There Is" (1948).[14] Here he argues that names need not be part of one's canonical notation; in fact, whatever scientific purposes are accomplished by names can be carried out just as well by the devices of quantification, variables and predicates. To see how Quine dispenses with names we must have recourse to a contribution by Russell, his theory of definite descriptions. This theory has been called a paradigm of contemporary analytic philosophy, and in it we have a brilliant example of the use to which quantificational notation can be put. Part of Russell's achievement was to provide an analysis of sentences like 'The father of Charles II was executed'. The phrase 'The father of Charles II' is called a definite description. Russell proposed construing such sentences as a special kind of existential generalization, one in which we say that there exists a father of

Charles II and at most one father of Charles II and that he was executed.

There are three components in the resulting sentence.

Existence:	There exists a father of Charles II and
At most one:	there is at most one such father and
Predication:	he was executed.

In canonical notation it appears as:

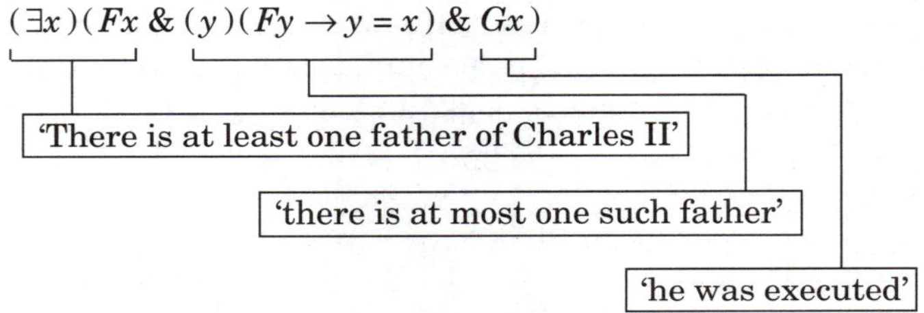

This analysis provides a contextual definition of definite descriptions. That is to say, any sentence with a definite description can be translated (paraphrased) into another sentence from which the definite description has been eliminated. Russell has shown that the job of definite descriptions can be accomplished merely by adhering to a canonical notation of truth functional connectives (conjunction and conditional signs), quantifiers and the sign for identity.

This theory was designed in part to solve a problem concerning non-being. Consider the following sentence and the accompanying argument.

> 'The present king of France is bald.'

The definite description here is a vacuous expression. It does not refer to any existing thing, since there is no present king of France. Now, this problem of non-being can be generated by the following argument. The sentence is meaningful and thus is either true or false. If true, then it is true of something, namely, the present king of France, and if false, then it is false of something, namely, the present king of France. So whether the sentence is true or false, there is a present king of France. But this conclusion conflicts with our assumption that there is no such being.

Russell's solution consists in pointing out that in its analysed form the sentence really says

Existence:		There is a present king of France, that is,
		$(\exists x)(x$ is a present king of France . . .
	and	at most one
	and	he is bald).

However, the existential generalization of a conjunction is false if one of its conjuncts is false. Since the existence clause, '$(\exists x)(x$ is a present king of France$)$', is false, the entire sentence is false. If we negate this false but meaningful sentence the result is a true one: it is not the case that there is one and only one present king of France and he is bald.

Russell's theory provides a way of defining away definite descriptions. Quine extends it as a way of defining away names. The idea is quite simple. Wherever we have a name, we supply a corresponding description. For 'Socrates' in 'Socrates is human', we supply 'the teacher of Plato', and for 'Pegasus' in 'Pegasus is a flying horse', we provide 'the winged horse of Bellerophon'. If we do not have a description to fit the name, we can always manufacture one in the following way. From names like 'Socrates' and 'Pegasus' we form the verbs 'to socratize' and 'to pegasize'. The above sentences with names can be replaced by 'The one and only x which socratizes is human' and 'The one and only x which pegasizes is a flying horse.' In canonical notation they appear as

$$(\exists x)(x \text{ socratizes } \& \ (y)(y \text{ socratizes} \rightarrow y = x) \ \& \ x \text{ is human})$$
$$\text{pegasizes} \qquad\qquad \text{pegasizes} \qquad\qquad \text{is a flying horse}$$

Thus, in Quine's most austere canonical language, there are no names, only variables, predicates, quantifiers, truth functional connectives and identity signs. Russell shows us how to eliminate the terminology of definite descriptions from our basic vocabulary; Quine improves upon this practice by showing us how to dispense with names by assimilating them to definite descriptions. David

Kaplan has put this well: "Quinize the name and Russell away the description."

The importance for ontology of the elimination of names is that the referential, that is, the ontologically significant function of language, is accomplished without names. Ontological commitment is a matter of variables and the objects which serve as their values, and not of names and the objects they name. To elaborate, let us make a survey of a variety of existence claims. These can be divided into singular and general assertions.

General existence claims like

'There are brown cows' (assertion of existence)

and

'There are no purple cows' (denial of existence)

appear in canonical notation as

'$(\exists x)(x$ is brown & x is a cow$)$', that is, there exists an x, such that x is brown and a cow,

and

'$\sim(\exists x)(x$ is purple and x is a cow$)$', that is, it is not the case that there is something that is both purple and a cow.

Singular existence claims and sentences with definite descriptions like

'Socrates exists'
'Pegasus does not exist'
'The present king of France doesn't exist'

are paraphrased as

'$(\exists x)(x =$ Socrates$)$', (that is, there exists an x such that it is identical with Socrates)

'$\sim(\exists x)(x =$ Pegasus$)$'

'$\sim(\exists x)(x =$ the present king of France$)$'

and appear ultimately in the austere canonical notation as

'$(\exists x)(x$ socratizes & $(y)(y$ socratizes $\rightarrow y = x))$', (that is, there exists exactly one thing which socratizes)

'$\sim(\exists x)(x$ pegasizes & $(y)(y$ pegasizes $\rightarrow y = x))$'

'$\sim(\exists x)(x$ is a present king of France & $(y)(y$ is a present king of France $\rightarrow y = x))$'.

Notice that the canonical notation in which we express our existence claims contains only variables, predicates, truth functional connectives and quantifiers. Thus Quine can truly say that "Quantification is the ontic idiom *par excellence*."[15]

In modern logic, it has become customary to present a logical system by first specifying the syntax (grammar) of the language and then providing a semantics (a list of truth conditions) for the sentences of the language. The syntax of Quine's canonical notation comprises a vocabulary containing

- variables: 'x', 'y', 'z', etc.
- predicates: e.g. 'is human', 'is taller than', etc. (schematized as 'F', 'G', etc.)
- logical constants: the truth functional connectives, the quantifiers, and the identity sign.

Rules are given which define the combinations of these signs that result in grammatically well-formed sentences. For example, the rule for negation states that a negation sign placed in front of any sentence yields a well-formed negative sentence. Once we have defined all the allowable well-formed formulas of the language, it is the business of semantics to show how we assign truth values to these sentences, for example, to conjunctions, to existential and universal quantifications and so on.

Until now we have been examining how Quine has used somewhat informally the notions of naming and predicating to explain under what conditions sentences of quantificational form are true. However, there is another and much more formally scientific way of specifying the truth conditions for sentences of one's language and in particular quantificational ones. In 1933, Alfred Tarski, in his paper "On the Concept of Truth in Formalized Languages", attempted to transform the discipline of semantics (in the sense described above) into a science as exact as that of mathematics.[16] As the title suggests, Tarski provides a definition of truth for sentences of exactly the type of language which Quine takes as canonical. Tarski's procedure consists in starting with propositional functions, that is, open sentences like '*x* is human' or '*x* is taller than *y*'. Objects (or more precisely sequences of them) are said to satisfy propositional functions. Thus the objects Socrates, Plato and others (but not Rover) satisfy the open sentence '*x* is human.' The sequence of objects Mount Everest and Mount McKinley (those objects in that order) satisfies the relational open sentence '*x* is taller than *y*'. The sequence containing Mount McKinley and Mount Everest, in that order, however, does not satisfy it. By treating sentences with no free variables, for example, 'Socrates is human', 'Everything is in space or in time', as a special kind of limiting case of open sentences, Tarski is able to provide an exact definition of truth.

The notions of naming, predicating and satisfaction (and even truth) have something important in common. They are all semantic relations, relating words to objects, that is, names to the objects named, predicates to the objects they apply to, open sentences to the sequences satisfying them. They can all be used to define a concept of truth according to which a sentence is true precisely when the objects described in it are just as the sentence describes them. The key idea is that it is the things in the world, that is, the way the world is, that make a sentence true. Philosophically this is a semantic variant of a very old theory: the correspondence theory of truth. According to this theory, a sentence is true when it corresponds, or is adequate, to reality.

Tarski conceived of this very correspondence concept of truth as a constraint (he called it a material adequacy condition) on his definition; moreover, he succeeded in formulating the intuition behind the traditional conception in a far clearer and less problematic manner than had hitherto been achieved. The following is his example of how this constraint should be formulated.

'Snow is white' is true   if and only if   snow is white.

The sentence on the left appears in quotation marks, which serve to indicate that we are referring to the sentence itself. We then predicate truth of it exactly on the condition that what the sentence says is so. In the traditional statement we would have said something like 'Snow is white' is true if and only if 'Snow is white' corresponds to reality. But it is precisely this traditional version which has been subject to serious criticism. After all, what does one mean by 'correspondence' or by 'reality'? Tarski's treatment, which Quine warmly espouses, avoids these criticisms by avoiding any but transparent notions, namely, some device for referring to the sentence itself and the 'if and only if' locution of our canonical notation. In an essay dealing with semantical relations of the type we have been considering, Quine says:

> Tarski's construction of truth is easily extended to other concepts of the theory of reference . . .. We have general paradigms . . . which . . . serve to endow 'true-in-L' [truth] and 'true-in-L of' [denotation] and 'names-in-L' [designation] with every bit as much clarity, in any particular application, as is enjoyed by the particular expressions of L to which we apply them. Attribution of truth in particular to 'Snow is white', for example, is every bit as clear to us as attribution of whiteness to snow. In Tarski's technical construction, moreover, we have an explicit general routine for defining truth-in-L for individual languages L which conform to a certain standard pattern and are well specified in point of vocabulary.[17]

The semantic – correspondence inspired – theory of truth provides a perspective for viewing Quine's work, in particular the close interdependence of questions of truth and questions of ontology. To accept a correspondence theory is to be involved in problems of ontology. For, according to it, the truth of a sentence reflects the way the world is and truth claims are ontological claims. For instance, perhaps the best argument for a Platonic ontology of abstract objects consists in taking seriously the claim that what makes sentences about abstract objects true is the reality of abstract objects. The strength of Quine's position on the nature of ontological commitment lies in its connection with this eminently defensible realist theory of truth. Sentences are true because of the way in which they reflect reality and the quantificational sentences are simply the ones which most explicitly reflect what there is. Whether Quine describes quantification in terms of naming, predicating or Tarskian satisfaction does not matter, in a sense; all of these provide arguments for the existential significance of quantification and do so as part of a modern version of the correspondence style account of truth.

Challenging Quine on expressing existence

Although there are many ways in which Quine has been questioned on his views on ontological commitment, I will focus on one strand: the Frege–Russell–Quine tradition of explicating existentials in terms of quantification. As mentioned earlier in this chapter, an older view of existentials connected them with the copula. In the twentieth century, this copula view of existence is best represented by Lesniewski's work and his followers, most notably, Lejewski. Let us first sketch and contrast the copula and the Quinian copula view and then see how they fare when dealing with the problem Quine dubbed "Plato's beard".

Both the quantifier tradition and the copula tradition endorse the slogan "being is not a predicate", and in doing so they share a further feature in common. They agree that it should be taken as meaning that existence sentences are translatable by contextual definitions into sentences in which the grammatical predicate 'exists' no longer appears. In these replacement/definiens sentences, existence is expressed not by a predicate but by a logical constant. The logical constant is the quantifier in the Frege–Russell–Quine tradition and the copula in Kant–Lesniewski–Lejewski. For Lesniewski and his followers, a formal logical system (named "Ontology") is set up with a singular form of the copula 'est' as a primitive logical constant, for example, 'Socrates est man'. It goes between nouns of all sorts to form a well-formed formula and its truth condition says that it is true only when the subject term refers to (denotes) a single object and that object is one of the objects the predicate noun refers to (denotes). In this framework neither the natural language quantifier 'Some' nor its counterpart in the language of logic '$(\exists x)$' has existential import, that is, are read as expressing existence. An object is said to exist if and only if Something is (est) it. The existential force is in the copula 'is' / 'est' and not 'Something'. In general:

$$\boldsymbol{b} \text{ exists} \quad \text{if and only if} \quad (\exists \boldsymbol{a})\boldsymbol{a} \text{ est } \boldsymbol{b}$$

in which the bold letters are variables for noun positions.

But why might one prefer the Lesniewskian view to the Frege–Russell–Quine one? Let us compare the two on the problem Quine calls "Plato's beard". In one form, the problem is that of arguing from a true premise concerning non-existent objects such as Pegasus or

Vulcan (a hypothesized planet which turned out not to exist)

1 Pegasus/Vulcan does not exist.

to the conclusion

2 Something does not exist.

On Quine's quantificational account, which equates 'Some', '$(\exists x)$' and 'There exists', the conclusion is tantamount to saying that there exists an object that does not exist. As Quine puts it, 2 is a contradiction in terms. Quine's Russell-like strategy in solving this problem consists of translating 1 into his canonical notation in which names do not occur; in their place definite descriptions are utilized. The sentence containing the definite description is then contextually defined in terms of Russell's theory of descriptions. The result, first in canonical notation and then paraphrased in English, is:

1′ $\sim(\exists x)(x$ pegasizes and $(y)(y$ pegasizes $\rightarrow y = x))$.

1″ It is not the case that there is one and only one object that pegasizes.

The conclusion in canonical notation appears as

2′ $(\exists y) \sim (\exists x)(x = y)$.

In this way of dealing with the problem, although the premise is true, the argument is not valid. There is no way of going from the true premise to the conclusion. It is not a matter of simply applying the logical rule of generalization that ordinarily lets you validly reason from a singular sentence to a particular "some" generalization. Moreover, the conclusion as stated in Quine's canonical notation according to his views is false in a rather deep way. The conclusion clashes with the following natural language claim, which Quine accepts:

3 Everything exists.

In canonical notation, 3 appears as

3′ $(y)(\exists x)(x = y)$.

Claim 3′ follows from the logical truth $(x)(x = x)$ and the canonically stated conclusion 2′ is inconsistent with 3′.

In summary, by Quine's solution, the original argument is invalid. In addition, the English conclusion is a "contradiction in terms", and when the conclusion is stated in canonical notation it is inconsistent with Quine's account of the logic of identity.

On the Lesniewskian view, the English argument fares quite differently. It is a sound argument with a true premise and a true conclusion following a valid principle of reasoning. The premise is taken as true but without dispensing with names. The conclusion is also taken as true since we do not equate the English quantifier expression 'Some' with 'There exists', or give it any existential force. In the formal Lesniewskian system, there is no conflict with the Lesniewskian laws of identity. And on the Lesniewskian account, the conclusion follows validly by that rule of generalization mentioned above, from --- a --- , $(\exists x)($--- x ---$)$ follows validly. Truth conditions can be provided that were inspired by Tarski's work but differ in important ways (see Challenging Quine, Chapter 3). On this account the argument is sound and not just valid. If the reader feels that the Lesniewskian solution does justice to the Plato's beard problem better than the Quinian solution, then Quine is challenged. If the conclusion in English, "Something does not exist", is not paradoxical, then there is something wrong with an account such as Quine's that makes it seem so. The appearance of a contradiction in terms occurs only when we add existential force to 'some'. The existential reading of the quantifier initiated by Frege and adopted by Quine is the cause of the problem. It requires reading the original unproblematically true sentence as though it is a contradiction in terms.

Another point worth considering is that the premise contains a name, an empty one. On Quine's view, names have no role in the canonical notation. However, if whatever benefits Quine derives from dispensing with names can be achieved with names and if names have functions not performed by corresponding descriptions, then there is a case favouring accounts that don't dispense with names.

There is much more to be said on these matters. Quine follows well-known principles for choosing between theories. One of these principles is known as conservatism. It is a maxim of minimal mutilation, stating that of competing theories, all other things being equal, choose the one that violates the fewest background beliefs held. That is, be conservative in revising background assumptions. If our pre-theoretic intuitions are that the original argument is sound, then keeping this background assumption warrants not following Quine's solution to the "Plato's beard" problem where an otherwise equally good alternative is available.

Chapter 3

Deciding on an ontology

Some rival twentieth-century ontologies

To appreciate Quine's own ontological commitments, it would be helpful to review some alternatives that were accepted by his contemporaries. These will be discussed in three groups: (1) different kinds of concrete individuals, (2) different objects for mathematics and set theory and (3) the positing of intensional objects.

Among the different candidates for being a concrete individual, two stand out. Some philosophers hold that phenomenal objects are the basic individuals, whereas others maintain that physical objects are the concrete values of our individual variables. Theorists of the first group have been called phenomenalists and its members included Berkeley, Hume and Mill. In the twentieth century, Russell, Carnap, Ayer and Goodman have held this view. The phenomenalists' individual is an appearance or sense datum. An example would be the brownish appearance associated with the desk before me. One of the basic problems for the phenomenalist is to explain other concrete objects in terms of his phenomenal ones, for example, to define physical objects such as the desk in terms of sense data. Thus J. S. Mill spoke of physical objects as permanent possibilities of sensation. Twentieth-century phenomenalists take a more linguistic approach to this problem: how can we translate sentences about physical objects, for example, 'This is a desk', into sentences (observation sentences) about phenomenal objects, for example, 'This is a brownish sense datum' or 'There is a brownish sense datum here and now'?

Theorists of the second group hold that physical objects are basic and do not need to be reduced to phenomenal ones. They start with objects like the desk rather than with deskish appearances. This position is a variety of realism and is sometimes called physicalism. Its answer to the question of the nature of the objects of perception is that we perceive physical objects and not their appearances. Popper, the later Carnap, Chisholm and Austin are some of the twentieth-century thinkers who subscribe to this view.

Another issue bearing on the question of the kinds of concrete individuals is the mind–body dispute, which arose out of attempts to explain the nature of human beings. Are we to adopt a dualistic ontology, as Descartes did, characterizing a person in terms of Bodies (physical objects) and Minds (a kind of non-physical, or spiritual, substance)? Although not discussed in quite so bold a form, part of the problem for contemporary philosophers is whether human behaviour can be accounted for in a language committed only to an ontology of physical objects or whether we must also refer to mentalistic entities.

One of the liveliest areas of ontological controversy in recent times is the philosophy of mathematics. The key question concerns the kind of objects required for the existential generalizations of mathematics. Dealing with geometry in terms of algebra (as is done in analytic geometry) makes mathematics collapse into the science of numbers. Now while it is possible to adopt an ontology of numbers, the history of mathematics in the past hundred years has frequently taken a different line. Instead of being considered as the basic mathematical entities, numbers have been defined in terms of sets. Frege provided the outlines of just such a definition for the natural numbers, that is, the whole numbers. Others have shown how the rational number system, that is, the whole numbers plus fractions, can be regarded as an extension of the natural numbers. Dedekind to some extent provided a definition, albeit controversial, of the real numbers, that is, all of the above numbers plus irrational numbers, such as the square root of 2, which cannot be expressed as rational numbers. For most of mathematics the real number system will suffice. This programme of reducing mathematics to something that either is set theory (numbers are all ultimately sets) or like it in power, explicitly advocated by Frege and worked out in greater detail by Russell and Whitehead in *Principia Mathematica*, is known as logicism. Its thesis is the reduction of mathematics to logic, if we construe logic broadly as the theory of truth functions and quantifiers as well as of sets or classes. On this conception, logic is the study of the properties of '~', '&', '(x)' and '∈'. The last is the symbol for 'is a member of', which is basic to set theory. (In what follows I shall use the terms 'set' and 'class' interchangeably; to remind the reader of this practice, at times I will write 'sets/classes'. While there are systems of set theory that distinguish the two notions, they will play no role in this work and so using the terms interchangeably will not pose any problems. Moreover, as we shall see in quoted material, Quine himself uses both expressions in this way where it does not matter.)

Quine has described the ontological options for the philosopher of mathematics as comparable to those facing a medieval thinker tackling the problem of universals.[1] The three modern alternatives are logicism, intuitionism and formalism. The logicist resembles the medieval realist in so far as he espouses an ontology of sets which are abstract objects of a sort. Following are some well-known reasons why sets are not concrete objects:

(1) In a number of versions of set theory, we are forced (on pain of inconsistency) to distinguish individuals from the sets of which they are members. Thus the set consisting of only one individual (called a unit set) must be distinguished from that individual. The concrete individual Socrates has to be distinguished from the abstract object, the unit set, containing only Socrates. It must be noted that this last point is not all that compelling a reason for making the distinction. There are other versions of set theory, Quine's "New Foundations" and his *Mathematical Logic*, for example, which are consistent and in which individuals are in fact identified with their unit sets.

(2) If objects are identical, then whatever is true of the one is true of the other. Thus a reason for distinguishing two objects is if something can be said truly of the one but not of the other. Now consider the unit set containing as its sole element my body and compare it to the set containing as its elements my head, trunk and four limbs. By the above principle of identity these are two different sets. The first has only one member, while the second has six members. Here we have two different objects, that is, two sets, where there is only one concrete object, that is, my body. So two such sets must be distinguished from the objects they contain.

(3) Even if there were only a finite number of concrete objects in the universe, with set theory one can construct an ontology of an infinite number of abstract objects. Imagine a universe contain-

> ing only one concrete object, for example, this desk. We could form the set containing only this desk, the set containing that set and so on *ad infinitum*. Where the medieval realist (the Platonist) said that universals have a real existence independent of concrete objects, the logicist says the same for sets.

Corresponding to the medieval view called conceptualism, which held that universals do not exist in reality but are mind dependent, is the current school of intuitionism. Both conceptualism and intuitionism hold that abstract objects (in the one case universals, in the other mathematical objects) are mental constructs and depend for their existence on the activity of some mind.

The last case, medieval nominalism, has its parallel in present-day formalism. The nominalist held that there are no universals, only concrete individuals. Whatever function universals have is accomplished by linguistic surrogates, that is, by the use of general words. Analogously, in mathematical philosophy formalists maintain that there are no sets or numbers but that mathematical discourse about such abstract entities can be paraphrased into discourse about language, for example, talk of numerals rather than numbers. Here numerals would have to be taken as tokens if they were to be concrete objects. Thus such a formalist alleges that his commitment is to just so many linguistic entities, which he must be careful to show are merely concrete individuals.

A fourth (and for us final) area of current ontological controversy concerns the need to introduce yet another kind of abstract object. An example would be properties (sometimes referred to as attributes). The property of being human is neither a concrete individual nor a set. Whereas Socrates was a concrete individual (as were his snubbed nose, his robes and so forth particular concrete objects), the property of being human is something shared by Socrates, Plato, you and me, and this property is not any one of these concrete objects. Properties, then, are presumably not concrete. However, they should not be confused with sets. Sets are identical according to whether they have the same members, but properties can differ even when they belong to the same individuals. The traditional way of making this point is with two coextensive class expressions which nonetheless represent different properties. Thus the classes of humans and of featherless bipeds are identical (every member of the one is a member of the other and vice versa). Nonetheless, the property of being human (humanity) is not the same as the property of being a featherless biped (featherless bipedity).

Properties are a variety of what are known as intensional objects and are distinguished from the equally abstract but extensional objects, sets. Intensional objects are sometimes spoken of as being meanings. Some philosophers take the meaning, intension or sense of the word 'human' to be the property of being human. On this view, two words can refer to the same objects but differ in meaning, that is, express different properties, as illustrated by the expressions 'human' and 'featherless biped'. Two expressions are said to be synonymous, to have one and the same meaning, when they are not merely coextensive but have exactly the same intension, that is, express the same property. Thus 'human' and 'rational animal', in addition to having the same extension, referring to the same objects, also express uniquely one and the same intension. A famous example of this point occurs in Frege's paper "On Sense and Reference", in which he distinguishes the meanings of expressions from their reference. His well-known example is that of the phrases 'the evening star' and 'the morning star'. The extension, the individual referred to by both of these, is the same, namely, the planet Venus. Although the reference is the same, the meanings expressed by the two differ. The moral is that one should not confuse meaning and reference.

Propositions are yet another kind of intensional object. 'Proposition' is usually used in present-day philosophy of language to refer to the meaning of a sentence as opposed to the sentence itself. For instance, the two distinct sentences 'Romeo loved Juliet' and 'Juliet was loved by Romeo' are said to have the same meaning, that is, express the same proposition. A proposition is what is expressed by a sentence; it is the sense or intension of the sentence. Ontologically, propositions are abstract objects of the intensional variety. Sentences, on the other hand, can be analysed as being either concrete objects (heaps of ink or sound waves) or abstract extensional objects (sequences of sets of ink marks).

Frege and his followers have a particularly rich ontology admitting both intensional and extensional objects. This wealth of objects can form the basis for a comparison with other more modest ontologies. To begin with, Frege assigns to each of the names, predicates and sentences of the new logic an intension (meaning) as well as an extension (referent).

Singular terms ('Socrates', 'the morning star')

Extension	Intension
the individual Socrates and the morning star	the individual concepts of Socrates and of the morning star respectively

Predicates ('is human')

Extension	Intension
the set of humans	the property of being human

Sentences ('Socrates is human')

Extension	Intension
the truth values, the True or the False	the proposition that Socrates is human

In contrast to this elaborate ontology are other more modest ones. Nominalists such as Nelson Goodman and Tadeusz Kotarbinski acknowledge only the existence of concrete individuals. Extensionalists such as Quine and Donald Davidson limit themselves to sets and individuals. Intensionalists like Frege, Rudolf Carnap, Alonzo Church, Ruth Marcus and Saul Kripke allow themselves ontologies consisting of some or all of the following: propositions, properties, individual concepts, the True and the False and sets, as well as individuals.

The reason given for introducing sets was to account for the truths of mathematics. What sort of reasons can be offered for introducing intensional entities? Here are some of the data which these entities are intended to account for:

(1) To begin with there is a cluster of notions connected with meanings in the sense of intensions; these include notions such as synonymy, translation, philosophical analysis as an attempt to capture the meaning of an expression, and analytic truth. For example, synonymy is said to consist of two expressions having the same intensions. Thus meanings, that is, intensional entities like individual concepts, properties and propositions, are used to explain synonymy. In so far as the notion of translation relies on synonymy, it too requires positing an ontology of intensional objects. One who thinks of philosophical analysis

as providing the meaning of a philosophical term can similarly be committed to meanings. The notion of analytic truth, that is, a sentence which is true in virtue of its meaning, is often explained in such a way that it relies on an ontology of meanings.

(2) Intensionalists will sometimes argue that the objects of which we predicate truth are propositions and not sentences. Consider the sentence 'He was snub-nosed'. It is true for Socrates but false for Plato. Since we do not want the objects of which we predicate truth or falsity to be both true and false, it appears that sentences are inadequate. By appealing to propositions, the intensionalist notes that the proposition that Socrates was snub-nosed is true while the proposition that Plato was snub-nosed is false. These two different propositions can both be expressed by one ambiguous sentence.

(3) There are contexts in which coextensive terms do not suffice for the same role. Consider the following argument. As the first premise we have a true identity statement,

'9 = the number of planets'

and the second premise is the true sentence,

'Of necessity 9 is greater than 7'.

Now, an otherwise accepted logical principle says that, given a true identity sentence, we may substitute one of the terms in that identity ('the number of the planets') for the other ('9'), so as to derive:

'Of necessity the number of planets is greater than 7'.

This conclusion is false. Some intensionalists argue that to substitute in contexts involving notions like necessity, we need something stronger than a true identity sentence. We need an identity of intensions and not just of extensions. Thus if instead of '9 = the number of the planets' we had used '9 = 3^2', we would have an identity of intensions and the conclusion 'Of necessity 3^2 is greater than 7' would be true. While this strategy is useful for modal contexts, it has its limitations for other intensional contexts.

'Necessity' is only one of numerous expressions that generate intensional contexts. Modal logic concerns itself with the properties of notions like necessity and possibility. Other words which form intensional contexts are those expressing propositional attitudes, for example 'knows', 'believes' and 'wishes'. Consider the following argument:

Electra knows her brother, Orestes.
Orestes is the stranger standing before her.

Therefore, Electra knows the stranger standing before her.

Some of the above intensionalists will similarly argue that a proper analysis of such contexts requires positing intensional objects in addition to extensional ones. However, the simple identity of intensions that worked for the above modal context will fail for belief contexts. So John, who knows the natural numbers and simple arithmetical relations, might believe that 9 is greater than 7, but since he knows nothing about squares of numbers he does not believe that 3^2 is greater than 7. In *Meaning and Necessity*, Carnap posited more complex intensional items to solve such problems. In doing so he introduced the notion of intensional isomorphism, which involves more sophisticated arrays of intensional objects than the simple identity of the intensions corresonding to '9' and to '3^2'.

As we mentioned in passing, Quine's own ontological commitments are restricted to extensional objects. He stands in opposition to the nominalist on the one hand and the intensionalist on the other. What sort of justifications can be given for the choice of an ontology, and in particular how does Quine justify his rejection of nominalism and intensionalism? In the next section we will explore the grounds for choosing an ontology; thereafter we shall describe Quine's own ontological preferences in greater detail and in the remainder of the book consider additional arguments for his case against his rivals.

Opting for an ontology: indispensability arguments

Not all quantificational discourse commits one to an ontology; for example, a piece of fiction like 'Once upon a time there was an F who . . .' does not involve us in assuming the existence of F's. We are, rather, committed by our most literal referential uses of language: those occurring in science. Hence the question of which ontology we accept must be dealt with in terms of the role an ontology plays in a scientific worldview. For Quine, ontological claims are parts of, and continuous with, scientific theory, and are thus to be judged by the relevant scientific standards:

> Our acceptance of an ontology is, I think, similar in principle to our acceptance of a scientific theory, say a system of physics: we adopt, at least insofar as we are reasonable, the simplest conceptual scheme into which the disordered fragments of raw experience can be fitted and arranged. Our ontology is determined once we have fixed upon the overall conceptual scheme which is to accommodate science in the broadest sense; and the considerations which determine a reasonable construction of any part of that conceptual scheme, for example, the biological or the physical part, are not different in kind from the considerations which determine a reasonable construction of the whole.
>
> . . . the question which ontology actually to adopt still stands open, and the obvious counsel is tolerance and an experimental spirit.[2]

The question of whether to be a nominalist or a realist is to be decided by comparing the two claims in a scientific spirit. Following scientific practice, we should evaluate the two hypotheses as to relative explanatory power, simplicity, precision and so forth. A theory with greater explanatory power (greater generality) can explain more phenomena than its rival. Of two theories, other things being equal, the simpler makes fewer assumptions. Newtonian mechanics and the Copernican hypothesis are the standard textbook examples of generality and simplicity respectively. Newton showed how previously disparate laws of motion for terrestrial and heavenly bodies could both be explained by a more general set of laws. Copernicus's view that the planets orbit about the Sun opposed the rival Ptolemaic theory of the Sun and the planets orbiting the Earth. At the time there were no observed differences between the two theories. However, the Copernican hypothesis explains the same observational data with simpler assumptions.

As an example of how the standards of generality (explanatory power) and simplicity bear on the choice of an ontology, consider how the debate between a nominalist and an intensionalist would be formulated. The nominalist will have to try to show that an ontology of individuals is all that is needed for science, states Quine:

> As a thesis in the philosophy of science, nominalism can be formulated thus: it is possible to set up a nominalistic language in which all of natural science can be expressed. The nominalist, so interpreted, claims that a language adequate to all scientific purposes can be framed in such a way that its variables admit only of concrete objects, individuals, as values – hence only proper names of concrete objects as substituends. Abstract terms will retain the status of syncategorematic expressions, designating nothing, so long as no corresponding variables are used.[3]

An intensionalist like Alonzo Church will argue that nothing less than an ontology comprising an infinite number of intensional entities has the necessary explanatory power.[4]

In his *The Web of Belief,* Quine discusses six virtues that make for a better hypothesis.[5] Three of these, namely, generality, simplicity and precision, are especially relevant to judging ontological hypotheses. So far we have commented only on generality and simplicity. The virtues are not independent: in some cases they overlap, while in others they clash. For instance, there is a sense in which generality implies simplification. A scientific law is a generalization which covers many instances and in doing so it simplifies. This simplicity is not an accidental feature of the scientific enterprise. In some cases, however, simplicity is sacrificed for the virtue of generality. A scientist may posit a new type of entity, thus increasing the complexity of a theory, so long as it also increases the theory's explanatory power. Examples of this abound. As cited above, Newtonian mechanics is just such a case, according to Quine:

> He [Newton] showed how the elliptical paths of heavenly bodies and the parabolic paths of earthly projectiles could be accounted for by identical, general laws of motion. In order to achieve this generality he had to add a hypothesis of gravitation; and the generality gained justified adding it.[6]

In general, theories that posit unobservable entities are less parsimonious than ones that do not, but they are preferable when they explain more.

The use of simplicity as a criterion for deciding between different philosophical theories has a long tradition. In one version it is known as Occam's razor, which says that entities should not be multiplied beyond necessity. In another it is known as the principle of parsimony. Russell's variant asserts that "wherever possible, logical constructions are to be preferred to inferred entities".[7] Quine warmly subscribes to these methodological maxims. Examples of simplicity abound in logical theory. In Quine's canonical notation, for instance, we need not begin by assuming all of the truth functional connectives but can start with just negation and conjunction. The remaining connectives can be introduced derivatively as notational abbreviations. For example:

> 'If *p* then *q*' is short for 'Not both (*p* and not *q*)'
>
> '*p* or *q*' is short for 'Not both (not *p* and not *q*)'

Here we are constructing conditionals, disjunctions and the remaining complex sentences rather than treating them as assumed. In fact, the logic of truth functions is reducible to a single connective, joint denial, that is, 'neither *p* nor *q*'. This provides one of the simplest approaches to the logic of the truth functions. As for the quantifiers, either one can be used to define the other:

> '$(x)Fx$' is short for '$\sim(\exists x)\sim Fx$'
>
> 'Everything is in space' is short for 'It is not the case that at least one thing is not in space'.

In its most austere, that is, simplest, form, Quine's canonical notation contains only joint denial, one of the quantifiers, individual variables and predicates. Another example of simplification is Quine's distinctive claim in his elimination of names via an extension of Russell's theory of descriptions. Throughout Quine's work, especially in his ontological decisions, we will find him appealing to the maxim of simplicity.

A word of warning is necessary. By 'simplicity' we do not mean some psychological trait such as being easily understood or being easy to work with. Indeed, a theory of truth functions that starts with more connectives is easier to understand and to work with. Nonetheless, it is not simpler in the sense with which we are concerned, because it starts with a larger number of assumptions.

Of Quine's remaining virtues for determining the superiority of hypotheses, an important one to note is precision. The more precise a hypothesis is, the more readily it can be confirmed or refuted. Vague declarations like 'When it's cloudy, it rains' or 'When their heads feel warm, they are ill' are not testable because of the imprecise notions of cloudiness and feeling warm. Contrast these with 'When the saturation point is reached, it will rain' and 'If a human being's temperature is above 101 degrees, then he is ill'. The quantitative notions of saturation point and temperature are precise enough to test. Quine considers two ways in which hypotheses can be made more precise. The first consists of introducing quantitative terms which make measurement possible. Examples of these have just been furnished. The second way, as described by Quine, is more relevant to our present concerns.

> Another way of increasing precision is redefinition of terms. We take a term that is fuzzy and imprecise and try to sharpen its sense without impairing its usefulness. In so sharpening we may effect changes in the term's application; a new definition may let the term apply to some things that it did not formerly apply to, and it may keep the term from applying to some of the things to which it had applied. The idea is to have any changes come in harmless cases, so that precision is gained without loss. It is to be noted that hypotheses briefly expressible in everyday terms and purporting to have broad application rarely turn out to be unexceptionable. This is even to be expected, since everyday terms are mainly suited to everyday affairs, where lax talk is rife.
>
> When philosophers give a precise sense to what was formerly a fuzzy term or concept it is called *explication* of that term or concept. Successful explications have been found for the concepts of deduction, probability, and computability, to name just three. It is no wonder that philosophers seek explications; for explications are steps toward clarity. But philosophers are not alone in this.[8]

Other examples of successful philosophical explications are Tarski's semantic definition of truth and Russell's theory of definite descriptions. Equally illustrative is the Frege–Russell–Quine explication of 'existence' in terms of '$(\exists x)$' and the accompanying logic of the quantifiers. In *Word and Object* (1960), Quine singles out the explication of the notion of an ordered pair as a paradigm case of philosophical explication.

Precision is an extremely important factor in Quine's evaluation of philosophical claims. His stance is comparable to the scientist's suspicions of such things as the concept of witches or the idea of a "vital spirit" in living beings which purports to explain their distinctively goal-directed behaviour. Scientists forego expanding their ontology to include witches or vital spirits because these entities have defied clear analysis. Similarly, Quine rejects the introduction of objects for which no clear theory can be provided. To paraphrase a slogan, "no clear entity without a clear theory". This consideration is a significant factor in Quine's sceptical attitude towards intensional notions.

However, the thrust of the requirement that philosophical analyses be precise is not merely negative, that is, to eliminate concepts which defy precise analysis. The positive side of such a successful analysis can result in the reduction of one sort of object to another. In this sense, the virtue of precision overlaps with that of simplicity. An example of this is the analysis of numbers as sets/classes.

It is most interesting that precision in many cases functions as a double-edged sword, dispensing with fuzzy overtones of a concept while improving on other facets. Thus psychologists ignore the supernatural connotations associated with purported witches and instead concentrate on analysing the unusual human behaviour involved, according to the most precise body of psychological theory available. The biologist refrains from ascribing intellectual or spiritual features to living beings, explaining their goal-directed behaviour in terms rather of the science of feedback systems. Similarly, Quine recognizes that in analysing/explicating the concept of number we discard certain connotations and clarify others. Thus, as we shall see, Quine can both discard intensional notions and attempt to find precise behavioural approximations to them.

In this section we have attempted to clarify Quine's appeal to scientific methodology to solve problems of ontology. This appeal illustrates one of his most important naturalist themes, that philosophy is continuous with science. Philosophical questions are decided by the same considerations as scientific ones. Philosophy differs from the sciences merely in the breadth of its categories.

Quine's ontology

For Quine, only two kinds of things exist: physical objects and sets/classes.

> Looking at actual science as a going concern, we can fix in a general way on the domain of objects. Physical objects, to begin with – denizens of space-time – clearly belong. This category embraces indiscriminately what would anciently have been distinguished as substances and as modes or states of substances. A man is a four-dimensional object, extending say eighty-three years in the time dimension. Each spatio-temporal part of the man counts as another and smaller four-dimensional object. A president-elect is one such, two months long. A fit of ague is another, if for ontological clarity we identify it, as we conveniently may, with its victim for the duration of the seizure.
>
> Contrary to popular belief, such a physical ontology has a place also for states of mind. An inspiration or a hallucination can, like the fit of ague, be identified with its host for the duration . . .. It leaves our mentalistic idioms fairly intact, but reconciles them with a physical ontology . . .. As seen, we can go far with physical objects. They are not, however, known to suffice. Certainly, as just now argued, we do not need to add mental objects. But we do need to add *abstract* objects, if we are to accommodate science as currently constituted. Certain things we want to say in science compel us to admit into the range of values of the variables of quantification not only physical objects but also classes and relations of them; also numbers, functions and other objects of pure mathematics. For mathematics – not uninterpreted mathematics, but genuine set theory, logic, number theory, algebra of real and complex numbers, differential and integral calculus, and so on – is best looked upon as an integral part of science, on a par with physics, economics, etc., in which mathematics is said to receive its applications.
>
> Researches in the foundations of mathematics have made it clear that all of mathematics in the above sense can be got down to logic and set theory, and that the objects needed for mathematics in this sense can be got down to a single category, that of *classes* – including classes of classes, classes of classes of classes, and so on. Our tentative ontology for science, our tentative range of values for the variables of quantification, comes therefore to

> this: physical objects, classes of them, classes in turn of the elements of this combined domain, and so on up.[9]

As Quine notes, the adoption of an ontology is tentative in exactly the same sense as is the adoption of any scientific hypothesis. In his earlier work he did not consider the claims of physical objects to be much stronger than those of sense data.[10] At that time he conjectured the feasibility of reducing physical objects to phenomenal ones and compared the relative simplicity of this hypothesis with one which assumed an ontology of physical objects only. In his more recent writings the case for physical objects appears to be overwhelming.[11] Let us summarize some of the reasons for this change of view.

By the 1950s, most philosophers agreed that the phenomenalists' programme to reduce physical objects to sense data did not work. If we began with sense data, sooner or later additional objects – physical ones – would have to be introduced; if the latter could not be dispensed with, then we would have done better to assume them from the start. Moreover, Quine maintains that we can explain everything that sense data have been introduced to deal with purely in terms of physical objects. Sense data theorists account for items like illusions in terms of the awareness of sense data. Quine suggests explaining such illusions as part of a general theory of propositional attitudes, namely, an analysis of intensional contexts such as '*x* believes that ----' and 'It appears to *x* that ----'. Where a phenomenalist's ontology seems doomed to require two sorts of objects – physical as well as phenomenal ones – Occam's razor dictates that we should try to get along with only one.

Quine's rejection of sense data is in keeping with his doctrine of naturalized epistemology.[12] The functions performed by sense data in the theory of knowledge are taken over by observation sentences (already part of our ontology, e.g. sentences like 'This is brown') and sensory stimulation (physical processes, i.e. nerve hits such as light rays striking the retina as opposed to appearances such as the red sense datum). Both observation sentences and physical processes are well within an ontology of physical objects and sets. The epistemological side of this will be elaborated upon in Chapter 8.

Quine's conception of man as a physical object is strikingly revealed by the following passage.

> I am a physical object sitting in a physical world. Some of the forces of this physical world impinge on my surface. Light rays

> strike my retinas; molecules bombard my eardrums and fingertips. I strike back, emanating concentric air waves. These waves take the form of a torrent of discourse about tables, people, molecules, light rays, retinas, air waves, prime numbers, infinite classes, joy and sorrow, good and evil.[13]

Quine's physical objects are not, however, simply those of the naive realist. His physical objects are theoretical posits, posited by common sense as well as by Einsteinian science. Common sense is construed as a theory and one continuous with the more systematic theories of science. From the vantage point of recent science, especially relativity physics and the canonical notation of the new logic, the physical objects which serve as values of variables are, according to Quine,

> thing-events, four-dimensional denizens of space-time, and we can attribute dates and durations to them as we can attribute locations and lengths and breadths to them . . .
>
> Physical objects conceived thus four-dimensionally in space-time, are not to be distinguished from events or, in the concrete sense of the term, processes. Each comprises simply the content, however heterogeneous, of some portion of space-time, however disconnected and gerrymandered.[14]

The reality of theoretical objects is part of Quine's pervasive scientific realism. Some philosophers of science have espoused phenomenalist or instrumentalist stances with regard to the more ambitious theoretical constructs of science. On their view, talk of electrons, neutrinos, quarks and so forth has no ontological significance. For some phenomenalists, talk of electrons serves as a convenient shorthand way of talking of complexes of sense data. For the instrumentalist, such talk is merely a convenient instrument for making predictions. Both of these treat '$(\exists x)Tx$', where T is a theoretical predicate, as not having the existential force that a scientific realist accords it. Quine consistently maintains the view that scientific discourse even at its most unobservable extremes makes the same claims on reality as our talk of ordinary objects.

As already indicated, Quine acknowledges the need for classes to account for mathematical science. He is a Platonic realist of a sort in that he admits a variety of abstract objects as part of his universe. His acceptance of this view was made reluctantly and only after he had explored alternatives. In an autobiographical piece he states, "Already in 1932 and in 1933 in Vienna and Prague . . . I felt a nominalist's discontent with classes".[15] This dissatisfaction gave way eventually to resignation, and Quine may be described as being a reluctant Platonist.

Throughout his career, Quine has tried to explain as much as he can while assuming as little as possible. Nominalism, with its scant ontology, was and remained an object of fascination. In 1947 he and Nelson Goodman co-authored the paper "Steps Towards a Constructive Nominalism". It remains one of the most serious attempts to implement the nominalist's programme. The opening boldly proclaims:

> We do not believe in abstract entities. No one supposes that abstract entities – classes, relations, properties, etc. – exist in space-time; but we mean more than this. We renounce them altogether.
>
> . . . Any system that countenances abstract entities we deem unsatisfactory as a final philosophy.[16]

The paper can be divided into two parts. In the first, the authors provide ways of construing some realistic talk of classes as talk of concrete individuals. They note, for instance, that the statement 'Class A is included in class B' can be paraphrased as quantifying only over individuals, that is, 'Everything that is an A is a B'. Goodman and Quine also provide substitute definitions which do some of the work of definitions that rely on the notion of classes. In these definitions they rely on the relational predicate 'x is a part of y'. The objects to which this predicate applies are concrete individuals. This theory of the part–whole relation was systematically worked out by Goodman. It had already been worked out by Lesniewski in the system he named "Mereology". This theory has had a history of being exploited by nominalists to achieve some of the effects of set theory. Goodman and Quine describe the limited extent to which mathematics is reducible to part–whole talk.

In the second part of "Steps Towards a Constructive Nominalism", the authors attempt to provide a nominalistic way of talking about the languages of logic and set theory. They maintain that, with this nominalistic syntax, one can discuss merely the sentences and other expressions of mathematics, for example, numerals, expressions for sets or the membership sign, as opposed to mathematical objects, for example, numbers, sets or membership. They then proceed to construct mathematics instrumentally.

> This syntax enables us to describe and deal with many formulas (of the object language) for which we have no direct nominalistic translation. For example, the formula which is the full expansion in our object language of '$(n)(n + n = 2n)$' will contain variables calling for abstract entities as values; and if it cannot be translated into nominalistic language, it will in one sense be meaningless for us. But, taking that formula as a string of marks, we can determine whether it is indeed a proper formula of our object language, and what consequence-relationships it has to other formulas. We can thus handle much of classical logic and mathematics without in any further sense understanding, or granting the truth of, the formulas we are dealing with.[17]

Shortly after publishing this paper, Quine abandoned the nominalist programme. By contrast, Nelson Goodman continued to work along its lines. What reasons did Quine give for this abandonment? Later, in *Word and Object* (1960), he tells us that the motivation for introducing classes into one's ontology is no different from that for introducing any theoretical object. We posit physical objects because they simplify our common-sense theories, and molecules and atoms because they simplify special sciences. Classes are similarly posited because of their explanatory power and the relative simplicity of the systems in which they function. As scientific realists we should be committed to the values of the variables of mathematical science in precisely the same way as we are to those of physical or biological science. It just happens that the only values necessary for mathematical variables are ultimately classes. With the membership predicate '$x \in y$', and classes as the values for its variables, we can reduce an ontology of numbers to one of classes. Particular natural numbers such as 1 or 5 are classes of all classes of a certain sort. It is precisely when we quantify over classes, as in phrases like 'all classes' in the preceding sentence, that classes are added to our ontology.

One of Quine's favourite examples of the systematic power of sets is Frege's definition of the ancestor relation.[18] Frege defined ancestorship by appealing to the parenthood and membership relation and by quantifying over classes. Thus 'z is an ancestor of y' means that z is a member of *every class* that contains as members *all parents* of its own members and of y. If we replace the parent relation with the addition relation (which is itself definable in terms of membership and standard logical theory), we define the successor relation of mathematics. With successorship in hand, we can define the notion of a natural number in the general case, that is, not just 1 or 5 but a natural number in general. Note that the italicized positions in the above definition of ancestor would be the places in the parallel definition of successorship where we would quantify over classes.

But if we must have classes to simplify theory, then might not Quine have abandoned nominalism for conceptualism–intuitionism rather than for realism? The answer is no, for the intuitionist's ontology of abstract objects is too slight to serve the needs of classical mathematics. A crucial point occurs in dealing with the real number system, including irrational numbers like the square root of 2, which are not straightforwardly definable in terms of natural numbers. The intuitionists will not admit any numbers which are not properly constructed out of the natural numbers. One effect of this is that they sanction only denumerable totalities such as those constituted by the natural numbers and properly constructed extensions of them. However, classical mathematics appeals to the real numbers (a non-denumerable totality) in notions such as that of a limit. Dedekind did offer a definition of the real numbers but in doing so he quantified over totalities of numbers which are non-denumerable and thus not recognized by the intuitionist. Quine, needing a theory adequate to classical mathematics, does not limit himself to an intuitionist's ontology.

As early as 1932, Quine expressed his dissatisfaction with Russell's theory of types.[19] What is this theory and why does Quine object to it? We have remarked that mathematics reduces to set theory. Frege had made most of the important reductions here. In doing so, he and others used a principle concerning sets which Russell demonstrated as harbouring a contradiction. The principle appears obvious, asserting that every predicate can be used to construct a set. Thus the predicate 'is human' can be used to form the class of humans and the predicate 'is greater than zero' to form the class of numbers greater than zero. Russell chose a rather special predicate and then, on examining the class it formed, noticed that it yielded a contradiction. Consider the predicate 'is not a member of itself'. The class Russell constructed from it is the class of all classes that are not members of themselves. Next he examined this class to see whether or not it is a member of itself. If it is a member of itself, then since by hypothesis it is the class of all classes that are not members of themselves, it is not a member of itself. On the other hand, if it is not a member of itself, then, by hypothesis, it is a member of itself. In summary, if it is, then, it isn't: if it isn't, then it is. This contradiction is known as Russell's paradox. The paradox is not a frivolous matter. If mathematics, via set theory, rests on the principle which gives rise to this contradiction, then mathematics is inconsistent.

Since Russell's statement of this paradox, several solutions have been proposed. None of them has gained universal acceptance. This is one of the several reasons why Quine does not regard mathematics as being certain or different in kind from the other sciences. The alternative solutions seem to him to bear close resemblance to alternative hypotheses in physical theory. Russell's way out was his theory of types, in which it is meaningless to speak of a set being a member of itself. Objects and the expressions referring to them form a hierarchy. Individuals, objects of the lowest level, type 0, can be members of classes (objects of type 1) but not members of individuals. Classes of type 1, which as such have individuals as their members, can themselves only be members of higher level classes (type 2). Classes form an infinite hierarchy of types and there can be no totality of all classes.

To make this theory appear more appealing, Russell presented analogous cases in ordinary language where we might wish to make type distinctions. Sentences like 'The number two is fond of cream cheese' or 'Procrastination drinks quadruplicity' are regarded by him as not false but meaningless. In the first, 'being fond of cream cheese', a predicate that sensibly applies only to concrete objects and to animate ones at that, is nonsensically applied to an abstract object. Similarly for the second sentence, the relational predicate 'drinks' meaningfully relates an animate object and a liquid. In the above sentence, though, 'drinks' is improperly used between two abstract terms. Finally, the predicate 'is a member of itself' used in arriving at the paradox yields meaningless phrases. The two terms it relates are of the same type and thus in direct violation of the theory of types. Russell's solution consists of restricting the principle that every predicate has a set as its extension so that only meaningful predicates have sets as their extensions.

Quine, among others, has voiced several objections to Russell's remedy. For one thing, the theory of types requires an enormous amount of duplication.[20] Russell required different variables for each type and the objects which serve as the values of these variables were also segregated into different types. A frequently noted drawback is that certain objects, such as numbers, will thus be duplicated. The number one, for instance, is a class of a certain type and there are classes of higher types perfectly analogous to it which define different number ones. In effect there appears to be an infinite duplication of number ones at different stages in the hierarchy of types.

Another drawback of the theory bears directly on Quine's programme for quantifiers and ontological commitment. In Russell's view, all the objects there are cannot be gathered into a single totality. There is no possibility of having a class containing all classes and individuals. Philosophically this means that the universal quantifier '(x)' for Russell is typically ambiguous and cannot apply to everything but only to all the objects of a single type. The existential quantifier is similarly restricted in its range of applicability. It no longer means that there is an x *simpliciter*, but, rather that there is an x of type n. In 1936, as Quine was settling down to his reappointment at Harvard as a Faculty Instructor, he began again to ponder over alternatives to Russell's theory.

> It was with a view to these courses that I tried to settle on a sanest comprehensive system of logic – or, as I would now say logic and set theory. One venture was "Set-Theoretic foundations for logic", 1936; a second was "New Foundations for Mathematical Logic", a few months later. In these at last I settled down to the neoclassical primitive notation that Tarski and Gödel had settled on in 1931: just truth functions, quantification, and membership. The one reform on which I was now concentrating was avoidance of the theory of types. I wanted a single style of variables, ranging over all things.[21]

Avoidance of Russell's version of the theory of types – with its different universes – allows Quine to let the individual variables 'x', 'y', 'z' and so on take as values individuals, classes, classes of classes and so on for all that there is.

Over the years Quine has put forward experimentally a number of logical systems and set theories. Many of these have in part been designed to avoid an ontology of segregated universes. The two most famous are developed in "New Foundations for Mathematical Logic"

(1937) and *Mathematical Logic* (1940).[22] "New Foundations" retains some of the benefits of Russell's theory without making all of its assumptions. In the Quinian system, the predicates used to determine classes are ordered, along the lines of type theory; Quine calls this "stratification". The classes which the predicates determine, however, are not ordered. That is to say, variables are part of the scheme of stratification but their values are not. The formula stating that a class is a member of itself is not stratified and cannot serve to determine a class. This eliminates the possibility of constructing the Russell paradox and does so without placing any undue constraints on Quine's programme for ontological commitment.

There is another important philosophical difference with Russell's approach. For Quine, sentences violating the principles of stratification are not meaningless. Thus "The number four is fond of cream cheese" is false. It is an unusually blatant falsehood, but it is a falsehood nonetheless. Quine holds that the motivation for declaring such sentences to be meaningless or category errors rests on the theory of types. Having given up this theory he is loath to declare syntactically well-formed sentences to be meaningless.

In the system of *Mathematical Logic*, Quine offers a variant of Zermelo's way of avoiding paradox. In both "New Foundations" and *Mathematical Logic* the quantifiers apply to a universe comprising all that there is. Russell wanted to use '$(\exists x)$' to express existence even when the objects that serve as the values of the variable 'x' must always be restricted to a single type. Thus '$(\exists x)$' used to quantify over individuals is distinct from '$(\exists x)$' used to quantify over classes of type 1. '$(\exists x)$' is thus systematically ambiguous. But since this quantifier is used to express existence, 'exists' is similarly systematically ambiguous. Quine, whose variables range over a single universe containing whatever exists, regards the doctrine of the ambiguous or equivocal nature of existence as a misconception fostered by type theory. When we say that Socrates exists, that is $(\exists x)(x = \text{Socrates})$, and that the set corresponding to the number four exists, there is no difference in existence, though there is a tremendous difference in the kind of objects said to exist. The first is a concrete individual and the second an abstract object.

In Quine's most distinctive systems there is but one style of variable, that of first order logic, for example, 'x', 'y' and so on. All the values of this style of variable are objects, although some are concrete and others abstract. There are concrete individuals, sets, and if one wishes to assert the existence of intensional entities such as properties, then properties would also be included among the values. This information can be put in a slightly different way. For Quine, the constants that can be substituted for this single style of variable are all singular terms. These can be names of concrete individuals like 'George Washington' and 'Mount Everest', or names of abstract objects. The latter abstract names can be class names like 'red' when used to name the class of red things, or property names like 'redness' for the property of being red.

Talk of properties brings us to the question of whether intensional entities have a place in Quine's ontology. His answer is no. Positing properties, propositions or the like in addition to individuals and classes serves none of the needs of science and philosophy. It is not just that properties are abstract entities, since classes are equally abstract. With properties the additional assumption is not warranted by a corresponding increase in explanatory power. Classes help to explain mathematical data, but Quine is sceptical as to the data which intensional entities are supposed to explain. A related criticism of the intensionalist hypothesis bears on the imprecise nature of the concepts employed. Quine finds that the explanations offered for intensional idioms fail to clarify them. In succeeding chapters we will present his criticisms of intensionalist analysis of topics such as:

(1) propositions as the bearers of truth;
(2) interrelated notions of meaning, synonymy, translation and analysis;
(3) the analytic–synthetic distinction;
(4) modality and propositional attitudes.

Conflict with Carnap over ontology

In commenting on Carnap's ontology, Quine says:

> Though no one has influenced my philosophical thought more than Carnap, an issue has persisted between us for years over questions of ontology and analyticity. These questions prove to be interrelated.[23]

To gain the proper perspective on this controversy, we must say a few words about Rudolf Carnap's views. He was one of the leading members of a group known as logical positivists or logical empiricists. This school developed as a reaction to the kinds of speculative metaphysics which dominated the continental, and in particular German-speaking, universities at the turn of the century. A group was formed which came to be known as the Vienna Circle; its members included, among others, Carnap, Otto Neurath, Moritz Schlick and Herbert Feigl. The Second World War saw some of these philosophers emigrate to the United States. In a number of cases it was through the efforts of Quine himself that they found positions at American universities. The positivists' reaction to speculative metaphysics led to their framing a test for meaningful cognitive discourse; this is their famous verifiability criterion of meaning which asserts that a sentence which has no possibility of being verified is a meaningless pseudo-sentence. Such sentences have the appearance of being cognitively meaningful but are not. According to this criterion, many of the pronouncements of speculative metaphysics are not merely false but meaningless. How ironic that Carnap, who helped frame such a test, should be charged by Quinians as holding a position with metaphysical assumptions of the Platonic sort. For if we apply the standard that to be is to be the value of a variable to Carnap's philosophical views, they appear to commit him to an ontology consisting of classes, properties, propositions and so forth.

Carnap was dismayed by the charge that he harboured metaphysical assumptions. Part of his response to Quine was terminological.

> I should prefer not to use the word 'ontology' for the recognition of entities by the admission of variables. This use seems to me at least misleading; it might be understood as implying that the decision to use certain kinds of variables must be based on ontological, metaphysical convictions. . . . I, like many other empiricists, regard the alleged questions and answers occurring in the traditional realism–nominalism controversy, concerning the ontological reality of universals or any other kind of entities, as pseudo-questions and pseudo-statements devoid of cognitive meaning. I agree of course, with Quine that the problem of "Nominalism" as he interprets it is a meaningful problem. . . . However, I am doubtful whether it is advisable to transfer to this new problem in logic or semantics the label 'nominalism' which stems from an old metaphysical problem.[24]

There is, however, a deeper non-verbal disagreement that has its origin in part in some ideas Carnap inherited from the early work of Wittgenstein. In his *Tractatus,* Wittgenstein declared that words such as 'object', 'thing', 'number' or 'individual' are pseudo-concepts.[25] Consider how they occur in the following sentences:

'For any individual *x*, if *x* is human then *x* is mortal'

'There is a number *x*, such that *x* is greater than 7'.

According to Wittgenstein, the sole function of the words 'individual' and 'number' should be limited to contexts such as these, where they serve to indicate certain restrictions on the range of the variable. Thus 'individual' limits the range of the variable to individuals, and 'number' to numbers. Attempts to use these words in other contexts, such as 'There are individuals' and '1 is a number', were declared nonsensical pseudo-propositions. Carnap incorporated these ideas into his *The Logical Syntax of Language* (1934). He called these expressions universal words. They either function dependently as auxiliary symbols for variables "for the purpose of showing from which genus the substitution values are to be taken" or independently as quasi-syntactical predicates in the material mode.[26] That is to say, sentences like 'The moon is a thing' and '1 is a number' are material mode counterparts of

' 'moon' is a thing word'

and

' '1' is a numeral or number word'.

Both of these uses of universal words, that is, in quantifying phrases and outside them, have a distinctively linguistic function. In connection with quantification they perform the semantical function of restricting the quantifier and in the other context they covertly make linguistic claims, for example, about the word for the moon as opposed to the moon itself.

In 1950, Carnap wrote a paper entitled "Empiricism, Semantics, and Ontology", in which he tried to distinguish his views from those of Quine and in which he relied heavily on the above account of universal words.[27] In that essay, Carnap distinguished two types of questions about existence: internal questions and external ones. Within a linguistic framework, one can ask internal questions about the existence of particular entities. External questions, however, are questions about the existence of the systems of entities as a whole. Thus, within the framework of a language of things, we can enquire about the existence of particular things like cows. The external question is whether to accept the linguistic framework of things at all. External existence questions about things are either meaningless metaphysical sentences or, in a more charitable interpretation, distinctively linguistic questions as to whether to adopt the language of things.

> To accept the thing world means nothing more than to accept a certain form of language, in other words, to accept rules for forming statements and for testing, accepting or rejecting them. The acceptance of the thing language leads, on the basis of observations made, also to the acceptance, belief, and assertion of certain statements. But the thesis of the reality of the thing world cannot be among these statements, because it cannot be formulated in the thing language or, it seems, in any other theoretical language.[28]

The earlier treatment of universal words when they occur outside quantifying phrases is now used to distinguish a special class of existence sentences (categorial existence claims), namely, existential sentences with universal words occupying the predicate position:

'There are things';
'There are numbers';
'There are properties';
'There are propositions'.

Carnap claims that if these are external existence claims, then they are either meaningless or, at best, linguistic proposals advocating respectively the adoption of the thing, number, property and proposition languages. As a linguistic proposal, 'There are properties' is a disguised way of saying 'Adopt the property language!' The latter is in the imperative mood and such sentences are strictly speaking neither true nor false; for example, consider the sentence 'Shut the door'. They can be justified only by their effectiveness as a policy.

When these external questions are decided affirmatively and the above sentences are construed as internal categorial existence claims, they turn out to be linguistically, that is, analytically, true. Their truth merely reflects our decision to adopt the linguistic framework in question. Externally, the question 'Will you adopt the language of numbers?' is answered affirmatively. Internally, in the language of numbers, 'Are there numbers?' is decided by appeal to the external linguistic decision. Carnap's point against Quine is that externally such existence claims are not true or false (not cognitively significant) but merely proposals about language, and internally these categorical existence claims are trivially true as merely having recorded certain linguistic decisions. In either case, existence claims containing universal words would not have the ontological character Quine maintains they do. Accordingly, Carnap does not regard himself as a Platonist even though he quantifies over classes and properties. For him the question of whether there are properties is either a disguised linguistic proposal or a consequence of a purely linguistic decision. Reasoning in this way, Quine's criterion of ontological commitment is significant only for internal existence claims with respect to non-universal words.

Quine's reply consists in part in refusing to distinguish universal words from the more ordinary sort of predicates and consequently categorial existence claims from other existence claims.[29] What is the difference between ordinary predicates like 'is a cow' or 'is odd' and the universal predicates 'is a thing' or 'is a number'? Quine finds that it is only a matter of greater generality. Ordinary predicates circumscribe subclasses of those corresponding to universal predicates. Cows are merely a subclass of things and odd numbers a subclass of numbers. Wittgenstein and Carnap proceeded on the assumption that when a certain degree of generality is reached the predicate involved performs a distinct function. On this view the only function that they concede to the most general predicates, that is, to universal words, is that of talking about language. Less general words are usually used for talking about non-linguistic objects. On this analysis, 'cows' straightforwardly refers to cows, while 'things' covertly refers to a language of things. Quine finds that this distinction is arbitrary, for one could just as well say that 'cows' makes a covert reference to the language of cows. Considerations of simplicity favour following Quine and saying that both expressions are used primarily to refer to non-linguistic objects and that 'thing' is the more general word.

Consequently for Quine there is no difference in kind between

$(\exists x)(x \text{ is a cow})$

and

$(\exists x)(x \text{ is a thing})$.

A theory implying the first is committed to an ontology of cows (to things as well, since all cows are things), and a theory implying the second is committed to things. Thus Carnap, his remarks to the contrary notwithstanding, is committed to abstract entities when he quantifies over them. Whether this situation sufficiently resembles an ancient tradition to be dubbed "Platonism" is a terminological matter. But even here Quine has the advantage, as the resemblance is quite strong.

Quine acknowledges that in disagreements over ontology the participants often find it convenient to talk about words rather than things. He calls this strategy "semantic ascent" and finds that its usefulness consists in allowing disputants to

> be able to discuss very fundamental issues in comparatively neutral terms, and so to diminish the tendency to beg questions. Naturally the strategy proves especially useful for issues of a broadly philosophical sort, ontological or otherwise. But the philosophical truths, ontological and otherwise, are not for that reason more linguistic in content than are the more sharply focused truths of the special sciences. Between ontology and the more local existence statements I recognize no difference of kind.[30]

Thus in a discussion about physics the talk may turn to the word 'simultaneity' in place of the object simultaneity and in philosophy to singular terms in place of individuals. But the convenience and frequency of semantic ascent in philosophy does not signify that philosophy is concerned with linguistic questions. Witness the feasibility of doing the same for 'cows' or 'molecules'. This does not signify that animal husbandry or physics is primarily concerned with a linguistic subject matter.

Nor does semantic ascent require that the truths involved be linguistic truths. In subsequent chapters we examine Quine's attack on the notion that there are two kinds of truths: one factual, that is, synthetic, and the other linguistic, that is, analytic. Carnap's position that very general ontological claims are essentially linguistic relies very heavily on the assumption that there are distinctively linguistic truths. If Quine's critique of such truths were effective, then it would further undercut Carnap's views on ontology.

Quine's views on ontology represented a serious concern in twentieth-century philosophy with metaphysical questions. In this respect he is closer to Russell and the Polish philosopher–logicians than to the antimetaphysical strains in twentieth-century thought, whether these had their roots in logical positivism or in a philosophy of ordinary language. The metaphysical tradition of which Quine is a part partly grows out of a concern for logic, in his case directly out of the logic of existence sentences. This tradition can be traced back to Plato, Aristotle, Aquinas, Occam and others. Indeed, in some respects, a medieval metaphysician and logician such as Occam or Buridan would probably be more at home with Quine's writings than with those of most nineteenth-century metaphysicians. The excesses of speculative metaphysics which the positivists attacked are not to be found in Quine's work. In his departure from the confines of a narrow positivism he has breathed fresh air into recent Anglo-American philosophy. The concern for a logic with a bearing on questions of ontology has been healthy in at least two ways. First, logic, by the breadth of its categories, provides a sound basis for metaphysical speculation. Second, metaphysics rooted in questions of logic may, hopefully, maintain the high critical standards of its sister discipline and thus avoid the excesses it has succumbed to in the past.

Inscrutability of reference

Quine recognizes two different sorts of indeterminacy and warns us not to confuse them:

> there is a deeper point, and Orenstein has done well to expose it. The indeterminacy of translation that I long since conjectured, and the indeterminacy of reference that I proved, are indeterminacies in different senses. My earlier use of different words, 'indeterminacy' for the one and 'inscrutability' for the other, may have been wiser.[31]

The two indeterminacy claims are of reference and of meaning. Referential indeterminacy is also known as inscrutability of reference and as ontological relativity. Meaning indeterminacy is referred to as indeterminacy of translation and as a thesis about radical translation. In this section we examine inscrutability and in Chapter 6 the indeterminacy of meaning/translation.

An important feature of Quine's views, which surfaces in his paper "Ontological Relativity", is the recognition that empiricism does not uniquely determine which objects are required as the values of our variables. There is an inscrutability or indeterminacy of reference that is in keeping with empiricist strictures on deciding which ontology to accept. This is of a piece with Quine's naturalistic empiricism and is later generalized into a view he refers to as global structuralism. It is only at the observation sentences, which Quine takes as indissoluble wholes, that is, holophrastically, that the system is, so to speak, externally constrained. There are equally plausible ways of meeting these observational constraints with quite different objects serving as the values of the variables.[32]

As an introduction, consider a situation in the philosophy of mathematics where quite different objects can be taken as the values of the variables for arithmetic and yet preserve equally well the truths of arithmetic. Numbers can be treated as Frege–Russell sets or as quite different Von Neumann sets. On the Frege–Russell account the number one is the set of all sets that are equinumerous with (i.e. can be placed in a one-to-one correspondence with) a set containing a single element; the number two is the set of sets corresponding to a set with two elements; and so on. Numbers in general are so-called higher order sets containing sets that correspond in this way to a given set. By contrast, von Neumann's numbers are constructed in terms of the empty/null set and sets of all sets of earlier numbers. Starting with zero as the null set, the number one is the set whose element is the set containing the null set (zero); the number two is the set containing the earlier numbers (zero and one); the number three is the set containing the numbers two, one and zero; and so on. For Quine and structuralists the question of whether we are really and truly committed to the set of all sets equinumerous to a given set as on the Frege–Russell account, or to a set comprising the null set as on Von Neumann's view, is a question without sense. We cannot sensibly ask which is the real number five, the Frege–Russell set or the Von Neumann one. The question is without sense in that there is no way of dealing with this question. There is no way in arithmetic for deciding between the two. For Quine this amounts to there being no empirical difference that would allow one to decide between the two. Reference is inscrutable.

There are other cases which furnish proof of the inscrutability of reference. One type is the gavagai–rabbit case. It is mentioned in "Ontological Relativity" and prefigured in *Word and Object*. The rabbit case is intertwined in *Word and Object* with the discussion of a linguist translating a native speaker's utterance of the one-word sentence 'Gavagai'. The evidence for the linguist's translation is limited to the native responding appropriately to the whole sentence 'Gavagai'. This leaves open what to take as the reference of the term 'gavagai'. There is no way of empirically deciding whether the term, the lower case 'gavagai', is used to refer to rabbits, rabbit parts, rabbit stages and so on. The empirical constraints cannot determine which of these diverse ontological items is correct. (Note that the upper case 'Gavagai' is a one-word sentence and the lower case 'gavagai' is a term or predicate.) The capitalized 'Gavagai' is the holophrastically construed observation sentence which has a determinate role as to stimulus and response. By contrast, the lower case 'gavagai' is the term or predicate and its reference is not determinate.

A later example of inscrutability of reference concerns proxy functions. For one type of proxy function Quine introduces the notion of a "cosmic complement". Consider how predicates applying to concrete objects (and the sentences containing them) can be reinterpreted in terms of different ontological items assigned as values of the variables. This can be done so that there is no empirical way of determining which is the correct one. As was seen in the mathematics case, the moral of inscrutability/structuralism is that it is an error to speak as though there were a uniquely correct referent. Consider the sentence 'This rabbit is furry'. It is true as usually interpreted about individual rabbits and individual furry things. This individual rabbit is assigned to 'This rabbit', the set of rabbits is assigned to 'is a rabbit' and the sentence is true since the assignment of the subject term is a member of the set assigned to the predicate. But we can reinterpret the sentence in terms of cosmic complements. The sentence remains true and there is no empirical way, if we do this uniformly, to say which is the correct ontology required for the truth of the sentence. Thus assign to 'This rabbit' the entire cosmos less this rabbit. This is the cosmic complement of this rabbit. (Imagine the universe as a completed jigsaw puzzle with one rabbit piece removed; the cosmic complement would be the puzzle without that rabbit piece.) Assign to the predicate 'is furry' the set of each of the cosmic complements of individual furry things. The sentence 'This rabbit is furry' is true under such an interpretation because the cosmos less this rabbit is a member of the set of cosmic complements of individual furry things (i.e. that set includes the cosmic complement of that individual rabbit). One can extend this treatment of singular sentences to the remaining referential sentences. (To see how this works on the puzzle analogy, assume that there are only two individual rabbit pieces. The cosmic complement of rabbit 1 – the entire puzzle without rabbit 1 – is a member of the set containing the complement of rabbit 1 and the complement of rabbit 2.)

In essence, then, inscrutability of reference is the phenomenon that, given an empiricism with its observational base made up of holophrastically construed observation sentences, the question of the referents required to account for the truths we accept in terms of this base turns out to be whatever objects will serve to preserve these truths. Proxy functions show that entirely different objects fulfil this role of assigning the needed referents to preserve the truths.

Perhaps one can extend the argument and present other cases than those Quine offers. Quine might regard these extensions as challenges to his own view. Consider, for instance, debates about when a singular sentence is true. Different accounts invoke different ontologies which make no observational difference. Nominalists require only concrete individuals to account for the truth value of 'Socrates is human', that is, the subject's referent is identical with one of the predicate's referents. Platonists' proposals vary from the extensional, the subject's referent is a member of the set referred to by the predicate, to the intensional, the subject's referent has the property referred to by the predicate. Montague offered another ontological alternative: the property referred to by the predicate is a member of the set of properties referred to by the subject. Would Quine accept these cases as supporting ontological relativity and global structuralism? Would he say that the question as to what really and truly makes a singular sentence true is without sense as he does for other cases? Global structuralism, argued for in terms of the various accounts that can be given of truth conditions for singular sentences, was in a way an option considered by Hugh Leblanc and me when discussing Leblanc's truth-value semantics. In such a semantics one only assigns truth values to singular sentences and puts aside the further question of which ontological items account for the truth values.[33]

Challenging Quine: indispensability arguments

We can distinguish a number of factors in deciding on an ontology: the epistemological evidence side, the semantical (truth condition) aspect and the ontological commitment side. Indispensability arguments are central to Quine's view of how these factors relate to each other. We are ontologically committed to those objects that are indispensable in the explanations given by our best-evidenced theories. One type of indispensability argument is reasoning to the best explanation.[34] For Quine it does not matter whether the explanation posits genes, neutrinos or mathematical objects such as numbers or classes. He does not discriminate, for ontological purposes, between the use of indispensability arguments in connection with concrete though theoretical objects which are indispensable for biology and physics and abstract objects, the numbers and classes required for the mathematics essential to biology and physics.[35]

Several authors who each accept indispensability arguments in their own way challenge Quine here. Hartry Field appeals in part to the fact that genes, neutrinos and so on play a causal role in our explanations, and numbers and classes do not. Field also argues that what is indispensable about the mathematics is not that its principles are true, but merely that they are consistent. On such grounds as these, Field distinguishes the use of inference to the best explanation in the two cases. Given the different explanatory role of mathematical entities and physical entities,[36] he acknowledges commitment to the existence of genes and neutrinos, but is agnostic as to numbers. Field goes on to offer a "fictionalist" account of mathematics. It avoids commitment to the abstract objects which mathematics as a body of truths might commit one to, and puts in its place mathematics as a consistent body of principles. What is indispensable about mathematics is that it be seen as a consistent story and this is preserved on a fictionalist account. For Field "mathematical claims are true only in the way that fictional claims are true".[37]

Other empiricists argue against Quine's holism and its bearing on indispensability arguments and inference to the best explanation.

So, in different ways, Elliot Sober and Penelope Maddy argue that observation determines which parts of science we accept as true and not whole systems indiscriminately. Sober argues that, contrary to Quine's picture, unobservable posits such as genes and quarks differ from unobservable posits such as numbers.[38] Sober maintains that there are alternative or "contrasting" theories for such concrete theoretical objects and in the face of observation they are dispensable in a way that mathematical objects are not. In a word, for Sober we can conjecture different competing theories for genes and quarks in a way that we cannot for numbers and the truths of arithmetic. He points out that observations are not relevant to accepting the mathematical components of a theory. Quine, commenting on Sober, acknowledges that "mathematics [implies] observation categoricals without enhancing its own credibility when the credibility is confirmed".[39] The mathematical and the non-mathematical cases are indispensable in quite different ways. Penelope Maddy also argues that although both components are indispensable, in practice we take a realist stance on the posits of physics and biology but only an instrumentalist stance on those of the mathematics involved in biology, physics and so on.[40] Bas Van Fraassen rejects inference to the best explanation.[41]

Some see the restriction of logic to first order logic as questionable (see Chapter 5, Challenging Quine). Others (Feferman, Wang, Parsons Chihara, etc.) propose substitutional and other treatments of the quantifiers so that quantifying into positions that Quine would say commits us to the existence of sets are freed of such ontological commitment.[42] The issues in connection with substitutional quantification are rather complex. With respect to our commitment to sets, a crucial question is whether the mathematics required for our best scientific theories is impredicative or not.[43] Impredicative concepts have an air of circularity about them. Impredicativity can arise when a quantifier requires a substitution instance that involves that quantifier. This defies the substitutional account of quantifiers, which requires that the substitution instances are not themselves quantificational. As an example consider the following example of an impredicative claim.

Napoleon had all the properties that every great general has.

$(F)[(x)(Gx \rightarrow Fx) \,\&\, Fn]$

The (F) quantifier (substitutionally construed) requires every instance of the (x) quantifier, which requires every instance of the (F) quantifier. The issues are substantial questions in the foundations of mathematics as to how much of the mathematics indispensable for our best science can be accomplished employing only predicative concepts.

As a case in point, Quine mentions a proof concerning the real numbers. On a predicative approach the proof that the real numbers are dense (roughly speaking, that there is continuity, in that between any two real numbers there is another real number) is not available.[44] This factor was one that led Russell to abandon a predicative approach.

The conflict is that if these sentences are known independently of experience, then they constitute an exception to the principle of empiricism and thus furnish a refutation of it. One traditional solution is rationalism, which accepts the existence of a priori knowledge and denies that all knowledge is empirical. Philosophers of this persuasion, from Plato through Russell, have explained such knowledge in terms of non-empirical modes of cognition. For example, in Plato and Russell there is an appeal to an intuitive recognition of a priori truths. Needless to say, this intuition is not to be confused with the observation, perception and experience the empiricist relies upon. From the standpoint of ontology, the objects known by intuition are non-empirical and are in fact some variety of the abstract objects we mentioned in Chapter 3.

Another solution was offered by John Stuart Mill. As a thoroughgoing empiricist, Mill denied that there is a priori knowledge and then attempted to explain the purported instances of it in a manner in keeping with the principle of empiricism. Thus he claimed that all the truths of logic such as 'All men are men' and the truths of mathematics like '2 plus 2 equals 4' are inductive generalizations from experience. They differ from 'All men are under seventeen feet tall' and 'There are at least nine planets in the solar system' only by virtue of the overwhelming evidence in their favour. The purported a priori truths are confirmed in every instance at hand, for example, all things, let alone men, are found to be identical with themselves, and wherever we find two collections of two objects we actually find four objects. For Mill, concrete empirically known individuals confirm the principle of identity as well as the laws of arithmetic.

Neither of the above solutions was acceptable to twentieth-century empiricists. The school of logical empiricists or positivists associated with the Vienna Circle and, in particular, with Wittgenstein, Carnap and Ayer rejected the account of a priori knowledge provided by the rationalists and by Mill. As strict empiricists, they denied not just the existence of non-empirical knowledge as described by rationalists but also the sense of the doctrine. Yet granted that there is a priori knowledge, the positivists were compelled to offer an account of it. Mill's solution was open to numerous criticisms. For one thing, Mill failed to account for the purported necessity of a priori truths. That is to say, the principle of identity and the truths of mathematics do not just happen to be true, are not merely contingent, but must be true. Even if one could learn that everything is self-identical by inductive generalizations from experience, one cannot learn that of necessity everything is self-identical in that way. David Hume had already made the general point that experience does not provide the basis for judgements of necessity, and it remained only for the positivists to apply this general maxim to Mill's account of necessary truths. Rationalists like Plato and Russell had posited their realm of necessary objects available to non-empirical faculties to account for this necessity.

The positivists were thus left to feel the full brunt of the problem of a priori knowledge. They took seriously our knowledge in logic and mathematics and were aware of the profound advances made in these subjects. Their solution was to account for the a priori and the necessity connected with it in a non-empirical but nonetheless innocuous manner. Like the rationalists they insist that there is knowledge of necessary truths, but unlike them they attempt to provide a naturalistic and mundane explanation of this knowledge. The a priori–empirical distinction is primarily epistemological and concerns different kinds of knowledge. The positivists invoked and revitalized another distinction, that of analytic and synthetic truths. This is a distinction with regard to language and in particular with regard to two types of sentences. As made by Kant, it served to distinguish analytic judgements whose predicate concept is already included in the subject concept, for example, 'All unmarried men are men', from synthetic sentences whose predicate concept is not already included in the subject concept, for example, 'All unmarried men are under seventeen feet tall'. The truth of analytic sentences is a matter of redundancy: one who understands the subject term simultaneously recognizes the truth of the predication. Wittgenstein marked this distinction by saying that these sentences are tautologies. A synthetic sentence requires more than an understanding of the subject term's meaning in order to evaluate the sentence's truth, that is, after understanding the subject 'unmarried men' we must do something else in order to determine whether these men are under seventeen feet tall.

The positivists, however, would not accept the way in which Kant made this distinction. For one thing, Kant's distinction applied only to subject–predicate sentences. The positivists employed a broader use of 'analytic'. Analytic truths were identified with linguistic truths, many of which are not subject–predicate in form. An analytically true sentence is true in virtue of the meaning of the expressions in it. 'All unmarried men are unmarried' is analytic because of the identity of meaning of part of the subject and the predicate. The positivists' definition goes beyond Kant's and applies to sentences that are not of the subject–predicate form. Thus, 'It will rain or it will not' is analytic, that is, true because of the meanings of 'or' and 'not'; '2 plus 2 equals 4' is analytic because of the meanings of '2 plus 2', 'equals' and '4'. For one to recognize the truth of an analytic sentence, it suffices to understand the language, that is, the meanings of expressions. For a synthetic sentence like 'Some unmarried men are over six feet tall' it is necessary but not sufficient in discovering its truth to understand the meanings of the words involved. We must first understand the meanings of the words, but then we must take a look and make the appropriate observations; only then are we in a position to judge the truth-value of the sentence. Similarly, to find out whether it will rain or snow we must do more than understand the meanings of the words involved, as contrasted with knowing whether it will rain or it won't.

The positivist invokes the linguistic, analytic–synthetic, distinction to solve the epistemological problem of a priori knowledge. The solution offered is that all a priori knowledge is merely analytic. All the knowledge that we have which is not grounded in experience is, contra Mill, genuine, but is, contra the rationalists, vacuous. The rationalist who claims to know non-empirically that 2 plus 2 equals 4 is right in denying that we learn this by experiencing pairs of two objects, but wrong in providing a faculty of intuition: '2 plus 2 equals 4' is not an empirical but a linguistic truth. No experiment or experience can falsify this sentence because we will not let it. If we placed two objects and another two objects together and then discovered only three objects, we would not let this count as evidence against '2 plus 2 equals 4'. Thus '2 plus 2 equals 4' is necessarily true because it reflects our conventions for the meanings of the words involved. Its necessity is not a mystery requiring the positing of a realm of necessary objects but merely a reflection of the element of convention in language.

The analytic–synthetic distinction becomes the distinction of linguistic and factual truths. This bifurcation is in turn used to account for the a priori–empirical difference. All a priori knowledge is analytic or linguistic. Here is another point of contrast between the positivists and Kant. Kantians spoke of synthetic a priori truths and meant by this sentences like '7 plus 5 equals 12' and 'Nothing is taller than itself'. For Carnap and Ayer, all a priori knowledge is true in virtue of the meanings of the words involved, that is, analytic, and the above sentences are no exception. There is no synthetic a priori knowledge. Analogously, the distinction of necessary from contingent truths is also explained in terms of the analytic–synthetic distinction. For Carnap, all necessary truths are analytic, requiring not a special ontology of necessary objects but a foundation in truths of language. Although there are many variations in the treatment of the analytic–synthetic distinction it became a cornerstone of twentieth-century empiricism. It is no wonder, then, that an attack on it by Quine, a fellow member of the empiricist camp, should cause such an uproar.

Duhemian–Holistic empiricism and the dogma of reductionism

Quine's rejection of the positivists' brand of empiricism can be divided into two parts. In the first place he agrees with Mill that there is no a priori knowledge; however, his reasons for arriving at this conclusion are quite different from Mill's. Quine espouses a holistic theory in the tradition of Pierre Duhem and he interprets the principle of empiricism, that all knowledge is grounded in experience, in such a way that the purported examples of a priori knowledge are shown to be spurious. In the second place, when Quine argues that there is no a priori knowledge he is questioning the very data for which the analytic–synthetic distinction is to account. If there are no data, one becomes sceptical about the existence of a distinction which explains them. This is a bit like denying that there are witches and then rejecting the "theory" of demonology invoked to explain them. In this chapter we will examine Quine's rejection of a priori knowledge, and in later chapters we will turn to his scepticism about the analytic–synthetic distinction and related notions from the theory of meaning.

Empiricism is the thesis that our knowledge is justified by experience, by our observations. The classical British empiricist spoke, in the manner of Hume, of ideas having empirical content. Hume himself talked of our ideas being copies of corresponding impressions. There are two points to notice here: (1) empiricism is being presented both as a genetic thesis about the origin of knowledge and as a logical thesis about the justification of knowledge; and (2) the vehicle or unit of empirical significance is an idea. The linguistic counterparts of ideas are terms (general and singular) and for linguistically oriented empiricists the term 'cat', and not the idea of a cat, is what has empirical content. More recent empiricism has clarified its status as a thesis about the justification of knowledge, and it has shifted the burden of empirical significance from terms to sentences.

Pragmatists, among others, have insisted that a hypothesis be justified not in terms of its origins, but in terms of its consequences. Hence a hypothesis may have originated in any manner, even as a product of pure imagination; its cognitive value depends on its having the right sort of observable consequences, that is, on what happens when it is tested. As William James quipped, "By their fruits ye shall know them and not by their roots".

A prominent example of the view that sentences and not terms are the units of empirical content is found in the positivists' verifiability criterion. Recall that its purpose was to provide a test of the meaningfulness of cognitive discourse. According to the verifiability theory, a sentence is empirically meaningful only if it is logically possible for there to be observation sentences – sentences recording our experience – which would furnish evidence for or against the sentence. If a sentence has no observable consequences and is not analytic (a truth based on language), then it is pronounced cognitively meaningless. The point to be emphasized here is this theory's assumption that we can examine isolated individual sentences for empirical content. Now it is precisely this aspect of empiricism that Quine rejects and refers to as the dogma of reductionism.

> But the dogma of reductionism has, in a subtler and more tenuous form, continued to influence the thought of empiricists. The notion lingers that to each statement, or each synthetic statement, there is associated a unique range of possible sensory events such that the occurrence of any of them would add to the likelihood of truth of the statement, and that there is associated also another unique range of possible sensory events whose occurrence would detract from that likelihood. This notion is of course implicit in the verification theory of meaning.
>
> The dogma of reductionism survives in the supposition that each statement, taken in isolation from its fellows, can admit of confirmation or infirmation at all. My countersuggestion . . . is that our statements about the external world face the tribunal of sense experience not individually but only as a corporate body.[2]

To appreciate Quine's position we must take a closer look at the concept of testing. Testing, after all, is precisely the case where experience, that is, observable consequences, is appealed to. Quine will claim that empirical evidence is always for or against systems of sentences and never for single isolated sentences. In other words, his brand of empiricism is holistic. He takes whole systems of sentences and not individual ones as the units of empirical significance. According to the view that Quine is combating, the logical structure of the test of a hypothesis is as follows. We have a hypothesis to be tested and some sentences describing certain initial conditions, and from these we derive some observable consequences.

Hypothesis
Initial conditions

---

therefore, Observable consequences ('therefore' represents the use of principles of logic and mathematics to carry out the derivation).

If the observable consequences fail to occur, this failure is taken as empirical evidence refuting the hypothesis in question. The pattern of a test so construed consists in the observable consequences being implied by the hypothesis and the statement of the initial conditions. Falsity of the conclusion is taken as evidence of the falsity of the premise serving as the hypothesis. As an example, consider a test of the hypothesis that the Earth is flat (and without its end visible).

Hypothesis:	The Earth is flat.
Initial conditions:	A ship sails away from New York harbour in a straight direction.
therefore,	The ship should appear smaller and smaller as it recedes and finally disappears.

However, we actually observe the ship seeming to sink into the sea. The bottom sinks from view first and the top last. We conclude that the flat Earth hypothesis is false.[3]

Pierre Duhem (1861–1916), a physicist and historian and philosopher of science, pointed out that the logic of testing is not as simple as we have just suggested and that it is not possible to test empirically an isolated hypothesis.[4] Consider the above example again. Is there really only one hypothesis involved or are there many of them? For instance, does not the hypothesis that light travels in a straight line have to be added to the flatness hypothesis in order to derive that the ship will disappear all at once or top first? And if we are careful about the use of this additional hypothesis, must we not recognize that it is itself embedded in a theory or system of hypotheses about light? Thus a more realistic picture of the logic of testing would be:

> Hypothesis 1
> Hypothesis 2
> . . .
> Hypothesis *n*
> Initial conditions (and any hypotheses they harbour)
> ―――――――――――――――――――――――――――
> therefore, Observable consequences.

Now, in the face of the conclusion being denied we cannot unequivocally tell which hypothesis ought to be rejected. No one isolated hypothesis has been rejected but rather a body of hypotheses have, and there is a certain amount of leeway as to which one we decide to discard. This point of Duhem's conflicts with the assumption of many empiricists that isolated individual sentences regularly have empirical, that is, testable, content.

Quine has elaborated on Duhem's idea, making explicit certain of its consequences; he examines and takes seriously all of the alternatives left open by a test situation as described above. We will discuss these options as pertaining to the hypotheses, the initial conditions, the observable consequences and the principles used to derive the observable consequences.

(1) In the face of the recalcitrant observation we can revise one or more of the hypotheses at stake. Depending on our relative confidence we could choose to reject the one in which we have the least confidence. Quine would invoke a principle of conservatism to retain those hypotheses that clash least with the rest of our body of beliefs. He has also colourfully called this a "maxim of minimum mutilation".[5]

(2) We can reject the statement of the initial conditions. In some experiments this is the course that is adopted. In the same sense in which a science teacher might reject the findings of a student because the experiment had not been properly set up, a

practising scientist might decide that there was something wrong with the conditions for making the test. This is frequently the case with testing in the social sciences, where a questionnaire used might not furnish the right controls for what is being tested.

Of equal interest here is the fact that the more sophisticated the science in which we are testing, the more likely it is that the description of the initial conditions will presuppose background theories. Imagine a test in physics using an ammeter (a device for measuring electrical current); this will presuppose additional hypotheses about electricity. There will usually be a number of auxiliary hypotheses associated with the instruments used in conducting experiments, and any one of these may be singled out for rejection.

(3) We could decide to reject, or at least reinterpret, the observed datum itself, which clashes with the conclusion. Quine speaks in this vein of "editing observation".[6] In common-sense cases we do not hesitate when the observation clashes with a large body of beliefs in which we have greater confidence. When a partially submerged oar is observed to be bent, rather than subscribe to the belief that oars bend upon submersion, we discount the evidence our eyes present us with. A similar tack is taken in more sophisticated scientific contexts. In a famous series of lectures, the physicist Richard Feynman presented the following case. From well-evidenced assumptions that play crucial roles in physical theory, it follows that in a photograph two stars should appear as far apart as *n* units:

*   *

However, on an actual photograph they appear to be only one half that far apart:

*   *

Since it would be less conservative to reject the laws of gravity and other associated principles, we deny that the photo furnishes unassailable counter-evidence and look for some way to edit the observational data.[7] To reject any or all of the laws of physics would involve much more far-reaching changes in our system of beliefs than editing the data presented by the photograph. In this case physicists accounted for the apparent proximity of the two stars in the photograph as an effect of the distance from the stars and the angle from which the photo was taken.

Once again it must be noted that in so far as instruments, for example, telescopes or ammeters, are used to make observations, the auxiliary hypotheses associated with these instruments, for example, the theories of optics or electricity, must be taken into account. Thus in a test where the observations made to determine the correctness of some prediction rely on instruments which presuppose background theories, the option remains open to revise this group of background assumptions.

(4) The last alternative available to us in testing is to question the principles of logic and mathematics involved.[8] Thus the testing in which Newtonian physics was replaced by Einsteinian physics resulted in, among other things, the replacement of Euclidean geometry by a non-Euclidean variety. In somewhat the same experimental spirit it has been suggested that the logical principles used for quantum mechanics should be those, not of two-valued logic, but of a many-valued logic. Now while this proposal has by no means met with general support, its importance lies in the fact that it can be made, that is, that in the face of negative findings an alternative, albeit not a very likely one, would be to revise the standard principles of logic. Quine's principle of conservativism explains why we are least likely to revise the principles of mathematics or logic. Their revision would have the most far-reaching effects and would involve changing the largest number of our other beliefs.

We are forced to recognize that from the fact that sentences cannot be tested in isolation but only as parts of systems of sentences, it follows that every sentence at all logically relevant to a test risks the danger of experimental refutation. There are, in principle, no sentences immune to experimental rejection, and every sentence has some empirical import as part of a system; the system is the primary vehicle of empirical significance. With this Duhem–Quine variety of empiricism in mind let us reconsider the problem of a priori knowledge. The principle of empiricism – all knowledge is justified in terms of experience – is now interpreted by Quine as asserting that it is the whole system of our beliefs which has empirical significance and that every belief within it shares in this empirical significance:

> The totality of our so-called knowledge or beliefs, from the most casual matters of geography and history to the profoundest laws of atomic physics or even of pure mathematics and logic, is a manmade fabric which impinges on experience only along the edges. Or, to change the figure, total science is like a field of force whose boundary conditions are experience. A conflict with experience at the periphery occasions readjustments in the interior of the field. Truth values have to be redistributed over some of our statements. Re-evaluation of some statements entails re-evaluation of others, because of their logical interconnections – the logical laws being in turn simply certain further statements of the system, certain further elements of the field. Having re-evaluated one statement we must re-evaluate some others, which may be statements logically connected with the first or may be the statements of logical connections themselves. But the total field is so undetermined by its boundary conditions, experience, that there is much latitude of choice as to what statements to re-evaluate in the light of any single contrary experience. No particular experiences are linked with any particular statements in the interior of the field, except indirectly through considerations of equilibrium affecting the field as a whole.[9]

No sentence can be singled out as being in principle incorrigible; for in the attempt to fit theory to observation, any one sentence may become a candidate for revision. Logic, mathematics and all other purported a priori knowledge are parts of our system of background assumptions and are, in principle, open to revision. If a priori knowledge is knowledge that is justifiable independently of experience, then Quine denies that there is any. Our choice of a system of logic or mathematics is dependent on the same sort of broad empirical considerations as our choice of a system of physics. We use the simplest systems of logic and mathematics which coheres with the rest of our sciences; should empirical findings require a change in either logic or mathematics for the benefit of the overall system, then it would be incumbent upon us to provide such a change.

To gain some perspective on Quine's view of what is purported to be a priori knowledge it would be helpful to make certain comparisons. To begin with, while Quine is definitely an empiricist, he (like Plato and Russell) acknowledges the existence of abstract objects which serve as the ontological basis for the truths of mathematics.

Ontologically he could be described as a reluctant Platonist, admitting only as many abstract objects, such as sets, as are indispensable for the business of science. Unlike Mill, Quine recognizes the truth of '2 plus 2 equals 4' not because it corresponds to pairs of concrete objects but because it is an abbreviated way of describing certain relations which obtain between certain sets.

Even though Quine's ontology is that of a Platonist, his epistemology is not. Where Plato, Russell and other rationalists account for our knowledge of the truths of logic and mathematics in terms of non-empirical modes of cognition such as intuition, Quine is an empiricist, although in a strictly holistic Duhemian sense. The decision to introduce abstract objects is no different in principle from the decision to introduce other non-observable theoretical objects. It is made on the grounds of the explanatory power and relative simplicity of the systems they are part of. Where Mill sought to establish logic and mathematics on the basis of an overwhelming amount of direct evidence, Quine appeals instead to the overwhelming amount of indirect evidence. Mill attempted to justify so-called a priori knowledge empirically by appealing to rather simple and naive inductive procedures. He spoke of examining so many instances of the principle of identity and then inductively generalizing. The more sophisticated twentieth-century methodology places relatively less stress on the force of direct evidence than it does on that of indirect evidence. Science is not just a collection of sentences, each one of which has been separately established in the above inductive manner. Rather, science is a web of logically interconnected sentences. One does not have to subscribe to the Duhem point (although it helps) to recognize that evidence, especially for the more theoretical parts of science, for example, '$E = mc^2$' or molecular theory, is not direct. Such evidence draws consequences from those theories. These consequences in turn eventually yield other and more observable consequences that provide indirect tests for those theories. In this web of beliefs, logic and mathematics play a central role. To reject a random observation has few consequences; to revise a theory such as that of molecules has more widespread consequences for all chemical phenomena; and to revise a principle of mathematics or logic has the most far-reaching consequences.

The positivists' rejection of Mill's view of mathematics and logic as empirical was that we do not and would not apply empirical methods to these sciences. This rejection has force only against naive accounts of empirical methodology. The positivist misses the mark because he has failed to establish that mathematics and logic are not guided by the same broad theoretical considerations as physics. Quine's case is that mathematics and logic are like the more theoretical parts of physics. They are capable of being tested although, like the tests for physical theory, these tests are indirect. To complain that '2 plus 2 equals 4' or 'All *A*'s are *A*'s' are not established by simple induction and hence are not empirical would sanction the argument that since '$E = mc^2$' and 'Photons behave like waves' are not inductive generalizations, then they too are non-empirical.

In another objection to Mill, Ayer claims that '2 plus 2 equals 4' is not susceptible of experimental refutation because he, Ayer, believes that its truth is a matter of linguistic convention. For Ayer, the truths of arithmetic are not falsifiable, because we will not allow them to be falsified.[10] Quine goes one step further than the positivist and notes that in the context of a test situation we have the leeway to save "by convention" any sentence, that is, any hypothesis or statement of initial conditions, and not just sentences of logic and mathematics. As a thesis accounting for the necessity, that is, the non-refutable character of certain sentences, conventionalism is bankrupt, because every sentence on the Duhemian model is equally endowed with the possibility of being saved by patching up the system somewhere else. This point provides a *reductio ad absurdum* of the claim that certain sentences have a privileged status by showing that all sentences have this status. In principle, no sentence is irrefutable, and in this sense Ayer is wrong. By adopting a naive model of testing one may be led to this false belief but, as we have seen, any sentence can be revised. Quine's position in this respect resembles the view that Peirce labelled "fallibilism".

The effects of dispensing with the a priori

One of the goals of this chapter has been to undercut the analytic–synthetic distinction by arguing that one of the most important reasons for introducing it, namely, to explain a priori knowledge, loses all its force with Quine's denial that there is such knowledge. But we cannot hope to do justice to Quine's thought without saying more on the subject of analyticity. Much of Quine's philosophy of logic and language has been presented in the context of discussions of sentences presumed to be analytic. These analytic sentences can be analysed as falling into two categories: those that are logical truths in Quine's strict sense of the term; and those that are part of a broader class which, although not such logical truths, are nonetheless considered to be analytic.

<u>Logical truths</u>

'It will rain or it won't'
'All unmarried men are unmarried men'

<u>The Broader Class</u>

'All bachelors are unmarried men'
'Vixens are female foxes'
'Every event has a cause'
'Nothing is taller than itself'

We already know that Quine maintains that the justification of these sentences constitutes no exception to empirical methodology. In Chapter 5 we turn to Quine's philosophy of logic, beginning with his conception of the nature of logical truths (sentences listed in the first category above). In succeeding chapters we will examine Quine's thoughts on the remaining collection of analytic sentences.

Challenging Quine: naturalism and the a priori

Several authors question the Quinian position that there is no a priori knowledge. I will consider three forms of this challenge. George Rey provides a thought experiment that serves as a useful foil for making a number of distinctions. The second challenge is from one of the most serious contemporary attempts at a rationalist's reply to Quine (Laurence BonJour) and the last is from Hartry Field. I recommend that the reader read or skim at this juncture and then return to it after going through the remaining chapters.

While working within the confines of a naturalized epistemology (see Chapter 8 for a survey of naturalism in epistemology), George Rey offers an account of how one might allow for the a priori.[11] He presents a thought experiment which is a naturalist's version of an older rationalist theme of innate ideas and innate knowledge. Consider the possibility that there is a module in our cognitive capacities (perhaps in the brain) and that it generates theorems of logic. One such theorem might be that if snow is white, then either snow is white or roses are red. Since the theorem is generated by an innate capacity, Rey proposes that it serve as a candidate for a priori knowledge. However, as we shall see in Chapter 8, Quine does not deny the possibility of innateness. Indeed, Quine maintains that we have an innate capacity (a gene determined disposition) to spot perceptual similarities. Let us try to get clear about what is to count as a priori knowledge.

At the outset we should distinguish genetic rationalism from at least epistemological rationalism. Just as empiricism is an epistemological doctrine about the evidence for beliefs and not about their origins, the same should be said for genetic rationalism's relationship to rationalism as an epistemological view. Being born with information or acquiring it after birth are both questions of genesis and as such are not addressing the issue of evidence and justification. As mentioned above, Quine acknowledges, without the use of thought experiments, that people are born with cognitive abilities that are not acquired.

If some sentences are generated innately, then the question remains of what makes them authoritative, that is, true. Quine is a realist on truth, holding a Tarskian correspondence realist-style account of truth. So even if sentences/theorems of logic were generated innately as in Rey's thought experiment, the question would remain of what makes them authoritative/true. This problem assumes even greater force when applied to claimants for the a priori which, even if they are generated innately, are not theorems of logic.

However, even if these sentences/theorems are known and hence authoritative/true they are not distinct in their being authoritative, their being true or simply in being known. They would be true in the same Tarskian correspondence sense that the rest of our knowledge is. And while the truths of logic can be axiomatized (some statements are taken as basic to derive the others) and a foundationalist account of them can be given, this is not distinctive of the truths of logic (see Chapter 5). We can also axiomatize branches of non-a priori knowledge. Furthermore, this foundationalist strategy of axiomatizing does not exist for other claimants which are not truths of logic to be a priori, for example, 'No bachelors are married', 'Nothing is taller than itself'. On the question of delineation, in Chapter 5 we shall see that although the truths of logic can be precisely defined/delineated, this does not account for their truth.

Moreover, no such precise delineation of the broader conception of the a priori has been given.

The issue seems to come down to the following. Even if we assume that the claimants to the a priori are known and true, the remaining issue is how these claimants differ from non-a priori knowledge. Laurence BonJour and Hartry Field address these issues, although not as just stated.

BonJour separates Quine's critique of analyticity from his critique of a priori knowledge. If we assume that the function of the analytic–synthetic distinction is to explain a priori knowledge, the critique of analyticity provides reasons for scepticism about the a priori. But even if we assume that the notion of being analytic could be properly explicated, the question remains whether all a priori knowledge is knowledge of analytic truths.

But what of Quine's holistic empiricism and the Duhemian argument that there is no a priori knowledge? BonJour defends a rationalist position that there is a priori justification. However, unlike traditional rationalists, he gives up on the quest for certainty and offers a fallibilist version of rationalism wherein rational insight as a special non-empirical way of knowing is fallible. The issue then is not whether claimants to be a priori can be rejected. For BonJour, the crucial issue concerning a prioricity is whether BonJour's rationalist notion of justification or what he sees as Quine's is correct. He says that

> What follows from the Duhemian view is only that the revisions prompted by recalcitrant experience need not be confined to the observational periphery . . . But to conclude from this that any sentence can rationally be given up . . . it must be assumed that *epistemic rationality is concerned solely with adjusting one's beliefs to experience* . . . the claim of the proponent of a priori justification is . . . precisely that there are propositions . . . that it is justifiable . . . to accept . . . or irrational to give up, for reasons that have nothing to do with adjusting one's beliefs to experience.[12]

BonJour believes that the only source of revision Quine does (or can?) allow is "adjustment of beliefs to experience", that is, the relation of sentences to observation sentences. This is not quite accurate since Quine appeals to logical consistency, simplicity, conservatism and so on. The issue then becomes whether these are justified a priorily, that is, in some rationalist way. BonJour claims that they are and that Quine presupposes such a priori justification.[13] While it may be possible to construct a revisionist rationalist version of Quine along such lines, there is no reason why a Quinian would have to pursue this path. Quine would not deny that in arguing about revising our beliefs, even the possibility of revising our logic, we are appealing to principles. But it does not follow from this that these background assumptions are justified in some special rationalist way.

But BonJour does more than make the above unproven charge. He goes on to address the case for the special character of a priori justification. As I see it both BonJour and Quine are realists about truth-authoritativeness. I construe Quine as saying that there is no plausible rationalist account of why claimants to be a priori are justified that distinguishes them from the rest of our knowledge. BonJour offers a positive account of what is distinctive about such knowledge. BonJour's rationalism is that of a realist: a priori knowledge is rational insight into necessary features of reality. It is not a dogmatic but a moderate rationalism in that claims to a priori knowledge are fallible and corrigible. His positive account involves presenting and then examining what he takes to be intuitive cases of a priori knowledge and justification, such as knowing that nothing red all over is green (or not red all over). His rationalist solution is that the necessary features of reality in what is known a priori are not extrinsically (contingently/empirically) related to content; instead mental content consists of the very stuff that has the necessity. Properties are both really in the world and in the content as well. The problem of how to make the rational real and the real rational is bridged by identifying them – uniting them as being constitutive of extra-mental reality as well as of rationality, that is, mental content. On BonJour's account, the content of the rational insight into the necessity that nothing is both red and not red (e.g. green) is at one with the objects constituting the reality in question. The properties/universals having the necessary connection are part of the content. The objective necessity, exclusion of the property of being red from the property of being not-red (e.g. green) contains components, that is, the properties/universals that are also components of the content of the proposition involved in having that insight. So BonJour's positive account comes down to the acceptance of intuitions as to the existence of a priori knowledge and the explanation of how such intuitions are possible.

The rationalist–realist proponent of a priori knowledge as rational insight into necessary traits of reality faces the problem of how a mind can come to knowledge of necessary traits of reality. It is a special case for the rationalist–realist bearing on a priori knowledge of the more general problem of our knowledge of the external world. How can a mind come to know necessary traits of extra mental reality in an a priori fashion? Quinians are not likely to credit the intuitions BonJour cites that a priori knowledge exists. They would also raise questions about the positive account given of such purported knowledge.

In the above we have, for the most part, confined ourselves to logic as the paradigm of a claimant to be known a priori. In turning to Hartry Field's ideas let us explicitly restrict ourselves to logic and consider whether it constitutes a priori knowledge.[14] Field's points apply in the first instance to the rules and not to the principles, laws or what have so far been spoken of as the "truths" of logic. Rules are not strictly speaking true or false. Given sentences of the forms

If *p* then *q*
p

we can derive sentences of the form

q.

This rule may be useful or satisfactory but it is not the right kind of object for being true or false. Field conceives of logic, his candidate for the a priori, along anti-realist lines as rules rather than as truths. On the surface this allows Field to sidestep the question of what makes logic authoritative, where "authoritative" is construed as true in some realist sense. However, the question remains as to why these rules work and if they work, Field has to describe how they work in a different way from other rules. For example, we might set up a branch of science as a system of rules. We would then ask what makes that system work and whether the way that it works is different from the way logic as a system of rules would.

Field's answer is that logic as a system of rules is a priori in that it is presupposed in a special way. It is indefeasible. By this Field means that it is assumed (or in some special sense must be assumed) in our inductive procedures.[15] Logic is naturalistically a priori in the sense that it is in a special sense indefeasible and in addition believable independently of the facts.[16] As such logical rules are independent of the facts of empirical science. What the a prioricity of logic comes down to on this view is (a) indefeasibility (logic has to be – in some sense must be – assumed/presupposed when we do science) and (b) logic is at the same time independent of the claims of any particular scientific theory. Quinians might try to contest the indefeasibility point. While it does seem as though some logic must be assumed, doesn't this still leave open the questions of just which system of logic to choose?

Chapter 5

The nature of logic

Analyticity as logical truth

Some define an analytic truth as one the denial of which leads to a contradiction. Kant, for instance, supplemented his well-known treatment of analyticity in terms of the predicate concept being already included in the subject concept in this way. The problem in such a definition is the phrase 'leads to'. The intent is that logical principles applied to the denial of a sentence will suffice for deriving a contradiction. Thus interpreted, the above definition is equivalent to a more affirmative statement: a sentence is analytically true precisely when it follows from the principles of logic alone. But since what follows here are the theorems or laws of logic, then analytic truth in this sense is the same as logical truth. We must turn here to examine Quine's thoughts on analyticity as logical truth. To begin with, we will present a distinctively Quinian definition of logical truth. This will lead us to consider the bounds of logic, that is, where does logic end and mathematics begin? We will take note of the way Quine expresses the principles of logic, and we will then consider some criticisms of the attempts to ground logic and mathematics non-empirically.

The definition of logical truth

Consider the logical truth

Brutus killed Caesar or Brutus did not kill Caesar.

The schema for this sentence is:

> *p* or not *p*

Such truths are distinguished by the fact that they remain true no matter what expressions we, taking care to be grammatical, put in the place of the non-logical parts. In the above schema, the non-logical parts are indicated by *p*. Whatever sentence we put for *p* or, in particular, 'Brutus killed Caesar', the resulting compound sentence will remain true. Non-logical truths do not have this property. Consider 'Brutus killed Caesar or Portia killed Caesar'. It is true since one of the disjuncts (the first) is true. Its schema is *p* or *q*. If we vary 'Brutus killed Caesar' and put in its place the false sentence 'Calpurnia killed Caesar', then the ensuing disjunction 'Calpurnia killed Caesar or Portia killed Caesar' is false. In other words, a logical truth cannot be changed into a falsehood when we vary the non-logical expressions, whereas an ordinary truth can be so changed. Logical truths depend solely on the logical words they contain. (In this sense they are said to be formal or to depend solely on their logical form, which is indicated by the schema '*p* or not *p*'.)

Quine has formulated this by saying that for logical truths the role played by logical constants is "essential" while that played by non-logical expressions is that of "vacuous variants":

> A logically true statement has this peculiarity: basic particles such as 'is', 'not', 'and', 'or', 'unless', 'if', 'then', 'neither', 'nor', 'some', 'all', etc. occur in the statement in such a way that the statement is true independently of its other ingredients. Thus, consider the classical example:
>
> (1) If every man is mortal and Socrates is a man then Socrates is mortal.
>
> Not only is this statement true, but it is true independently of the constituents 'man', 'mortal', and 'Socrates'; no alteration of these words is capable of turning the statement into a falsehood. Any other statement of the form:
>
> (2) If every -- is -- and -- is a -- then -- is -- is equally true, so long merely as the first and fourth blanks are filled alike, and the second and last, and the third and fifth.

> A word may be said to occur essentially in a statement if replacement of the word by another is capable of turning the statement into a falsehood. When this is not the case, the word may be said to occur vacuously. Thus the words . . . 'Socrates', 'man', and 'mortal' occur vacuously in (1). The logical truths, then, are describable as those truths in which only the basic particles alluded to earlier occur essentially.[1]

This is not Quine's only definition of logical truth, but it is his most distinctive one. The same concept of logical truth, although Quine was not aware of it when he formulated his version, is to be found in the writings of Bernard Bolzano (1781–1848) and Kazimierz Ajdukiewicz (1890–1963). One of its virtues lies in what it does not say. Many textbooks of logic explain logical truth and related notions in modal terms. Logical truths are said to be distinguished by being "necessary" or "true in all possible worlds", and a valid argument is defined as one in which if the premises are true, then the conclusion "must be true" or "cannot possibly" be false. Such accounts make elementary logic presuppose modal logic. Quine's definition leaves logic autonomous in this respect. He is sceptical about explanations of necessity and related modal notions. Quine has provided some of the most telling criticisms of modal logic.[2] A valid argument in his terms is one in which the premises "logically imply" the conclusion. Implication is defined in terms of the logical truth of a corresponding conditional. Thus, the premises

All men are mortal
Socrates is a man
―――――――――

logically imply the conclusion

Socrates is mortal.

In canonical notation the argument appears as

$(x)(x \text{ is a man} \rightarrow x \text{ is mortal})$
s is a man
―――――――――
s is mortal.

This implication holds because the corresponding conditional:

If $(x)(x \text{ is a man} \rightarrow x \text{ is mortal})$ & s is a man then s is mortal,

is a logical truth. The schema corresponding to this conditional is

$$[(x)(Fx \rightarrow Gx) \,\&\, Fa] \rightarrow Ga$$

Varying other predicates for F and G and names for a in the original true conditional will yield only true conditional sentences.

If logical truths are those in which only logical constants occur essentially, then the question of the scope or extent of logic depends on what we take to be a logical constant. Quine lists as the logical constants the truth functional connectives 'not', 'and', 'or', 'if, then' and 'if and only if'; the quantifiers 'all' and 'some'; and the identity predicate '$a = b$'. Logical truths in which the truth functional connectives occur essentially are the subject of the logic of sentences or truth functional logic. For this, the basic part of logic, there are decision procedures, that is, mechanical methods or algorithms, for discovering these logical truths. The method of truth tables is one such procedure. Quine himself has developed algorithms of this sort. The best known of these are in his textbook *Methods of Logic* (1950). Sentential logic has been proved consistent and complete; its consistency means that no contradictions can be derived, and its completeness assures us that every one of the logical truths can be proved.

The full logic of quantification supplements the truth functional connectives with quantifiers, predicates and individual variables. Alonzo Church has shown that, unlike truth functional logic, the full theory of quantifiers and relational predicates can have no decision procedure. However, even though there is no mechanical procedure for establishing the quantificational truths of logic, we are guaranteed, by the completeness of quantificational logic (established by Kurt Gödel in 1930), that all such logical truths are provable.[3]

Quantificational logic is also known as first order or elementary logic. The question of whether to count '=' as a logical constant is answered affirmatively by Quine. One of his reasons is that first order logic plus the principles of identity are complete (as established by Gödel).[4] Another reason is the topic neutrality of the identity predicate. It is used in all the sciences and the variables it requires are like those of logical theory in that they range over all objects. A last consideration is that a case can be made for reducing identity to the other notions of quantificational logic. In summary, for Quine logic is first order logic with identity.

Quine falls squarely in the camp of Frege, Russell and Whitehead in holding that mathematics is reducible to set theory, the theory of the "is a member of" predicate, the sign for which is '∈'. We would write

'Socrates is a member of the class of man'

as

'$s \in \{x \mid x \text{ is a man}\}$', that is, Socrates ∈ the class of men.

Given the theory of membership and the theory of first order logic plus identity, Quine and his logicist predecessors introduce all mathematical notions as definitional abbreviations, for example, a number is defined as a special set, addition as a special function on these sets, and so on. The question to be posed here is whether '∈' should be considered a logical constant, that is, does logic include set theory? Frege, Russell and Whitehead held that it did.

More recently, many philosophers, Quine among them, have come to restrict the word 'logic' to first order quantificational theory plus identity exclusive of set theory.[5] Among Quine's reasons for this restriction are the following. First, the presence of paradoxes in intuitive set theory, especially the Russell paradox mentioned earlier, has led to axiomatized set theory. The principles of the latter are designed to avoid these paradoxes and are far from obvious. Set theory in this respect differs from first order logic in that its principles are not obvious. There is a general consensus about elementary logic, which is lacking in the case of set theory. Alternative set theories have the status of so many tentative hypotheses. This, by the way, gives credence to Quine's view that mathematics based on set theory is not so very different from other sciences, whose theoretical foundations are not as well established as we might wish.

A second reason for distinguishing set theory from logic is provided by Kurt Gödel's proof of the incompleteness of systems as powerful as set theory. Gödel established that any system (such as set theory) powerful enough to derive the truths of elementary arithmetic is, if consistent, incomplete. That is to say, there are arithmetical truths which are not derivable within this system. The incompleteness of set theory contrasts sharply with the completeness of elementary logic. Yet another difference between set theory and ordinary logic bears on the ontological commitments of these two. While the variables of logic range over all sorts of objects, those of set theory have sets as their distinctive values. That is to say, the ontology of set theory is somewhat more restrictive. In his earlier writings, Quine spoke of a broader and narrower conception of logic. He spoke in this way because the issue of what to count as a logical constant is in good part terminological.[6] Frege defined analyticity as logical truths enriched by definitions. By 'logic' Frege meant a theory that does similar work as set theory, and he could claim that Kant was wrong in thinking that the truths of arithmetic, for example, '7 + 5 = 12', are synthetic. Quine, using 'logic' differently from Frege, can agree with Kant that the truths of arithmetic are not truths of logic. That the borderline between logical truths and others is arguable is not an embarrassment. Indeed, it is in keeping with Quine's position of gradualism that the differences between logic, mathematics and theoretical science are not as hard and fast as one would make them seem: one can balance the differences between logic and mathematics noted above with similarities. For instance, mathematics, like logic, is universally applied; that is, every science makes use of both logic and mathematics.

Expressing the principles of logic and set theory

Accepting Quine's construal of logic as the theory of truth functions, quantification and identity, we now turn to the question of how he expresses its principles, a matter of no small ontological significance, as we shall soon see. To realize the virtues of Quine's approach, we shall begin by contrasting it with the sort of presentation found in most ordinary textbooks. Let us consider truth functional logic and, in particular, the following principle: $p \vee {\sim}p$.

To the present reader versed in questions of ontology, the above expression should be cause for bewilderment. What type of expression is '*p*'? Many ordinary logic texts would answer that it is a variable: some say it is a propositional and others a sentential variable. But, if '*p*' is a variable, what sort of object is its value? When one subscribes to the dictum that to be is to be the value of a variable, the admission of a new style of variables has consequences for one's ontology. Let the reader open any logic text to examine the statement of the theories of logic, and he will be forced to reckon with the question of what these expressions mean.

Authors treating '*p*' as a variable have in the main taken four different courses. The first involves an intensionalist ontology in so far as it construes '*p*' as a propositional variable. For example, at times Church has taken this course.[7] To quantify here and assert $(\exists p)(p \vee \sim p)$ is to say that there is a proposition such that it either is or is not the case. More specifically, '*p*' is a variable which takes sentences as its substituends, for example, 'Brutus killed Caesar'. And these sentences in turn name propositions which are the values of the variables in question.

Quine rejects this approach for two reasons.[8] The first is ontological while the second might be thought of as semantic. If we must expand our ontology to include new types of entities (let alone intensional ones), we should do so not at the outset but only after failing to find an alternative, less costly solution. This is but another application of Occam's razor: entities should not be multiplied beyond necessity. Quine does indeed offer a less costly solution – the use of schemas to be explained below.

The semantic reason for not treating '*p*' as a variable is that Quine thinks this approach rests on a mistake. For Quine, the position taken by variables is one suitable to names. For the variable '*x*' in '*x* is a man' we can sensibly write the name 'Socrates'. The values of the variable '*x*' can be thought of as the objects named by the substituends of '*x*'. But if names are the suitable substituends for variables, then reconsider '*p*'. For '*p*' in '$p \vee \sim p$' we could sensibly put the substitution instance 'Brutus killed Caesar' (yielding 'Brutus killed Caesar or Brutus did not kill Caesar'). If '*p*' is a variable, then its values are the *objects named by the sentences* that are substitution instances. The mistake here is in the supposition that sentences name objects. Sentences are meaningful parts of speech but they are not names. So while Quine acknowledges that on other grounds one may argue that sentences express a proposition or that propositions and not sentences are true or false, it is simply false that sentences like 'Brutus killed Caesar' are names. Even if there are propositions, sentences do not name them; they convey them as their meanings.

A second course was taken by Frege. He construed quantification over sentential positions as quantification over truth values. The values which variables like '*p*' ranged over were the special objects, the True and the False; '*p*' and '*q*' so construed might be called truth-value variables. Accordingly, the substituends 'Brutus killed Caesar' and 'Portia killed Caesar' were treated as names for one of these two objects. The admission of the True and the False does mean a major increase in one's ontology. But unlike propositions, the True and the False are extensional objects: the identity condition '*p* = *q*' (construed as truth-value variables) is simply that '*p*' and '*q*' refer to the same truth value. (More than this identity of truth-values is required when '*p*' and '*q*' are interpreted as propositional variables.)

Nonetheless, Quine would still rather not increase his ontology to include additional and rather unusual objects such as the True and the False. They serve no theoretical purpose that cannot be accomplished by more conservative means.[9] In addition, the semantic point noted in connection with propositional variables applies with equal force to treating '*p*' and '*q*' as truth-value variables. The sentence "Brutus killed Caesar", which can serve as a substitution instance for '*p*', is said to be true, but this is quite different from saying that this sentence names a special object called the True. To repeat a point, sentences are not names.

A third approach is that given by Quine in *Mathematical Logic*. In this work he avoids the above difficulties by expressing the principles of logic metalogically. Throughout his career Quine has fastidiously distinguished the different levels at which language can be used. To say that Boston is a city is to use the word 'Boston' to refer to some non-linguistic object located in Massachusetts. To say that 'Boston' is a word with six letters is to *mention* the word. The above distinction between language that refers to non-linguistic objects and language that refers to linguistic objects is one facet of what is known as the use–mention distinction. Tarski, speaking of the same phenomenon, distinguishes *object-language expressions* about non-linguistic objects like Boston from *metalinguistic expressions* about the expression 'Boston'. In *Mathematical Logic*, Quine presents his system, which includes truth functional logic, metalinguistically.[10] To avoid confusion, Greek letters 'Φ' and 'Ψ' are adopted as sentential variables. 'Ψ' is a metalinguistic variable having as its values sentences of the object language. The substituends for such variables are not the sentences of the object language but rather the names of such sentences. By ascending to this metalinguistic approach we avoid the two types of difficulties that accompany the adoption of either propositional or truth-value variables. The ontological commitment of metalinguistic quantification is to a realm of linguistic entities, namely, the expressions of the object language in question. Ontologically such a course is irreproachable, since whatever our views are, we expect to be committed to the existence of linguistic entities anyway. Moreover, the semantic problem, which arises for the object-language variables we have so far considered, does not arise here. The substituends for the variable 'Φ' are truly names. They are metalinguistic names of sentences of the object language. 'Brutus killed Caesar' is the sentence within the single quotation marks. That is to say, one way of forming names of expressions – mentioning expressions and thereby ascending to the metalanguage – is to place them in quotation marks. Consider the following sample object-language sentence: Brutus killed Caesar. Its name is 'Brutus killed Caesar'.

A fourth and last alternative in treating 'p' as a variable consists of a non-Quinian approach to quantification which has come to be known as substitutional quantification.[11] Indeed, Quine has been concerned with stressing the differences between the substitutional and other approaches, and with exploring their relative advantages. He refers to his Tarskian oriented approach as referential or as objectual.[12] Recall that for Quine '$(\exists x)(x$ is a man$)$' is true when an object that is a value of the variable 'x' happens to be a man; he has coined the terms 'objectual' and 'referential' quantification for his interpretation. This idea provides the basis for saying quantification furnishes a clue to existential–ontological questions. The substitutional view of quantification explains '$(\exists x)(x$ is a man$)$' as true when '$(\exists x)(x$ is a man$)$' has a true substitution instance, as in the case of 'Socrates is a man'. Hence for proponents of this view, '$(\exists x)$' can be read as 'Sometimes true' and in particular in the above example as 'It is sometimes true that x is a man' or 'In some instances x is a man'. Where the existential–referential view of quantification invokes an object as a value of a variable, the substitutional view invokes a substitution instance (substituend) of a variable.

The substitutional theorist explains the use of variables for sentence positions, for example, 'p' in '$(\exists p)(p \vee {\sim}p)$' as follows. It merely says that in some instances '$p \vee {\sim}p$' is the case and '$(p)(p \vee {\sim}p)$' says that '$p \vee {\sim}p$' is true for all instances, that is, is always true. No mention is made of values of variables, thereby initially avoiding the question of ontological increase when quantifying with respect to new styles of variables. Note that here 'p' is still an object-language variable. It is a mistake to confuse the variables of substitutional quantification, which might have no ontological import, with the variables of "referential" metalinguistic quantification, such as 'Φ', which commit one ontologically but just happen to be at a metalinguistic level of language.

The semantic point which Quine applied to propositional and truth-value variables does not apply to the substitutional interpretation of '*p*'. On the substitutional account, a sentence such as 'Brutus killed Caesar' is a substituend for '*p*' but no further assumptions are made about this substituend naming values or about the mistaken view that sentences are names.

Quine's attitude toward substitutional quantification is ambivalent. On the one hand, it appears to offer exciting prospects for the would-be nominalist. In this direction, Quine explored how far one can go in avoiding referential quantification over abstract objects by having recourse to the substitutional view.[13] On the other hand, the substitutional approach clashes with Quine's programme to explicate ontological commitment. In the substitutional view the treatment of '*p*' as a quantifiable variable needn't have ontological significance; in fact, quantification of any sort whatsoever might be construed substitutionally as having no ontological significance.[14] For Quine to adopt a substitutional view is to cease directly talking of objects and hence to cease expressing an ontological position. Substitutional quantification, though, has its share of problems.

One line of criticism of the substitutional view that Quine has explored concerns quantification with regard to objects that do not have names.[15] There are physical objects such as grains of sand, atoms and electrons which are without names. In such cases referential quantification can refer to the objects without recourse to names. Substitutional quantification, where the substituends are names, would be at a disadvantage. It differs from objectual–referential quantification when we have more objects than substituends to name them. In these cases substitutional quantification does not enable us to express certain types of generalizations. This is but one of Quine's indications of the shortcomings of substitutional quantification. However, the would-be nominalist might at this point propose retaining referential quantification for physical objects and adopting substitutional quantification for abstract objects. But Quine has pointed out that the prospects even here are quite dim. Of special significance is the fact that substitutional quantification is not capable of expressing the impredicative notions which are an integral part of classical mathematics. By contrast, the referential variety of quantification is quite compatible with impredicativity. The issue of dispensing with impredicative notions was mentioned in Chapter 3 in connection with alternatives to being committed to sets in using mathematics.

We have considered four ways of understanding logical principles such as '$p \vee {\sim}p$' where 'p' is taken as a variable, namely, as a propositional, a truth value, a metalinguistic and a substitutional variable. However, Quine's most distinctive and best-known approach, to be found, among other places, in his "Set Theoretic Foundations for Logic", *Elementary Logic*, *Methods of Logic*, "Logic and the Reification of Universals", *Philosophy of Logic* and elsewhere, differs from all four of these. Quine does not take 'p' as a variable at all but as a schematic letter. A most important difference between variables and schematic letters is that variables can be quantified over. This is what, in Quine's referential view of quantification, gives quantification its ontological significance (indicating how many values of the variables are referred to). A schematic letter, however, is a dummy expression; in its place we can put appropriate parts of speech. Thus 'p' in '$p \vee {\sim}p$' indicates where sentences must be inserted. The schema can be instructively contrasted with a resulting sentence: 'Brutus killed Caesar or Brutus did not kill Caesar'. This is a true sentence, in fact a logical truth. The schema '$p \vee {\sim}p$' is not even a sentence, but merely a pseudo-sentence. Unlike the Brutus sentence, a schema is not capable of being either true or false. Moreover, schemas ought not to be confused with the metalinguistic expression '$\Phi \vee {\sim}\Phi$'. Again, a schema is not strictly speaking a part of a language (even a metalanguage); it is a dummy expression – a placeholder for "real" expressions. However, there are important relations between schemata and logical truths; for instance, a schema such as the one above is said by Quine and his followers to be "valid" when it is the schema of a logical truth.

So far we have concentrated on expressing the principles of truth functional logic. Similar remarks are in order for quantificational logic. The principle '$(x)(Fx \vee {\sim}Fx)$', which corresponds, for example, to 'Everything is either yellow or not yellow' raises analogous questions about the letters 'F' and 'G'. If they were treated as variables, then, if referentially construed, they would be either intensional property variables or extensional class variables. In *Mathematical Logic*, Quine uses special metalinguistic variables to express such principles, whereas substitutional quantification theorists would make do with predicates providing substitution instances. Once again Quine's more distinctive attitude is to regard '*F*' and '*G*' as schematic letters and not as variables at all. Thus '*F*' is a dummy expression indicating where a genuine predicate can be placed, for example, 'is yellow' can be put in the above positions and thus yields '$(x)(x$ is yellow or $\sim x$ is yellow)'.

The logician who objectually, that is, referentially, quantifies over predicate positions, for example, '$(\exists F)(Fx)$' (this step results in what is called higher order logic, as contrasted with first order or elementary logic where the quantification is confined to individual variables), leaves himself open to the same sort of criticisms raised earlier. What sort of objects are the values of the new variables? Such quantification increases one's ontology to include properties or sets. Of the extensional construal of '$(\exists F)(Fx)$', Quine has said that it is semantically misleading and is "set theory in sheep's clothing".[16] In addition there is the semantic error of treating predicates as names. If '*F*' is a referential variable, then its substituends, for example, 'is yellow', should name a value of the variable. But 'is yellow' is a predicate and not a name. Some would say that 'is yellow' expresses or has a property as its intension, or that 'is yellow' circumscribes or has a class as its extension. However, this is beside the point since 'is yellow' is not a name, not even of either of the property yellowness or the class of yellow objects.

For Quine, all logic is first order logic. It provides us with a canonic notation. If one wishes to talk about abstract objects (sets, properties, propositions, truth values, etc.) it is more perspicuous to do so via the variables '*x*', '*y*', '*z*'. These variables of first order logic can have individual concrete objects as their values as well as abstract objects such as properties, sets and so on. In this respect Quine's slogan "To be is to be the value of a variable" could be misleading; it would be more accurate to say that to be is to be the value of a variable of first order logic.

Thus the underlying logic in Quine's most famous systems – "New Foundations" and *Mathematical Logic* – is first order logic. To reduce mathematics to logic and set theory, first order logic must be supplemented with special axioms for sets. These axioms are stated in the language of first order logic with only one style of variable. The substituends for these variables are singular terms: concrete singular terms, for example, 'Socrates', for concrete individuals; and abstract singular terms, for example, 'the class of even numbers', that is, '$\{x \mid x$ is divisible by $2\}$', for sets or classes. Where Quine conjectures, as he sometimes does, the introduction of intensional objects, he accordingly develops a notation for the abstract singular terms, for example, 'the property of being red', that refer to them.[17] The underlying logic remains the same. In summary, Quine's canonical notation recognizes only one style of variable; it suffices for reference to any sort of entity and need not be supplemented when we try to express the principles of logic, set theory or even theories of properties, propositions or anything else.

Are logic and mathematics true by convention?

With our newly acquired information on the scope and nature of logic, we are ready to state Quine's criticisms of the attempt to justify logic and mathematics (the latter via set theory) in a different manner from that of other sciences. Following him, we will refer to this attempt as the linguistic doctrine of logical truth. Prominent among the varieties of this doctrine is the notion that logic and mathematics are in some sense true by convention and that physics and other natural sciences are not. Quine first published his doubts about the "difference" in epistemological grounding for the so-called "formal" and "factual" sciences in the essay "Truth by Convention", which appeared in 1936 in a Festschrift for Alfred North Whitehead.

In this early essay we find his scepticism about the analytic (linguistic) and synthetic (factual) distinction – later dubbed one of the dogmas of empiricism – addressed exclusively toward the claim that logic and mathematics are analytic. In the later "Two Dogmas" essay, his scepticism is extended to other forms of analyticity, and whereas the early essay argues for the common epistemological character of all the sciences, no reference is made to holistic empiricism. In 1954, Quine submitted the paper "Carnap and Logical Truth" for a prospective volume on Carnap; here he refined and supplemented the earlier criticisms of truth by convention.

The terms "convention" and "conventionalism" have been bandied about in twentieth-century philosophy. Quine examines various versions of the claim that logic and set theory are true by convention. There are as many of these versions as there are different senses of "convention". Conventionalism can be construed as a matter of: (1) definition; (2) arbitrary axiomatization; (3) formalization-disinterpretation; and (4) arbitrary hypothesizing. Quine finds that these claims (a) are based on confusions, or (b) are not distinctive of any one science, or (c) are void of empirical significance.

Ever since the second half of the nineteenth century, there has been a great deal of investigation into the nature of deductive systems. At the risk of oversimplifying, we can say that the discovery of paradoxes and anomalies was a significant factor which led to reformulating the paradox-laden disciplines as deductive systems. The situation was particularly acute in mathematics, for example, the development of consistent non-Euclidean geometries and the discovery of paradoxes concerning numbers and sets. If a contradiction is demonstrated in a science, it is natural to order the sentences of that science so as to locate the source of the contradiction. The method of axiomatization is just such a procedure. The axioms of a system are those sentences which are used to prove all the other sentences (these are called theorems). Should our theorems contradict each other, we can then try to locate the source of this in one or more of our axioms. The guilty axiom is revised and the paradox removed. Thus Russell's paradox has motivated different axiomatizations of set theory.

A more sophisticated approach to the treatment of a deductive system is formalization. A formalized deductive system is one in which the expressions occurring in the system are stripped of their significance and regarded as so many distinct deposits of ink. The idea is that by disinterpreting the signs of the system, we can be more explicit and concentrate more easily on the purely formal or syntactical relations. Deduction is one such formal relation, that is, the notion of deduction or proof is susceptible of a purely formal definition. We can treat the proof of a sentence as a sequence of well-formed deposits of ink, generated according to rules, with the sentence proved as the last well-formed deposit. In this way David Hilbert formalized geometry and propositional logic and thus was able to prove certain important results about them, such as their consistency and completeness.

Axiomatization and formalization are by now well recognized and quite universally accepted procedures, but they are not distinctive of logic and mathematics. Although branches of mathematics and logic were among the first to be axiomatized and/or formalized, these methods can be, and have been, applied to physics, biology and the study of parts and wholes, as well as other subjects. Furthermore, neither of these procedures gives credence to the notion of truth by convention.

In axiomatizing a given subject we somewhat arbitrarily choose certain sentences to serve as axioms from which to derive the others.

One sense then given to the expression 'truth by convention' is that axioms are true by convention in that they are arbitrarily chosen. But this picture of the matter is confused. In axiomatizing, we are merely sorting out among the truths of a science those which will play a special role, namely, serve as axioms from which we derive the others. The sentences sorted out are already true in a non-conventional or ordinary sense.

The fact that there are frequently different ways of axiomatizing the same subject and hence that there is a certain leeway or choice or arbitrariness bears only upon the matter of ordering already true sentences. Quine calls this point of axiomatization 'discursive postulation':

> Discursive postulation is mere selection, from a preexisting body of truths, of certain ones for use as a basis from which to derive others, initially known or unknown. What discursive postulation fixes is not truth, but only some particular ordering of the truths, for purposes perhaps of pedagogy or perhaps of inquiry into the logical relationships.[18]

The thesis that a formalized discipline, in virtue of its being formalized and not merely axiomatized, is true by convention seems to be that in a system whose signs have been freed from their ordinary meanings we are free to do with such signs what we will. The rules for manipulation and/or interpretation of the expressions are open to choice and are, in this sense, a matter of convention. But this again is a confusion. If we disinterpret a sentence and thereby ignore what it means or refers to, then we are left with a deposit of ink marks which are no more true or false than a geological deposit is. The truth-value of a sentence is essentially connected with its reference, and to formalize and put aside matters of reference is to put aside all questions of truth-value. Suppose we formalize the sentence 'Socrates is mortal or Socrates is not mortal'. To help us abstract the words from their customary reference, let us use a circle, ○, for 'or', △ for 'not' and a vertical bar, '|', for 'Socrates is mortal'. If one now says that '|○△|' is true by convention – since we can choose as we wish the rules for manipulating or interpreting the signs – then we must reply that in so far as the string '|○△|' has no meaning, is uninterpreted, it is neither true nor false in any sense; in so far as it is interpreted, it is true or false in some ordinary non-conventional sense. To paraphrase Quine, in disinterpretation there is no truth by convention because there is no truth.[19] For Quine, as for Frege, Russell–Whitehead, Lesniewski and others, logic and mathematics are fully interpreted systems.

The thesis that logic and/or mathematics are true by convention sometimes takes the form that their sentences are true by definition. But to define an expression is to show how to translate it into other expressions. For example one can define the conditional sign '$\rightarrow$' in terms of the signs for negation, '~', and conjunction, '&': thus '$\sim(p \ \& \sim q)$' defines '$p \rightarrow q$'. Given a suitable number of primitive defining expressions ('~', '&', '(x)' and '=' will do for logic), we can introduce by definition other logical signs, for example, '$\rightarrow$' or '$(\exists x)$'. The thesis that the truths of logic are true by definition and in this respect a matter of convention has quite limited force. It merely tells us that the logical principle '$p \rightarrow p$' is true by definition relative to its being a definitional transcription of '$\sim(p \ \& \sim p)$'. But what then accounts for the truth of '$\sim(p \ \& \sim p)$'? Since it is already in primitive notation, it cannot be true by definition but must be true in some other presumably non-conventional sense. Hence truths by definition are at best true relative to truths in the ordinary sense.[20] In other words, given a logical or mathematical truth in primitive notation, its truth is not a matter of definition; and given a second sentence that by definition is equivalent to the truth in the primitive notation, the truth of the second sentence is not merely a matter of definition but rests on the non-definitional truth of the first sentence. We hasten to add that such relative truth by definition is found in any discipline in which there are definitions, and is not peculiar to logic or mathematics.

Yet another way of stating the doctrine of truth by convention is in terms of the arbitrary element in framing hypotheses. Various proposals have been made for different systems of set theories designed to avoid Russell's paradox. There is an element of latitude in producing and deciding among the different hypotheses. (Quine reminds us that this latitude is not peculiar to logic and mathematics but occurs in other disciplines such as physics.) Furthermore, the element of arbitrariness or conventionality is a property of the act of hypothesizing and not of the hypothesis itself. To confuse the mode of genesis of a hypothesis with its cognitive value, that is, the grounds of its truth, is a mistake which pragmatists have labelled the genetic fallacy. The grounds for the truth of a hypothesis are independent of its origin (whether it is adopted in a spirit of convention or in any other fashion). Quine speaks of the act of hypothesizing in cases like the above as legislative postulation:

> The distinction between the legislative and the discursive refers thus to the act, and not to its enduring consequence, in the case of postulation as in the case of definition. This is because we are taking the notion of truth by convention fairly literally and simplemindedly, for lack of an intelligible alternative. So conceived, conventionality is a passing trait, significant at the moving front of science but useless in classifying the sentences behind the lines. It is a trait of events and not of sentences. Might we not still project a derivative trait upon the sentences themselves, thus speaking of a sentence as forever true by convention if its first adoption as true was a convention? No; this, if done seriously, involves us in the most unrewarding historical conjecture. Legislative postulation contributes truths which become integral to the corpus of truths; the artificiality of their origin does not linger as a localized quality, but suffuses the corpus.[21]

Quine's thoughts on the grounding of logical truth are too numerous for us to go into all of them, but we can examine three more in this chapter. Some adherents of the linguistic theory of logical truth say that a sentence like 'Everything is self-identical' is true purely in virtue of the language in which it is couched, that is, solely in virtue of the meaning of '='. However, one could just as well claim that the sentence in question reveals a self-evident trait of the nature of the world. Quine's point is that these claims about the grounds for this truth from the logic of identity are empirically indistinguishable. As William James put it in a now famous story:

> Some years ago, being with a camping party in the mountains, I returned from a solitary ramble to find every one engaged in a ferocious metaphysical dispute. The corpus of the dispute was a squirrel – a live squirrel supposed to be clinging to one side of a tree trunk, while over against the tree's opposite side a human being was imagined to stand. This human witness tries to get sight of the squirrel by moving rapidly around the tree, but no matter how fast he goes, the squirrel moves as fast in the opposite direction, and always keeps the tree between himself and the man, so that never a glimpse of him is caught. The

> resultant metaphysical problem now is this: Does the man go round the squirrel or not? He goes round the tree, sure enough, and the squirrel is on the tree; but does he go round the squirrel? In the unlimited leisure of the wilderness, discussion had been worn threadbare. Everyone had taken sides, and was obstinate; and the numbers on both sides were even. Each side when I appeared therefore appealed to me to make it a majority.
>
> Mindful of the scholastic adage that whenever you meet a contradiction you must make a distinction, I immediately sought and found one, as follows: "Which party is right," I said, "depends on what you practically mean by 'going round' the squirrel. If you mean passing from the north of him to the east, then to the south, then to the west, and then to the north of him again, obviously the man does go round him, for he occupies these successive positions. But if on the contrary you mean being first in front of him, then on the right of him, then behind him, then on his left, and finally in front again, it is quite as obvious that the man fails to go round him, for by the compensating movements the squirrel makes, he keeps his belly turned towards the man all the time, and his back turned away. Make the distinction, and there is no occasion for any farther dispute. You are both right, and both wrong according as you conceive the verb "to go round" in one practical fashion or the other.[22]

In such circumstances the correct conclusion to draw is that both formulas – that logical truth depends on language alone and that logical truth depends on the structure of reality – are empty verbalisms with no explanatory power.[23]

The obviousness of the truths of logic comes to play an important role in Quine's demarcating of logical truth.[24] Logical truths, exclusive of set theory, are either actually obvious or potentially so. The completeness of first order logic guarantees that starting from actually obvious axioms we can proceed by actually obvious rules of inference to establish all the remaining truths. However, this obviousness should not be construed as evidence for the linguistic theory of logical truth. Were someone to deny an obvious truth such as 'It is raining' while standing in the rain or the logical truth 'If Brutus killed Caesar, then Brutus killed Caesar', we would most likely take this as evidence that he misunderstood the sentences, that is, the language involved, and perhaps that he meant something else. The denial of obvious truths is so basic a form of disagreement that it appears to count as evidence for what language means and hence that the truth of the sentence involved is merely a matter of language. However, if the denial of an obvious truth counts as evidence for the truth being linguistic, then we would be led to the absurdity that "It is raining" is a linguistic truth.

A similar point about the obvious nature of logical truths can be made by considering the role of such truths in constructing translations. A basic premise for translating one language into another is to save the obvious. This amounts to no more than arguing that obvious truths are a crucial part of the data to be explained. One reason that logical truths are so central to language – and perhaps a reason for thinking that they are linguistically based – is precisely that they are obvious. Every translation must preserve them. In this sense "save the logical truths" is a convention but it is a rather special case; it is the convention underlying all science to "save the data" (which in linguistics in part means "save the obvious").

A last consideration which might deceive the unwary into holding the linguistic theory of logical truth is that the attempt to generalize about a logical truth frequently involves talking about language, what Quine has called semantic ascent. The linguistic theorist concludes from this talk of topics, such as logical validity as talk of language, that logical truths are merely truths of language. Let us recall that the logical truth 'Brutus killed Caesar or Brutus did not kill Caesar' is not readily generalized upon by the use of variables. '$p \vee {\sim}p$' where 'p' is a referential object-language variable involves an increase in ontology and in addition the error of confusing a sentence with a name. One solution to expressing the logical form of the above truth is to construe 'p' schematically. Schemas such as '$p \vee {\sim}p$' cannot be said to be true or false since they are not really sentences, but they can be said to be valid. Validity means simply that any sentence put in the place of the schematic letters will result in a logical truth. The notion of validity involves semantic ascent to the metalanguage where we speak of sentences replacing schematic letters. Thus, in simulating generalization about a logical truth via the notion of validity, we talk about language. The linguistic doctrine errs, though, when it concludes from this that logical truth or validity is simply a matter of language. The nature of a logical truth (and hence that of validity which depends on it) is that a sentence is a logical truth if it is true and remains true when we vary any of its non-logical parts. This definition circumscribes the logical truths as a subclass of the broader class of truths. The Tarskian-correspondence-type definition of truth applied to this broader class certifies the non-linguistic element in all truths: "Logical theory, despite its heavy dependence on talk of language, is already world-oriented rather than language-oriented; and the truth predicate makes it so."[25]

Challenging Quine: a broader conception of logic

For Quine, logic is first order predicate logic and quantifiers are limited to its singular terms. A case can be made that logic should also include quantifiers for other parts of speech such as predicates and sentences. Two arguments will be offered: (1) the naturalness of quantifying into predicate and sentence positions; and (2) problems concerning Quine's schema.

One reason for having quantifiers for predicate and sentence positions is that it is so natural an extension of first order logic as to appear inevitable.[26] Just as there are valid first order principles of generalization such as for arguing from

Socrates is human i.e. Hs

to

Something is human i.e. $(\exists x)Hx$,

there are corresponding principles for generalizing with regard to predicate, and to sentence positions. It appears to be as natural to validly reason from

Socrates is human i.e. Hs

to

Something is true of (or applies to) Socrates i.e. $(\exists F)(Fs)$.

There are a number of alternatives for providing truth conditions for these quantifiers. Such truth conditions will allow for the non-first order/non-Quinian quantifiers of this section. They also explain the non-existential account of quantification that was taken (Challenging Quine, Chapter 2) for solving the Plato's beard problem.

Moreover, the use of these quantifiers need not require additional ontological assumptions such as treating non-singular terms, for example, predicates and sentences, as singular terms. One type of truth condition would consist of combining a substitutional treatment with a non-substitutional one.[27] Another approach would revise and extend a method introduced by Benson Mates.[28] We can extend Mates's method to allow for empty names and for generalizing with regard to predicate and sentence positions. This will provide us with some advantages of substitutional quantifiers without taking on its problems. Quantification for predicate and sentence positions does not require taking those positions as though they involved singular terms as substituends and treating predicates and sentences as names. There need be no increase in ontological items since the substituends do not involve a commitment to new items. The predicates have their extensions but don't name them or properties. Sentences are true or false but don't require "Truth" and "Falsity" or propositions as their semantic values.

On our revision of Mates an atomic/singular sentence is true just in case the individual the singular term refers to is among the individuals the predicate applies to. On this revision atomic sentences are false when a singular term is vacuous. Generalizations (quantificational sentences) are true depending upon their instances being true when suitably reinterpreted, that is, given different semantic values. Thus, 'Vulcan exists' is false (it or the sentences that it might be defined in terms of, such as $(\exists x)(x = \text{Vulcan})$), since it contains a vacuous term. Its negation '~Vulcan exists' is true and serves as the premise of the Plato's beard puzzle considered at the end of Chapter 4. With this premise instance as true,

'Something does not exist' i.e. $\sim(\exists x)(x \text{ exists})$

is true as well. The premise is the instance that is required for the truth of the generalization. A "some" generalization has as its truth condition that an instance of it be true on at least one reinterpretation.

Given the truth of the instance

Socrates is human

the truth condition warrants the truth of the higher order generalization

$(\exists F)Fs$ i.e. Something is true of Socrates.

With relevance to Challenging Quine, Chapter 7, consider the following. From the instance

John believes that snow is white and so does Mary

it follows by natural rules of inference and is sanctioned by our truth condition that

$(\exists p)$(John believes that p and Mary believes that p),
i.e. There is something that both John and Mary believe.

A second reason for having quantifiers for various parts of speech and not just singular terms concerns being able to adequately express the principles of logic. Alonzo Church persuasively argued that just as arithmetic contains object-language generalizations, the same should be the case for logic.[29] We should be able to state object-language generalizations of instances of logical truths. Given the truth of particular cases of logical truth, such as "if it is raining, then it is raining", "if snow is white, then snow is white" and so on, we should be able to state the general case. Consider how when we have specific instances of truths of arithmetic such as $4 + 1 = 1 + 4$, $5 + 3 = 3 + 5$, we also have object-language generalizations: $(x)(y)(x + y = y + x)$. In order to attain a semblance of such generality for logic, Quine introduced his notion of schemas. Let us cast a critical eye on Quine's schema for sentence logic: $p \rightarrow p$ and for predicate logic: $(x)(Fx \rightarrow Fx)$. We are told that schematic letters, such as 'p' and 'F', are neither object-language expressions nor metalinguistic variables. This is only a negative characterization and out of keeping with Quine's requirement for being precise. Worse still, the introduction of schemas involves positing additional types of expressions and additional rules determining their well-formedness. This conflicts with the simplicity constraint and is particularly ironic considering the stress Quine placed on doing without names in his canonic notation. There seems to be no way in which Quine, who confines the language of logic to first order logic, can meet Church's challenge to express the truths of logic in their full generality and in the object language. It seems perfectly natural to think of schematic letters as object-language variables, although not along the lines Quine suggests. So, we might, in the object language, express what Quine has in mind by his schema $p \rightarrow p$ as the object language $(p)(p \rightarrow p)$. We can do this without treating the variable 'p' involved in the quantification as ontologically committing us to propositions or truth values. We might rely on our variant of Mates's truth condition.[30] Put rather sketchily, $(p)(p \rightarrow p)$ is true if and only if an instance of it remains true when the simple sentences involved are reinterpreted according to all the ways in which they can be true or false.

Chapter 6

Analyticity and indeterminacy

In Chapter 5 we considered logical truths, and the claims that such sentences are analytic and grounded in language. There are other sentences that are also said to be analytic and non-empirical in their foundation, even though they are not logical truths in the precise Quinian sense of this term. Such sentences as

> 'All bachelors are unmarried men.'

and

> 'Nothing is taller than itself.'

are purportedly different in kind from factual, empirically justifiable sentences. Although they too are said to be true in virtue of the meanings of their terms, they are not strictly speaking logical truths. To see this, we need merely apply the definition of a logical truth, that is, truths which remain true whatever replacements we put in for their non-logical parts. If, in the first sentence, we replace the non-logical part 'bachelor' with 'husband', we obtain the false sentence 'All husbands are unmarried men'. Similarly, in the second, when we replace the relational predicate 'is taller than' with 'is as large as', it yields the false sentence 'Nothing is as large as itself'.

Quine's approach to all the sentences called 'analytic' is to separate the logical truths from the others. However, this separation is primarily for polemical purposes. While he holds that no analytic sentence, logical truth or otherwise is non-empirically justified (the mistake in thinking so stems from the dogma of reductionism: the non-holistic view that empirical evidence does not apply to some sentences), he subjects the non-logical analytic truths to a further criticism. Where the class of logical truths is capable of precise definition and can be clearly distinguished, the other analytic truths defy any such analysis of their exact nature.

We will first consider Quine's critique of this distinction as the dogma discussed in the first part of "Two Dogmas of Empiricism". Later we will examine the criticisms that follow from the indeterminacy thesis Quine puts forward in *Word and Object*.

In Chapter 5 we examined analytical truths, where these were defined as truths the denial of which leads to a contradiction. Affirmatively put, these are the logical truths: the sentences that follow solely from the principles of logic. Quine's definition of a logical truth clearly and precisely defines exactly these truths. Granted the list of logical particles, we know exactly which sentences are logically true. Of course, this merely circumscribes a subset of a broader class of truths, and no evidence is found for any essential difference in their epistemological foundations. All truths are empirically justifiable holistically and among these the logical truths can be sharply distinguished. Can a similarly sharp distinction be made for another additional type of analytical truth?

Consider one of our examples of an analytic but non-logical truth. The first, 'All bachelors are unmarried', although not a logical truth, does bear a certain resemblance to one, namely, 'All unmarried men are unmarried men'. If the subject of this logical truth, 'unmarried men', is replaced by the synonymous expression 'bachelor', then we obtain a broader class of analytic truths. Following Quine we will characterize the additional analytic truths which form the broader class as those sentences which are the result of putting a synonym for its counterpart in a logical truth. The clarity of this definition and the distinction it is intended to express depend on the clarity of the definiens, for a definition is only as clear as the terms of its defining parts. Granted the clarity of the notion of logical truth, the brunt of Quine's criticism of this distinction, as we shall see, falls on the notion of "synonymy" and its presuppositions.

We turn now to Quine's criticisms of the analytic–synthetic distinction. Since we have already dealt with logical truth, in the remainder of this chapter 'analytic' will be used to refer mainly to the broader class of analytic truths.

We shall consider five ways of defining analyticity: (1) the appeal to meanings; (2) the appeal to definition; (3) the appeal to interchangeability; (4) the appeal to semantic rules; and (5) the appeal to the verifiability theory of meaning.

Dispensing with meanings

Perhaps the most common way of defining analyticity is as truth in virtue of the meanings of the words involved. Thus, 'All bachelors are unmarried men' might be regarded as analytic in so far as the meaning of the words 'unmarried man' is included in the meaning of 'bachelor'. This nearly amounts to a restatement of Kant's idea of the inclusion of the predicate concept in the subject concept. A slightly different approach would hypothesize the existence of meanings to explain synonymy and then use synonymy in turn to show how the above sentence is a synonymous instance of a logical truth. By positing meanings we can say that the words 'bachelor' and 'unmarried man' are synonymous, in that in addition to the fact that they refer to the same class of objects, they have exactly the same meaning. In general, one can say that two expressions are synonymous if and only if they share exactly one meaning. Some might also assert that 'Nothing is taller than itself' is analytic in the sense of being true in virtue of the meaning of the expressions involved, and that it is seen to be so by direct inspection of the meaning of the predicate 'is taller than'.

The success of the above explanations of analyticity and synonymy depends on the assumption of meanings. This assumption has its critics. Quine himself has examined several different theories of meaning and found them wanting. Many contemporary philosophers have voiced similar criticisms but they have not taken Quine's radical solution of dispensing with meanings altogether. Let us begin by taking up Quine's comments on three attempts at a theory of meaning: (1) referential theories, that is, meanings as referents; (2) mentalism, that is, meanings as ideas; and (3) intensionalism, that is, meanings as intensional entities.

A good part of the confidence people have that there are meanings rests on the confusion of meaning and reference. While there is no question that terms like 'Socrates' and 'bachelor' for the most part refer to objects (Socrates and individual bachelors, e.g. Elvis before Priscilla) as referents of the terms, these objects are not the meanings. Quine and others have repeated Frege's argument that meanings are not referents.[1] The word 'meaning' is ambiguous and we must remember that we are concerned here with meaning as it explains synonymy and analyticity. As Frege pointed out, since two coreferential terms, for example, 'the evening star' and 'the morning star', both of which refer to Venus, need not be synonymous (have the same meaning), then meanings, whatever they are, are not the same as referents. Quine observes this distinction by clearly divorcing the theory of reference from the theory of meaning.[2] In the former we investigate questions about reference, truth and ontology, whereas in the latter we investigate questions about meanings, synonymy, analyticity and so on. Quine takes it that notable advances have been made in the theory of reference, such as Tarski's semantic theory of truth and the Bolzano–Quine definition of logical truth. On Quine's view, work in the theory of meaning has not been met with such success. Quine, for one, has criticized the notions of meaning, synonymy and analyticity; a crucial question for the theory of meaning is precisely what meanings are.

A sense of security is engendered when one confuses meaning and reference. Meanings on this confusion are as mundane as any ordinary objects. Nothing could be more obvious than that there is a meaning for the word 'bachelor'; in fact, any unmarried man is, if meaning is the same as reference, part of that meaning. This false sense of security is shattered when we recognize that meanings and referents are distinct. We are left with the disturbing question as to what meanings are.

Mentalism, the view that meanings are ideas, has occurred prominently in pre-twentieth-century thought. On this view, 'bachelor' has as its meaning the idea present in the minds of users of the word. Ideas are mental entities and as such privately known only through the introspection of their owners. The tendency in late-nineteenth and twentieth-century psychology, linguistics and philosophy has been to dispense with talk of ideas in favour of more publicly observable phenomena. In psychology, external behaviour is studied and not internal mental states. Similarly, in linguistics, the appeal to meanings as ideas has come to be frowned upon. In philosophy, both pragmatists and students of the later Wittgenstein find the reference to ideas, especially in the philosophy of language, a source of difficulty. Quine is heir to all these traditions; his argument is in part that of a behaviourist, that private ideas are "pointless or pernicious" in the scientific study of language, and that we should dispense with them in favour of publicly observable linguistic behaviour.

> But even those who have not embraced behaviorism as a philosophy are obliged to adhere to behavioristic method within certain scientific pursuits; and language theory is such a pursuit. A scientist of language is, insofar, a behaviorist *ex officio*. Whatever the best eventual theory regarding the inner mechanism of language may turn out to be, it is bound to conform to the behavioral character of language learning: the dependence of verbal behavior on observation of verbal behavior. A language is mastered through social emulation and social feedback, and these controls ignore any idiosyncrasy in an individual's imagery or associations that is not discovered in his behavior. Minds are indifferent to language insofar as they differ privately from one another; that is, insofar as they are behaviorally inscrutable.
>
> Thus, though a linguist may still esteem mental entities philosophically, they are pointless or pernicious in language theory. This point was emphasized by Dewey in the twenties, when he argued that there could not be, in any serious sense, a private language. Wittgenstein also, years later, came to appreciate this point. Linguists have been conscious of it in increasing measure; Bloomfield to a considerable degree, Harris fully.
>
> Earlier linguistic theory operated in an uncritical mentalism. An irresponsible semantics prevailed, in which words were related to ideas much as labels are related to the exhibits in a museum [*the myth of the museum*]. To switch languages was to switch the labels. The uncritical mentalism and irresponsible semantics were, of course, philosophical too.[3]

A more sophisticated account of meanings is to treat them as abstract objects of the intensional variety. Unlike ideas, meanings in this sense are not mental entities although they are frequently said to be objects known by minds. Frege's writings provide the inspiration for this treatment. Having clearly distinguished the sense and reference of expressions, Frege provided a treatment of meaning as clearly distinguished from reference. Throughout the language of quantification he distinguished the sense and reference, that is, meaning and denotation, or intension and extension, of singular terms, predicates and sentences. Singular terms like 'the morning star' and 'the evening star' refer to one and the same planet but have different meanings (different senses). Predicates like 'is a bachelor' and 'is an unmarried man' have the same reference, that is, the class of individuals to which the predicates apply is the same; in addition they have the same meaning-sense, that is, they express the same intension or property. The two sentences 'It is raining' and 'Il pleut' have the same reference (the same truth value) as well as the same meaning-sense (the same proposition).

This approach commits one to an intensionalist ontology of individual senses or concepts, properties and propositions. On this view, to say an expression is meaningful is to say it has a meaning, that is, that there is an object which is its meaning-sense. Two expressions are said to be synonymous if they express the same meaning, that is, if there is a unique object which is their meaning. Thus, granted that the sentence 'Socrates is human' is meaningful, it follows on this account of meaningfulness that there is a meaning which this sentence has, that is, $(\exists x)(x$ is the meaning of 'Socrates is human'). Similarly, granted the synonymy of 'It is raining' and 'Il pleut', it follows that there is a proposition (a meaning) which is the meaning of the two expressions: $(\exists x)(x$ is the meaning of 'It is raining' and of 'Il pleut'). On this theory of language one is committed to recognizing meanings as intensions as values of the variables. Alonzo Church, for example, defended this Fregean theory of meaning and wrote on the need for such abstract entities in semantics.

Quine has raised numerous objections to the use of intensions in the philosophy of language. The most important of these are: (1) his reluctance to posit additional kinds of abstract entities if they are not really necessary; (2) the absence of a precise theory of intensions, especially the lack of an acceptable identity condition for intensional entities; (3) the problems that arise concerning what Quine has dubbed the referential opacity of discourse about intensions; and (4) Quine's view that meanings as posited entities (whether referents, ideas or intensions) perpetuate a myth of the museum view of language which falsifies and obscures the facts of language as they appear in an empiricist's (and a behaviourist's) philosophy of language. The last of these is bound up with Quine's much discussed conjecture as to the indeterminacy of translation, which appeared in *Word and Object* and his later works as well.

While Quine reluctantly acknowledges the need for admitting classes into his ontology on the grounds of their explanatory power, he questions the need for including intensional objects, such as properties and propositions. Church claimed that intensions are necessary as theoretical posits in an argument that is analogous to

Quine's recognizing the need to introduce classes.[4] The controversy between Quine and the intensionalists thus centres on the latter's claim that certain data require the introduction of intensions to explain them. Quine, however, argues that in some cases the data are questionable and in other cases other objects (non-intensional ones) will fulfil the explanatory role.

To begin with, Quine does not think the notion of meaning as a theoretical entity is required by linguists.[5] For him, the concepts of linguists, such as synonymy and meaningfulness, do not presuppose the existence of meanings. When the linguist investigates synonymy, he is concerned with how people use linguistic forms to correlate certain expressions with others. That is to say, the ontology required for linguistics comprises: (1) linguistic entities – sentences, predicates, singular terms and so on; and (2) human behaviour with regard to these linguistic entities. Quine does not see the need to posit meanings in addition to these. He is equally critical of a philosopher's notion of synonymy. He does not treat meaning in terms of the existence of a unique common meaning that two expressions have to each other, but rather in terms of human behaviour involving the expressions. In a parallel fashion, when a linguist investigates the meaningfulness or significance of expressions, he is concerned with grouping sequences of signs as significant in terms of behavioural responses towards them.

Quine has coined the term "the fallacy of subtraction" for the argument which moves from the meaningfulness or synonymy of expressions to the existence of meanings. According to Quine,

> it is argued that if we can speak of a sentence as meaningful, or as having meaning, then there must be a meaning that it has, and this meaning will be identical with or distinct from the meaning another sentence has. This is urged without any evident attempt to define synonymy in terms of meaningfulness, nor any notice of the fact that we could as well justify the hypostasis of sakes and unicorns on the basis of the idioms 'for the sake of' and 'is hunting unicorns'.[6]

Quine's point is that the mere occurrence of expressions like 'has a meaning' or 'has the same meaning as' does not necessitate an analysis which results in quantifying over (and hence hypostasizing) meanings. As a case in point, the common sentence 'Red is a colour' does not require an analysis, such as 'There is an x which is the property of being red and it is a colour', which involves us in an ontology of properties. 'Red is a colour' can instead be analysed as saying that all red things are coloured things, which involves quantifying only over concrete individuals. Thus, 'is meaningful' and 'is synonymous with' can be construed as predicates analysable in terms that require quantifying only over linguistic forms and human behaviour, but not intensions. But now the further question arises of the admissibility of a synonymy predicate even granted that when used it requires quantification only over linguistic forms and human behaviour. We shall see in the remaining sections of this chapter that the attempt to characterize synonymy precisely is in no better state than that of doing so for analyticity.

Some of the other data that intensions are intended to explain are translation, philosophical analysis, truth vehicles, modalities, propositional attitudes and, of course, analyticity. In *Word and Object*, Quine questions the place of meanings in giving an empirical account of translation. In the same book he explains that the process of providing philosophical analysis is never an attempt to capture the meaning of the expression being analysed.[7] He also argues that sentences do the job of propositions as the vehicles of truth and falsity.[8] Modal logic may require intensional objects, but Quine thinks that there are grounds for questioning the enterprise of modal logic. Where Frege, Church and their followers argue that propositional attitude ascriptions require the introduction of intensional objects, Quine maintains that other constructions, namely, extensional sentences not requiring reference to intensional entities, would do as well.[9] The details of some of these points will be explored in later sections and in Chapter 7. Let us now return to our more immediate concern, the introduction of intensions/meanings to explain analyticity. Since Quine is doubtful of the utility of introducing the analytic–synthetic distinction, this dubious distinction cannot itself be appealed to as data requiring the admission of meanings.

In Chapter 5 we touched on the question of providing an identity condition for intensional entities. Individuals are said to be identical when whatever is true of one is true of the other, and classes are said to be identical when they have the same members. These identity conditions are couched in relatively clear language; the notions of 'true of' and 'member of' must be contrasted with those used to characterize the identity of intensional entities such as properties. Recall that two properties are not identical if they merely belong to the same individuals, that is, if the expressions for the properties are merely coextensive. So 'human' and 'featherless biped' may stand for the same class of individuals but the properties of being human and of being a featherless biped are different.

Consider two attempts to provide identity conditions for properties. One is that properties *a* and *b* are identical if they not only belong to the same individuals but do so of necessity. Thus, while humanity and featherless bipedity belong to the same individuals, they do not do so of necessity, and hence, by this identity condition, they would be distinct properties. For Quine, who finds the notion of necessity itself in need of proper explanation, this attempt at an identity condition fails. As a second attempt one might say that *a* and *b* are the same properties if the statement '*a* is a *b* and *b* is an *a*' is not just true but is analytically true. Thus since 'Humans are featherless bipeds' is merely true, but not analytically true, the two properties involved are distinct. Here Quine points out: (1) 'Humans are rational animals' is not a logical truth, that is, is not a truth of first order logic, and so is not analytic in the sense of being a logical truth; (2) if 'analytic' means truth in virtue of the meanings involved, then the account is circular, that is, the identity condition for meanings as intensions relies on the concept of analyticity, which itself relies on the notion of meanings; and (3) if 'analytic' is used in some other sense, then, since Quine is sceptical that any precise analysis can be provided for the idea, he is equally suspicious of the use of this notion in any identity condition.

Another problem about intensional objects is shared by the intensional contexts connected with modalities and propositional attitudes. Talk of these yields "referentially opaque" constructions to which the ordinary logic of identity does not apply. The situation is further aggravated by the fact that classical quantification principles yield paradoxes in such contexts. In Chapter 7 we will discuss these matters.

Other attempts to explicate analyticity

So much for the attempt to explain analyticity by appealing to meanings. Quine proceeds to investigate whether a clear definition of analyticity, which relies on the notions of synonymy and logical truth, is achievable. Recall that the broader class of analytic sentences can be characterized as the result of putting synonyms for synonyms in logical truths. Thus, 'All bachelors are unmarried men' follows from the logical truth 'All unmarried men are unmarried men' when we replace the subject 'unmarried men' with its synonym. The success of this definition of analyticity hinges on the notion of "synonymy". In "Two Dogmas of Empiricism", Quine examines four accounts of 'synonymy' which are designed to explicate the notion of analytical truth and finds them wanting. They are appeals to (1) definition, (2) interchangeability, (3) semantic rules, and (4) the verifiability theory of meaning.

A first suggestion for explaining synonymy might be to appeal to definitions. But Quine maintains that when we examine all the different kinds of definition we find that they do not clarify synonymy, but either presuppose it or create it by conventional fiat. He classifies definition as reportive, explicative or stipulative. These categories are intended to cover all definitions. In reportive definitions, for instance as found in a dictionary, there is a description (or report) of the usage of two expressions which attempts to report a preexisting synonymy so that rather than explaining synonymy, the report presupposes it.

In explication, the purpose of the definition is not merely to report current usage but to improve upon it. The term 'explication' is Carnap's and the process of explication is the mainstay of philosophical analysis. Quine has adopted Carnap's term, although he provides an extensional account of its use in philosophy; for him analysis does not provide us with the meaning of the expression being analysed. Quine's scepticism about meanings leads him to avoid them in explaining philosophical analysis.

> We do not claim synonymy. We do not claim to make clear and explicit what the users of the unclear expression had unconsciously in mind all along. We do not expose hidden meanings, as the words 'analysis' and 'explication' would suggest: we supply lacks, we fix on the particular functions of the unclear expression that make it worth troubling about, and then devise a substitute, clear and couched in terms to our liking, that fills those functions. Beyond those conditions of partial agreement, dictated by our interests and purposes, any traits of the explicans come under the head of 'don't cares.' Under this head we are free to allow the explicans all manner of novel connotations never associated with the explicandum.[10]

For the present, we merely wish to show that explication does not explain synonymy. As a case of explication, take that offered for the conditional, or 'if-then', sentences of English in modern logic. In our definition we wish to report and preserve the usage according to which a conditional sentence is true when the antecedent and the consequent are true, and false when the antecedent is true and the consequent is false. Ordinary usage, however, says nothing about the two cases when the antecedent is false.

p	q	$p \rightarrow q$
T	T	T
T	F	F
F	T	?
F	F	?

Modern logic requires that some value be assigned to these cases and to this end we improve on usage by stipulating these values. The stipulation is governed by systematic considerations. We assign the value true to conditionals with false antecedents, because we want '$\rightarrow$' to be a truth functional connective and want sentences such as those of the forms '$p \rightarrow q$' and '$(p \;\&\; q) \rightarrow p$' to be true even when '$p$' is false and '$q$' true. Hence explication is in part a report of preexisting usage and in part a stipulation of usage; neither sheds light on synonymy. Reports of usage as in purely reportive definitions presuppose but do not explain synonymy. Stipulation that two expressions are synonymous creates synonymy and is definition by conventional fiat. But as we have seen (above and in Chapter 5), a close examination of the conventional character of definition reveals (1) that such legislative conventions are a feature of the act of adopting a sentence and not of the sentence or its truth per se, and (2) that such conventions are not in any sense distinctly linguistic, but can be a feature of the adoption of any kind of hypothesis.

The last type of definition, the purely stipulative, is involved when the term being defined has been created to fit the item described by the defining terms. Here is one example. In choosing a user's name for an e-mail account one is free to choose (within the limits of the programs involved) from among combinations of letters and numerals. Another example would be the beginning of the convention to use the ampersand, '&', as a sign for conjunction. Such pure stipulation is merely a limiting case of the stipulational element in explication. Aside from its rarity (confined as it is in most cases to technical rather than ordinary discourse), pure stipulation furnishes no explanation of ordinary cases of synonymy like 'bachelor' and 'unmarried man'. As was seen in its less extreme role in explication, it is not informative about the linguistic notion of synonymy.

A further attempt to define synonymy asserts that two expressions are synonymous if they are interchangeable. Now, interchangeability itself is as clear a notion as Quine could desire, being a variety of replacement of one expression by another, and thus similar to ideas involved in his definition of logical truth. But there are special problems in the case of synonymy. To begin with, note that an especially strong sort of interchangeability *salva veritate* is required. It is not enough to say expressions are synonymous when the interchange of the one with the other does not change the truth value of the sentences involved. Were we to apply interchangeability to non-problematic sentences such as 'George Washington was a man', interchanging 'featherless biped' with 'man', we would be led to the false view that 'featherless biped' and 'man' are synonymous. This definition of synonymy is too broad, since it leads to the incorrect treatment of merely coextensive terms as synonyms. An attempt to remedy this situation has led some to suggest that if the language were to include the right sort of necessity operator, then the failure of interchangeability *salva veritate* in a necessary truth would rule out the merely coextensive terms. Thus, that all men are rational animals is necessarily true, but that all men are featherless bipeds is not necessarily true. However, the reader is aware by now that given a sufficiently rich notion of necessity, analyticity can be defined, that is, necessity can be used to provide an identity condition, for meanings/intensions, and these in turn used to define 'analytic' as truth in virtue of meaning. The problem here is that of making sense of the notion of necessity, a question we will examine more closely in the chapter on intensional contexts. Indeed, the various different notions – meaning, analyticity, synonymy and necessity – are such that given any one of them you can define the others. Quine finds none of these sufficiently clear to serve as the basis for a definition and so requires that an adequate characterization of, say, analyticity must break out of this circle of intensional terms.

Yet another attempt to define analyticity in terms of synonymy with a logical truth is to appeal to the verification theory of meaning.

According to this theory, "the meaning of a statement is the method of empirically confirming or infirming it" and "statements are synonymous if and only if they are alike in point of method of empirical confirmation or infirmation".[11] Now Quine is quite sympathetic toward the empiricist aspect of this theory of meaning in so far as it provides the basis for a critique of language that purports to be informative but that has no testable content. In fact, this is the basis for his own positive approach to the notions of meaning, synonymy and analyticity, namely, to determine the empirical, and as such behavioural, grounds for these notions. However, the verifiability theory of meaning suffers from the dogma of reductionism: non-holistic empiricism. Once freed of reductionism, it does not provide the desired account of synonymy or analyticity. To begin with, recall that for Quine (following Duhem) we speak neither of terms nor individual sentences as having empirical consequences but rather of systems of sentences and, ultimately, the whole of our conceptual framework. In other words, we cannot speak of sentences as synonymous in virtue of their empirical significance because it is not individual sentences that are confirmed or infirmed, Quine explains:

> The dogma of reductionism survives in the supposition that each statement, taken in isolation from its fellows, can admit of confirmation or infirmation at all. My countersuggestion . . . is that our statements about the external world face the tribunal of sense experience not individually but only as a corporate body.[12]

Furthermore, the broader class of analytic truths also loses its special status once we adopt an empiricism without the dogma of reductionism. In the Duhem–Quine conception there is no reason to believe that there is a priori knowledge of any sort.

> Another . . . principle to view warily is "Every event has a cause." As a philosopher's maxim it may seem safe enough if the philosopher is willing to guide it around the recalcitrant facts. But this principle, in the face of quantum theory, needs extensive guiding. For if present physics is correct, there are events that are subject only to statistical and not rigidly determinate laws. This limiting principal can, like any other, be retained if one is willing to make enough sacrifices for it. But insofar as it purports to be a principle of physics, it cannot be counted as

self-evident even if it somehow survives modern quantum theory.[13]

There is one more approach to defining analyticity which Quine touches on in the "Two Dogmas" essay. This consists in constructing an artificial language and then defining 'analytic' for it. Carnap has taken this line. Recourse to such a constructed language can at times be helpful in defining or gaining insight into notions which are obscure in natural languages. For example, Tarski's definition of truth is for languages of this type, and Quine's characterization of 'existence' is carried out primarily for language transposed into a canonical notation of first order logic. The question then is whether Carnap has succeeded in clarifying the nature of analyticity relative to such artificial languages. The situation here is similar to the attempts to characterize the linguistic doctrine of logical truth, which we considered in Chapter 5. People have mistakenly argued from the fact that logic and mathematics are frequently treated more formally (that is, expressed as artificial rather than as natural languages and at times even fully formalized, i.e. axiomatized and/or disinterpreted) that the truth of these subjects is distinctively linguistic. We pointed out that formalization and/or axiomatization can be carried out for other sciences as well and so fails to distinguish logic and mathematics. In a similar vein, it is possible to construct a language and specify relative to it that 'All bachelors are unmarried men' and 'Nothing is taller than itself' are analytic. But this language-relative specification of analyticity does not really clarify analyticity, since it is neither sufficiently general nor truly distinctive of any set of truths. As to the matter of generality, Quine requires that we have more than a characterization of analyticity for language$_1$ and language$_2$ and so on. What we need is some characterization of analyticity which is common to all such purported reconstructions of analyticity: to analytic$_1$, and analytic$_2$ and so on. However, the appeal to artificial languages has failed to provide this characterization. Moreover, there is something arbitrary about Carnap's answer to the questions of which sentences are analytically true. The problem for Quinians is precisely why 'All bachelors are unmarried' is on the list and 'All men are mortal' is not. To be told that a sentence is analytic because it is on a list (even the list of an artificial language) provides no real distinction.

So far in this chapter we have traced Quine's sceptical attack on the theory of meaning as found in his criticisms of a purported distinction between two types of sentences. Quine's critics have responded along many lines. Some have attempted to show that the force of Quine's arguments does not apply to their own way of making the distinction, whereas others have attacked the standards Quine makes use of in his arguments. The debate in this area is ongoing and vigorous. One fact is certain though: the ease and confidence with which philosophers used to appeal to the analytic–synthetic distinction is a thing of the past.

Quine's critique of the theory of meaning has amounted to a challenge to provide precise accounts of its notions. What counts as precise could take the form of reducing intensional notions to extensional ones. His criticisms of modal concepts (see Chapter 7) has spurred a generation of responses in what is known as possible world semantics, which in one of its variations can be seen as trying to provide a reduction of intensional modal notions via extensional metalinguistic truth conditions for necessary truths. We will expand on this in Chapter 7. The success of this reduction is still challenged by Quinians.[14] More in keeping with Quine's challenge to explicate the theory of meaning is Davidson's work on letting a Tarskian theory of truth serve as a surrogate for a theory of meaning.[15] Another way that scepticism about the theory of meaning might be overcome would be by an empirical and behaviouristically constrained account of such notions. Carnap took up this challenge in his paper "Meaning and Synonymy in Natural Languages" and sketched a programme for empirically identifying meanings by testing translation hypotheses, e.g. a linguist's hypotheses for translating the term 'Pferd' from German to English as 'horse'.[16] Quine's response was the topic of radical translation and his conjecture of the indeterminacy of translation.

The indeterminacy conjecture

How much of language is susceptible to empirical analysis? Like Carnap, Quine takes the case of linguists hypothesizing about translation as the subject matter for empirical inquiry. Both take as their data a native speaker's response to appropriate stimuli. Quine introduces the concept of the "stimulus meaning" of a sentence for a person as the class of stimulations that would prompt the person's assent to it. He deals with the stimulus meaning of whole sentences, such as 'Here is a horse', and not terms, such as 'horse'. In addition,

Quine's sentence is for the most part taken holophrastically, that is, as an indissoluble or unstructured whole. Such a fused sentence might better be written as 'Here-is-a-horse'. It is these fused, holophrastically construed, sentences that are brought to bear in the test cases and not their component parts. Quine's linguist offers a hypothesis equating two such sentences (one is the native's and the other the linguist's) and checks it against a native speaker's assenting or dissenting to the native sentence in the presence of some non-verbal stimulus. Carnap considered translation for languages such as German and English, which are known to have much in common. Quine's most famous example is a thought experiment involving radical translation: translation between languages that may have very little in common. On the one hand we might have English, and on the other some exotic language called Jungle or the language of a Martian. The lessons learned from radical translation are then brought home to clarify the empirical basis of our own language, English. The indeterminacy of meaning is seen to apply to the home language of English as well.

In *Word and Object* Quine offered the thought experiment of radical translation. Think of a linguist among some radically foreign tribe. The linguist observes a certain correlation between a native utterance of 'Gavagai' and the presence of rabbits and proceeds to frame a hypothesis which equates 'Gavagai' and the one-word sentence 'Rabbit', short for 'Here's-a-rabbit' or 'Lo-a-rabbit'. The linguist could, on learning how to recognize the native's assent and dissent, question the native by uttering 'Gavagai' when a rabbit appears and seeing whether the native assents.

But how far does such evidence really go? All that we have as data are the native's expression and the rabbit stimulation. This merely yields the stimulus meaning determinate 'Gavagai' and the holophrastic 'Here's-a-rabbit'. Quine points out that on these limited grounds, these two observation sentences (in Quine's special sense of "observation sentence") are stimulus synonymous, and that one cannot go very far in translating other more theoretical non-observation sentences.

Carnap would presumably want this much to count as evidence that the terms 'gavagai' and 'rabbit', which are parts of these fused sentences, have the same meaning. But does the evidence really support this? All that we have as data are the native's fused sentence and the rabbit stimulation. Quine claims that on these grounds one could equally well translate 'Gavagai' as 'Here-is-a-rabbit stage' or

'Here-is-a-temporal-part-of-a-rabbit' or something else. For, wherever there are rabbit stimulations there are as well rabbit-stage stimulations, temporal parts of rabbits stimulations and so on. On what basis then would one decide between these different translations? At this point hypotheses less directly connected to the data – to the stimulus conditions – may be introduced by the linguist. These more theoretical assumptions, which Quine calls "analytical hypotheses", can be framed so as to do justice to quite different translations.

To illustrate this matter for the Gavagai case we must note that in order for the linguist to ask a question like 'Is this rabbit the same as that?' he must have decided on how to translate articles, pronouns, identity predicates and so on. To translate such a sentence into Jungle is to go far beyond the data provided by the stimuli. It involves selecting from different sets of analytical hypotheses, that is, from different possible manuals of translation. On one set of these we translate the question as 'Is this the same rabbit as that?' while on another as 'Is this rabbit stage of the same series as that?' Each of these translations is equally good at conforming to the stimulus conditions, yet they are mutually incompatible. Since neither of these has any immediate connection with the Gavagai stimulation there is no way of deciding between them. This is the indeterminacy of translation and of meaning.

Given the stimulus determinate meaning of a limited stock of observation sentences and some others, one could equally well translate in mutually incompatible ways the more theoretical non-observation sentences. On what basis then could one decide between these different translations? The thought experiment of radical translation provides evidence for the conjecture of the indeterminacy of translation and meaning. As we go further from observation sentences we cannot single out a unique translation, a unique proposition for a native's sentence to express.

A related question we may now ask is how far does the empirically determinable notion of stimulus meaning satisfy the philosopher's full-blooded notion of meaning? The answer is that stimulus meaning approximates to the more questionable notion of meaning only for those sentences which bear the closest relations to stimulus conditions. These turn out to be more like the one-word sentence 'Red', 'Rabbit' (or 'This-is-red', 'Here's-a-rabbit') than 'Bachelor' (or 'Here-is-a-bachelor') or 'Electron'. The latter sentences require background information and not merely present stimulation to prompt the speaker's assent.

Another way of putting the matter is that one could learn to use 'Red' correctly from someone who was merely pointing, that is, merely giving ostensive directions for its use. The speaker must also have a fund of "collateral information" in the cases of 'Bachelor' and 'Electron'. Two speakers might see the same person but because of their different background knowledge (collateral information) – one has the information that the person is not married and the other does not – the purely ostensive stimulation will not suffice for the learning of 'Bachelor'. In order for the second to learn that 'Bachelor' applies, he must acquire the appropriate collateral information. In the case of 'Electron', the collateral information is even more remote from the relevant stimulation (provided presumably by equipment in a physicist's laboratory) and encompasses a good portion of physical theory. The sentences which are least dependent on collateral information are Quine's observation sentences. For our present purposes, it is enough to recognize how small the class of observation sentences is in our language. For example, of the following sentences, how many could be learned purely ostensively (a prime trait of observation sentences)?

John's uncle is overweight.
Napoleon lost the Battle of Waterloo.
Heredity is a matter of genes.
Neutrinos lack mass.
2 + 2 = 4.

None of these qualify as observation sentences, because 'uncle', 'overweight', 'the Battle of Waterloo', 'genes', 'neutrinos' and '2' all require varying amounts of collateral information (even if construed holophrastically as one-word sentences doing the work of 'Here's-an-uncle'). Since most of our sentences are not observation ones, whose conditions for assent and dissent are exhausted in stimulus conditions, the attempt to provide an empirical account of meaning falls far short of its goal. Quine similarly introduces the notions of "stimulus synonymy" and of "stimulus analyticity" to see how far they take us toward the full fledged philosophical concepts of synonymy and analyticity. For synonymy and translation from one language to another, stimulus synonymy provides a surrogate of sorts only for those sentences directly connected with stimulus conditions (observation sentences). So far we have only discussed the concept of stimulus meaning for sentences and the attendant notion of stimulus synonymy for sentences. What of synonymy for terms that are parts of sentences? Quine reminds us of the lesson of the indeterminacy thesis – that far from being able to characterize synonymy empirically, we cannot even determine whether the terms 'gavagai' and 'rabbit' are coextensive. Writing on the sense in which language is public, Dagfinn Føllesdal points out that "Quine, more than any other philosopher, has made us see the far reaching implications of the public nature of language". Indeterminacy is a particularly striking case in point.[17]

In his later works, *Pursuit of Truth* and *From Stimulus to Science*, Quine puts the argument for meaning indeterminacy somewhat differently. He asks us to take as our thought experiment a situation where two linguists working independently of each other observe natives and their reactions to the presence of rabbits. Taking the natives' signs of assent and dissent to whole sentences as the observation base, we cannot conclude that the two linguists would come up with compatible manuals of translation.

> These reflections leave us little reason to expect that two radical translators, working independently on Jungle, would come out with intertranslatable manuals. The manuals might be indistinguishable in terms of any native behavior that they give reason to expect, and yet each manual might prescribe some translations that the other translator would reject. Such is the thesis of indeterminacy of translation.[18]

Indeterminacy provides further grounds for discrediting the philosophical notion of meaning. Philosophers have talked as if meanings are related to expressions somewhat the same way as paintings in a museum are related to their labels. Quine dubs this "*the myth of the museum*".[19] According to this view, two expressions are synonymous when they are related to a unique meaning, like two labels for the same painting. So two sentences are said to be synonymous when they express the same proposition. In the case of translation, one English expression is a translation of another in a different language when the two bear a relation to one and the same interlinguistic object which is their meaning. Quine is attempting to dislodge this model for thinking about language and to put in its place a more naturalistic and empirically based conception. According to the museum model, meanings have an absolute and not a relative status. An expression has its meaning, pure and simple, and two synonymous expressions relate to one meaning which, as interlinguistic, is independent of the languages in which it is expressed. What Quine has shown is that it makes no sense to speak of language-independent meanings. Translation from one language to another is relative to a set of analytical hypotheses. There is no independent meaning of 'Gavagai' which the linguist can link to 'Here-is-a-rabbit' and not 'Here-is-a-rabbit stage'. The linguist is at best in a position for saying that 'Gavagai', 'Here-is-a-rabbit' and 'Here-is-a-rabbit stage' are all synonymous in Quine's limited, ersatz sense of stimulus synonymous. Stimulus synonymy does not capture the full fledged notion of synonymy. As naturalists we have to study language in terms of linguistic behaviour in the face of stimulus conditions. In turn this behaviour must be interpreted in relation to more theoretical background assumptions, that is, analytical hypotheses. Following this naturalist empiricist programme does not yield the conception of meaning that philosophers have frequently assigned to them.

We have until this point been discussing the indeterminacy conjecture mainly in the context of radical translation. This can be misleading. The naturalistic constraints given in connection with that exotic foreign language are at work in our own home language as well.

> I have directed my indeterminacy thesis on a radically exotic language for the sake of plausibility, but in principle it applies even to the home language. For given the rival manuals of translation between Jungle and English, we can translate English perversely into English by translating it into Jungle by one manual and then back by the other.[20]

The myth of the museum and attendant philosophical notions suffer the same naturalist critiques for English as well as Jungle or Martian. Satires such as *Gulliver's Travels* and *Erehwon* make their points by being set in strange settings. These exotic settings highlight what may go unnoticed at home in everyday situations. In a similar way, the dramatic and exotic locale of radical translation and its indeterminacy lesson is intended to call our attention to what is going on in our home language of English.

With his indeterminacy conjecture Quine brings to bear the full weight of his naturalistic approach to the theory of meaning. Daniel Dennett takes the Gavagai case as a paradigm example of what he calls an "intuition pump". An intuition pump gets us thinking about a subject. Quine's thought experiment makes us realize what a naturalistic and empiricist account of language requires. Naturalism consists of adopting the outlook of the natural sciences when doing philosophy. So Quine looks at language, at home as well as abroad, from the standpoint of a fully self-conscious empiricist working with the assumptions of the best natural science. The data for language are public, as are the data of the natural sciences. We learn language and hypothesize about it on the basis of publicly available items, viz., behaviour. This behaviour consists of responding to stimuli. Human language, as a form of communication, is continuous with that of an ape's cry and a bird's call.[21] Such stimuli and responses are dealt with in dispositional terms that accord with the physicalist orientation of modern science. The dispositions in question are explained neurologically.

While Quine insists on behaviourism as the method for studying and acquiring languages, he is not a logical or ontological behaviourist; he is an evidential or methodological behaviourist. On the mind–body problem he endorses Davidson's anomalous monism: the view that our ways of speaking of the mental, for example, of perceptions and beliefs, cannot be stated in terms of the natural laws which govern the underlying physiological states, even though our mental states just are such neurological states. Quine construes the matter so that mental ascriptions play their role in everyday life and the social sciences, but cannot be precisely specified in purely physicalist terms.

Staying strictly in the bounds of such naturalistic constraints, a question remains as to just what the indeterminacy of translation/meaning amounts to. The indeterminacy conjecture shows that certain conceptions of meaning go beyond the bounds of a naturalistic approach. It remains for me to try to clarify this matter. I address this issue in the next section by exploring the difference between indeterminacy and the underdetermination of theory by evidence.

Contrasting indeterminacy and underdetermination

Several authors have presented views that challenge Quine on the relation of indeterminacy to the underdetermination of theory by evidence.[22] Chomsky, for instance, thought that the indeterminacy of meaning is no more than another case of underdetermination of a theory by evidence, viz., the underdetermination of a theory of translation by Quine's behaviourist evidence.[23] On numerous occasions Quine has denied this and tells us that with indeterminacy there is "no fact of the matter" whereas there is a fact of the matter for underdetermination.

> I developed a thought experiment in radical translation – that is, in the translation of an initially unknown language on the strength of behavioral data. I argued that the translations would be indeterminate, in the case of sentences at any considerable remove from observation sentences. They would be indeterminate in this sense: two translators might develop independent manuals of translation, both of them compatible with all speech behavior and all dispositions to speech behavior, and yet one manual would offer translations that the other translator would reject. My position was that either manual could be useful, but as to which was right and which was wrong there was no fact of the matter.
>
> My present purpose is not to defend this doctrine. My purpose is simply to make clear that I speak as a physicalist in saying there is no fact of the matter. I mean that both manuals are compatible with fulfillment of just the same elementary physical states by space-time regions.[24]

To understand Quine's view we must try to get clear about what he has in mind by the phrases 'underdetermination' and 'no fact of the matter'. Underdetermination is somewhat epistemological. Roughly speaking, a theory is underdetermined by the evidence when that evidence serves equally well to support another theory. This can be put better in terms of the concept of empirically equivalent theories.

> Physical theories can be at odds with each other and yet compatible with all possible data even in the broadest possible sense. In a word they can be logically incompatible and empirically equivalent.[25]

Quine's much discussed phrase 'no fact of the matter' should at the outset be taken metaphorically, since Quine is one of the foremost critics of positing facts as part of our ontology. If the phrase is to be taken figuratively, the question remains of what literal significance it should be understood as conveying. Some have taken it as having a methodological, epistemological or evidential significance: that there is no difference in evidence for the theories in question. But when we take this evidentialist stance, we seem to be interpreting indeterminacy of meaning as though it is no different from underdetermination. If underdetermination of theory is a matter of empirically equivalent theories, then indeterminacy construed purely evidentially amounts to nothing more than empirically equivalent manuals/theories/hypotheses of translation. Since this goes against Quine's stated intentions, it cannot be correct.

The correct solution is given in the following explanation of the phrase along ontological, and in particular, physical lines.

> Another notion that I would take pains to rescue from the abyss of the transcendental is the notion of a matter of fact. A place where the notion proves relevant is in connection with my doctrine of the indeterminacy of translation. I have argued that two conflicting manuals of translation can both do justice to all dispositions to behavior, and that, in such a case, there is no fact of the matter of which manual is right. The intended notion of matter of fact is not transcendental or yet epistemological, not even a question of evidence; it is ontological, a question of reality, and to be taken naturalistically within our scientific theory of the world. Thus suppose, to make things vivid, that we are settling still for a physics of elementary particles and recognizing a dozen or so basic states and relations in which they may stand. Then when I say there is no fact of the matter, as regards, say, the two rival manuals of translation, what I mean is that both manuals are compatible with all the same distributions of states and relations over elementary particles. In a word, they are physically equivalent. --- I speak of a physical condition and not an empirical criterion.[26]

As used here, 'facts of the matter' refers to the particular physicalist ontological commitments indispensable for translation. As explained in the previous section, the commitments required for a theory of translation are part of those that are required for natural science. The hypotheses bearing on translation require an ontology comprising dispositions to respond to stimuli. These are neurological items. Given such ontological items and their arrangement required by physical theory, there is no way of saying which of incompatible manuals of translation is correct. This would be the case even if we assumed that physical theory were determined. It is not as though the two manuals for translation are merely empirically equivalent in that there is no difference in evidence for them, and yet they do differ in underlying natural science. This epistemological/evidential situation is the case for empirically equivalent but incompatible theories. The two physical theories that differ, even if empirically equivalent, would differ at some points on different "truths" (so to speak "on the arrangement of ontological items"). By contrast, two different but empirically equivalent manuals of translation do not differ on the "arrangement of their ontological items". There are no physicalist items, or their arrangements, that is, facts/"truths" about dispositions, which they differ over. The translation manuals are empirically equivalent and incompatible, yet physically/ontologically equivalent. This is what 'no facts of the matter' comes down to and goes some way to explaining the special "speculative" nature of the philosophical conceptions of meaning revealed by the indeterminacy conjecture.

Contrasting inscrutability of reference and indeterminacy of meaning

In *Word and Object* we find an early statement of the indeterminacy of translation/meaning conjecture. Enmeshed in this statement is 'Gavagai' (the one-word sentence doing the same job as the stimulus synonymous fused sentence 'Here's-a-rabbit') as well as 'gavagai' (the term or predicate equated with 'rabbit', 'rabbit stage', etc.). We find here a semblance of the seeds for confusing two different indeterminacies: inscrutability of reference and indeterminacy of meaning. Several people mistakenly read Quine as though he were arguing from inscrutability to indeterminacy. This conflation has taken place in numerous lectures, private conversations, and in print. However, it is important for understanding Quine (as he informs us he wants to be understood) that we distinguish the two and view the case for indeterminacy of meaning without appealing to the gavagai/inscrutability case. Quine first proposed indeterminacy and only later did he come to present inscrutability explicitly and expressly as a separate theme.

> In my work the inscrutability of reference was one thing and the indeterminacy of holophrastic translation was another. The one admitted of conclusive and trivial proof by proxy functions, hence model theory, while the other remained a plausible conjecture.[27]

It might appear in *Word and Object* as if the argument for indeterminacy were from the inscrutability of reference; as though the problem of giving a unique manual of translation were based on the different referents that can be assigned to the term/predicate 'gavagai', viz., rabbits, rabbit stages and so on. However, this is not Quine's view. In his later works the two arguments are clearly separated. Indeterminacy of translation could, and perhaps should, have been argued for without appealing to the term or predicate 'gavagai'. (Perhaps it adds to the confusion that rabbits are also used when discussing inscrutability in connection with proxy functions.)

Inscrutability/indeterminacy of reference is also known as ontological relativity, and then as global structuralism. As mentioned above, it was first argued for via the terms (not sentences) 'gavagai'/ 'rabbit' in *Word and Object*. It was not clearly specified there as having a separate role apart from the indeterminacy of translation. It is still not completely distinguished in *Ontological Relativity*, when it was used to show that we cannot "settle the indeterminacy of translation between 'rabbit', 'undetached rabbit part' and 'rabbit stage'".[28] These uses are in connection with translation, and radical translation at that. By contrast, the argument for the inscrutability/ indeterminacy of reference via proxy functions concerns truths (perhaps science as a body of truths). The conclusion is that our theories do not have a determinate ontology. Proxy functions tell us that different items, for example, rabbits or their cosmic complements, fit equally well. And then structuralism says that it is meaningless to ask which one is really involved. Although it is an argument from the truth of sentences, the sentences have parts, terms or predicates, and it is to these that ontological items are assigned. Let us put aside the argument for inscrutability of reference via 'gavagai'/'rabbit' and focus on proxy functions. Proxy functions are more telling as to the nature of the inscrutability claim. Proxy functions and inscrutability bear on theories while indeterminacy bears on language.

Even more importantly, the argument for inscrutability (indeterminacy of reference) via proxy functions is a "constructive" proof while indeterminacy is only a conjecture. By "constructive" I mean that the proof depends on cases, such as the cosmic complements, which are provided and clearly specified. With inscrutability there are clearly established cases, for example, the various proxy functions that are appealed to and a proof (a deductive argument). By contrast, the argument for the indeterminacy of translation/meaning and of reference via radical translation is neither constructive nor a proof. It is more accurately described as being a conjecture. We are supposed to imagine an attempt at radical translation. The data are the stimuli or the responses, some of which are linguistic. The units of language initially involved are holophrastically construed observation sentences. These sentences are determinate in meaning. More theoretical sentences of a language do not have empirically identifiable meanings. 'Gavagai' and 'Here's-a-rabbit', taken as one-word sentences, have determinate meaning in Quine's sense of stimulus meaning and do not illustrate the indeterminacy of meaning/translation. However, there is so much leeway in translating other whole sentences (not to mention their parts) that there is little reason to think that they have determinate meanings. Concentrating on sentences and not their parts as the vehicle of meaning, the indeterminacy of meaning thesis is the inability to single out the propositions that the various sentences of the language are supposed to express.

> . . . my conjecture of indeterminacy of translation concerned not terms like "gavagai" but sentences as wholes, for I follow Frege in deeming sentences the primary vehicles of meaning. The indeterminacy ascribed to "gavagai" comes under the head rather of indeterminacy of reference, or ontological relativity. This indeterminacy is proved unlike my conjecture of the indeterminacy of holophrastic translation.[29]

The conjecture of indeterminacy is that there is no reason to think, given the empiricism/behaviourism involved in translation and its ontological underpinnings, that translation is determinate. Given the evidence, there is no good reason to think that a uniquely correct translation can be provided. Moreover there is "no fact of the matter". This conjecture is on quite a different footing from the proven inscrutability.

In the later work *Pursuit of Truth*, Quine clarifies the confusion concerning sentences and terms.

> The difference between taking a sentence holophrastically as a seamless whole and taking it analytically term by term proved crucial in earlier matters [learning language, observation sentences as evidence]. It is crucial also to translation. Taken analytically, the indeterminacy of translation is trivial and indisputable. . . . It is the unsurprising reflection that divergent interpretations of the words in a sentence can so offset one another as to sustain an identical translation of the sentence as a whole. It is what I have called inscrutability of reference; indeterminacy of reference would have been better. The serious and controversial thesis of indeterminacy of translation is not that; it is rather the holophrastic thesis, which is stronger. It declares for divergences that remain unreconciled even at the level of the whole sentence, and are compensated for only by divergences in the translation of other whole sentences.[30]

In explaining this passage I will repeat and reiterate some of the points made above. The distinction between taking sentences as seamless wholes and taking them term by term made at the outset of this passage refers to three roles played by holophrastic observation sentences: (1) as the entering wedge in learning language; (2) as the entering wedge in translation; and (3) as evidence in the sense of serving as an observational base. Terms and what referents are assigned to them come into play only: (1) at later stages of learning language than observation sentences; (2) at later stages in framing translations; and (3) at a more theoretical stage in theory construction.

> Proxy functions raise their ugly heads only when we take to philosophizing on the logic of scientific conjecture and experiment. It is there that we would learn that the reference of terms, in whatever language, can be varied isomorphically without prejudice to the empirical evidence for the truth of the scientific theory, . . .[31]

So, to begin with, one might distinguish indeterminacy from inscrutability on the basis of the different roles played by terms and assigning referents to them and that of the fused observation sentences containing those terms.

Moreover, Quine recognizes that if we take an analytic – term-by-term – approach to sentences, then, given the indisputable (proven) status of inscrutability, we also have indeterminacy of translation. Examples such as Harman's of interpreting numerals either in terms of a Frege–Russell ontology or a von Neumann one, provide vivid examples where inscrutability of terms would yield incompatible manuals of translation. Quine considers this type of argument from inscrutability to indeterminacy as trivial. It is not the serious argument he is interested in.

He would have us think of indeterminacy differently, presumably without appealing to inscrutability. What does this purer type of argument for indeterminacy (purged of any appeal to inscrutability) amount to, and why should Quine be so interested in taking it as representing his views? To begin with, the case for purely holophrastic indeterminacy is quite different from that for inscrutability. To repeat, Quine comes to realize that indeterminacy is a conjecture whereas inscrutability is proven.

> The indeterminacy of translation that I long since conjectured, and the indeterminacy of reference that I proved, are indeterminacies in different senses. My earlier use of different words, 'indeterminacy' for the one and 'inscrutability' for the other, may have been wiser.[32]

While there are several precise examples of inscrutability given in terms of proxy functions, indeterminacy, in this pure holophrastic form, "draws too broadly on a language to admit of factual illustration".[33] There are no straightforward instances of translations appealed to. Another important contrast is that purely holophrastic indeterminacy is directed at and is (at least at the outset) limited to sentences and sentence meaning, and does not go to the sub-sentential level of terms and their meanings or referents. If taken seriously, this tells us that Quine's indeterminacy conjecture is addressed primarily against the notion of a proposition as the meaning of a sentence and not at the meanings of terms. Furthermore the attendant criticisms of synonymy and analyticity would apply only in virtue of propositional meaning. In summary, holophrastic indeterminacy without inscrutability is a conjecture about translation, with little by way of example, and it applies primarily (if not exclusively) to propositions.

Challenging Quine: analyticity and indeterminacy

The history of those questioning "Two Dogmas" (Quine's most famous essay) and his scepticism about the analytic–synthetic distinction is long and complex.[34] For instance, over the years Jerrold Katz has steadfastly argued that notions such as meaning, synonymy and analyticity are data which linguists must explain. He offers accounts of these notions from the perspective of his own linguistic theory.[35] Another factor is the recognition on the part of many, especially given the influence of Kripke's *Naming and Necessity*, that the notions of a prioricity, analyticity and necessity must be clearly distinguished and that arguments concerning them addressed separately. The a priori is an epistemological notion, the analytic a semantic or possibly a logical one, and necessity a logical or a metaphysical one.

Possibly the best-known reply to Quine on analyticity is Grice and Strawson's "In Defense of a Dogma".[36] Grice and Strawson claim that there really is an analytic–synthetic distinction, that it is an ordinary non-technical distinction, and that it can even be taught. If we give someone sentences such as 'If it's raining then it's raining', 'All bachelors are unmarried', and 'Nothing is taller than itself' as samples, they will be able to distinguish further sentences that are of this type from others that are not. Gilbert Harman has critically discussed this reply to Quine.[37] Harman stresses that Quine is criticizing a technical philosophical distinction which is supposed to have explanatory power. For instance, it has been required that analyticity explain the notion of a priori knowledge. It was thought that a priori knowledge is supposed to be non-empirical in a harmless way: merely based on truths about meanings. Harman is critical on a number of grounds. To begin with, Grice and Strawson have left out the key explanatory role that intensional notions were to serve. Harman also goes on to offer an analogy. One could introduce in some non-technical sense a witch/non-witch distinction and teach people to use it. One would do this in the same way Grice and Strawson say one could, by the use of paradigm sample cases, teach students to classify sentences into analytic or synthetic. But this would have no explanatory value and it would only amount to a classification of what appears to be analytic and what appears to be a witch. The possibility of classifying sentences or people by how they appear does not guarantee that there is a real distinction present. A speaker's reference to a sentence by using the expression 'analytic' is as much beside the point as a Salem speaker successfully referring to a person with the words 'that witch'. The latter does not show that there really are witches and the former does not show that there really are cases of analyticity.

Much of Quine's sceptical attitude toward analyticity and the theory of meaning after "Two Dogmas" centred on his indeterminacy conjecture. There have been many different challenges to Quine's indeterminacy of meaning conjecture. Roger Gibson has provided a classification of several types of challenges.[38]

The first is that Quine's indeterminacy claim does not provide a proof of its claim. As mentioned earlier in this chapter, Quine offers indeterminacy as a conjecture and not as a thesis in the sense that it is to be proven.

A second challenge is to say that there is no special indeterminacy of translation. It is merely a case of underdetermination of theory. The rejoinder to this was provided in an earlier section.

The third type of challenge to indeterminacy is that there are factors in translations that render it determinate. Among such challengers are those who supplement what they see as the rather meagre appeals to behaviour and empathy that Quine restricts himself to and thereby argue that translation is determinate.

Chapter 7

Intensional contexts

Quine is one of the foremost exponents of extensionality.

> . . . A context is *intensional* if it is not extensional.
>
> Extensionality is much of the glory of predicate logic, and it is much of the glory of any science that can be grammatically embedded in predicate logic. I find extensionality necessary, indeed, though not sufficient for my full understanding of a theory. In particular it is an affront to common sense to see a true sentence go false when a singular term in it is supplanted by another that names the same thing. What is true of a thing is true of it, surely under any name.[1]

Two problematic varieties of intensional contexts are those representing modal notions and propositional attitudes. Two prominent modal functors/operators are those for necessity, i.e. Nec, and for possibility, i.e. Pos. Belief is the most discussed propositional attitude. Unlike extensional functors/operators, such as conjunction or disjunction, or quantifiers, when intensional modal or belief operators/functors are used to form complex sentences, certain replacement principles appear to fail. One of these replacement principles is Leibniz's Law. It states that given a true identity premise:

$$a = b$$

and another true sentence containing 'a', viz.,

--- *a* ---

they jointly imply a conclusion:

--- *b* ---

that is obtained by substituting/replacing '*a*' with '*b*'. Colloquially put, the idea is that equals can be replaced by equals.

However, consider what happens when one applies this rule in a modal and in a propositional attitude context.

From the true

It is necessary that 9 > 7, i.e. 9 is greater than 7

and the true identity claim that

9 is the number of the planets

by substitution we get the false

It is necessary that the number of the planets > 7.

This conclusion is false since there might have been fewer than seven planets.

In a similar fashion, some ancient Roman's cognitive state might be truly described as:

Julius believed that the morning star is the morning star

although it was true but not known to Julius that

The morning star is identical with the evening star,

it does not follow and would be false to say:

Julius believed that the morning star is the evening star.

Following in the footsteps of Frege, Russell and Carnap and along with figures such as Davidson, Kripke and others, Quine has devoted much effort to this topic. He refers to settings where replacement principles fail as "referentially opaque" contexts.

Modal logic

Modal logic is the study of implications holding between modal sentences and it comes in a number of forms. It can involve principles such as that a stronger modality implies a weaker one. Thus,

It is necessary that *p*   i.e. Nec *p*

implies

p

and

p

implies

It is possible that *p*   i.e. Pos *p*.

C. I. Lewis, one of Quine's teachers, was a prominent contributor to modal logic in the first half of the twentieth century. He developed five systems of propositional modal logic. These are known as S1, S2, S3, S4 and S5, and they contain successively stronger conceptions of necessity. In S4,

It is possible that it is possible that *p*

implies

It is possible that *p*.

In a stronger system, S5,

It is possible that it is necessary that *p*

implies

It is necessary that *p*.

From 1946 on, Rudolf Carnap and Ruth Barcan Marcus pioneered investigations into quantificational modal logic. Among the latter's contributions was a controversial formula known as the Barcan formula.

> If it is possible that $(\exists x)Fx$, then $(\exists x)$ such that it is possible that Fx
>
> i.e. $\text{Pos}(\exists x)Fx \to (\exists x)\text{Pos}Fx$

Quine has been sceptical of modal logic. Taking a serious risk of over-simplifying Quine's views, let me classify his criticisms as involving two themes: the quotation paradigm and essentialism.

The quotation paradigm

Consider the following silly syllogism:

> Pigs are dirty.
> Pigs is a four-lettered word.
> ———————————————
> So, some four-lettered words are dirty.

There are two ambiguities that this specious reasoning trades on. The one we are interested in concerns the use–mention confusion. The use–mention distinction dictates that we distinguish when an expression such as 'pigs' is being used in an object language to refer to the animals that oink and when the expression is functioning in a metalanguage to talk about itself. In the latter case the expression is said to be mentioned and not used. To distinguish the mention from the use case we use quotes for the mention case. With this convention in mind, the following are true

> Pigs are dirty.
> 'Pigs' is a four-lettered word.

and the following are false

> 'Pigs' are animals.
> Pigs are nouns.

As Quine tells it, a motive for C. I. Lewis developing modal logic was rooted in a use–mention confusion of the metalinguistic relation of implication with the object language sentence connective representing conditionals.[2] (Of course, this confused motive is not the only motive for investigating modal logic.) In English, conditionals are standardly expressed as 'If --- then ---' and in sentence logic as '→'. C. I. Lewis and others, such as Russell in *Principia Mathematica*, mistakenly read the conditionals

$$\sim p \rightarrow (p \rightarrow q)$$

$$p \rightarrow (q \rightarrow p)$$

as though these conditionals/→ expressed the metalinguistic relation of a sentence being implied (following logically or being a logical consequent). By doing this paradoxical claims (dubbed paradoxes of material implication) arose:

> A false statement (such as 'Monday comes directly after Friday') implies every statement ('2 + 2 = 4')
>
> A true statement ('2 + 2 = 4') is implied by every statement ('All men are mortal').

The paradox disappears when one observes the use–mention distinction and recognizes that implication is a metalinguistic relation between quoted/mentioned sentences stating that one sentence validly follows from others. By contrast, the conditional is a sentence-forming connective which goes between two sentences requiring for its truth that the consequent be true when the antecedent is. When the two sentences are at the object language level, the conditional formed is also at the object language level.

Quine sees Lewis as having been in the grip of this confusion. Lewis developed a modal notion, a connective, which he thought might escape the paradoxes. He called it "strict implication". This connective was to go between two sentences to form a more complex sentence. Its role was to capture the metalinguistic notion of implication as an object language connective.

> Socrates is human strictly implies that he is human or rational, i.e. p strictly implies p or q

but

> Socrates is human does not strictly imply that Socrates taught Plato, i.e. p does not strictly imply q.

Strict implication can be defined in terms of the modal functor of necessity and a conditional sign

> It is necessary that if Socrates is human, then he is human or he is rational, i.e. $\text{Nec}(p \rightarrow [p \text{ or } q])$

Quine's point is that modal logic as originally conceived by Lewis was poorly motivated, failing to recognize a use–mention confusion. The conditional

> If Monday comes after Friday, then 2 + 2 = 5

is a true conditional because of the falsity of its antecedent. However, the metalinguistic claim

> 'Monday comes after Friday' implies (has as a logical consequent) '2 + 2 = 5'

is false: '2 + 2 = 5' is not a logical consequence of 'Monday comes after Friday'.

Quotation is an important model in Quine's understanding of intensional contexts: referential opacity. He was not alone in thinking that statements of necessity had a metalinguistic aspect. At the time of "Two Dogmas" it was common to assume that

> It is necessary that bachelors are unmarried

was another way of saying

> 'Bachelors are unmarried' is an analytic truth.

With quotation contexts as a model for modal contexts we have a clear and ready explanation of the failure of substitutivity of identity. One cannot substitute one expression for another even when the two expressions have the same referent if the substitution is to take place in a context where the expression is mentioned and not used, i.e. the expression is being referred to.

> 'Plato' is a five-lettered expression.
> Plato is identical with the teacher of Aristotle.
> ______________________________
> So, 'The teacher of Aristotle' is a five-lettered expression.

De dicto and *de re* modality: quotation and essentialism

The *de dicto–de re* modality distinction dates back to Abelard. Commenting on Aristotle, Abelard indicated that the question of whether a man who was sitting might not be sitting is ambiguous and can be interpreted in two ways.

> It is possible that a man who is sitting is not sitting.

> Pos$(\exists x)(x$ is a man and x is sitting and x is not sitting$)$.

On this interpretation the modal functor governs the entire sentence and is said to be a *de dicto* modality. The sentence is false, as it is not possible for something to have the contradictory properties of sitting and of not sitting.

A second construal expresses the truth that

> A man who actually is seated might not have been seated.

> $(\exists x)(x$ is a man and x is sitting and Pos x is not sitting$)$.

The possibility functor governs an occurrence of the variable occurring once within its scope, that is, the part 'x is not sitting', and that variable also occurs outside that scope. This is a case of 'quantifying into' a modal context and is an explication of Abelard's notion of *de re* modality. Someone who sat down might not have sat down. The man, the object that is the value of the variable, who actually is seated is said to have the possibility of not being seated. So to speak, the object x referred to in the clause 'Pos x is not sitting' is what has that possibility. In the *de dicto* case the possibility concerns an entire statement (a closed sentence).

For this *de re* case the problem of substitutivity is one of whether an expression occurs within the scope of a modal functor. If it does, then it can be likened to the quotation context and substitution is not allowed. On this quotation model the *de dicto* cases are not especially problematic since all the terms occur within the scope of the modal operator. The failure of substitution is explained on the quotation model. All such *de dicto* sentences are definable in terms of variations on the following form

It is necessary that ----

which in turn is modelled on quotation contexts such as

'----' is analytic.

The issues are subtler when we turn to *de re* modalities. Two considerations come to the fore.

(1) When is substitution allowable? We must distinguish the scope of the necessity functor and occurrences inside and outside the scope of that functor.
(2) How should we understand expressions occurring both inside and outside the scope? Two approaches are: quotation (the same object under different descriptions) and essentialism.

We will examine these topics by considering the evolution of some of Quine's views. In his earlier writing on modal logic Quine discussed the following example:

Nec (9 > 7) i.e. (9 is greater than 7)
9 = the number of the planets
____
therefore, Nec(the number of the planets > 7)[3]

Quine has been challenged with regard to his use of this example.[4] Since 'the number of the planets' is a definite description when it occurs in a complex context (embedded in the necessity functor), such as in the conclusion, that sentence is ambiguous. On Russell's theory of descriptions, the sentence can be replaced in two different ways. In one, the new sentence will be *de dicto* in that the necessity operator/functor will occur in front of the entire sentence in which the defined away definite description occurred.

> It is necessary that (<u>the number of the planets</u> > 7).

So construed, the conclusion does not follow, since the term here underlined occurs within the scope of the opacity producing functor.

The second construal is as a *de re* modal claim with one occurrence (underlined) of the term outside the scope of the necessity functor and one inside it.

> <u>The number of the planets</u> is such that necessarily it (the number of the planets) > 7.

The conclusion does follow because it results from substituting in the first occurrence of the term. That occurrence is not in the scope of the necessity operator. To repeat, it is crucial to distinguish whether or not a term occurs within the scope of an intensional functor. When it does, one cannot substitute. When it is not embedded in the scope of such a functor the context is not intensional – it is extensional – and one can use ordinary replacement principles.[5]

Quine persists and asks how we should understand constructions such as Nec ($x > 7$), which occur in the *de re* reading. Which is the object x that is necessarily greater than 7? If it is 9, then since that is one and the same object as the number of the planets, we are left with the problem that its being necessarily greater than 7 is incompatible with the fact that there might not have been more than seven planets. Quine deals with this difficulty in terms of two strategies: the quotation paradigm and essentialism. On the quotation approach we can consider the *de re* claim in terms of the following claim

> The object described by 'the number of the planets' is necessarily greater than 7.

On this quotation model, modal truths depend on how you describe an object. Modalities such as necessity are not so much objective features of things but rather are language dependent. Claims of necessity do not depend on how objects are, but on how they are described. Described using the expression '9 ', that object is necessarily greater than 7. However, the same object described by the expression 'the number of the planets' is not necessarily greater than 7. Such an approach relativizes necessity to how we talk about objects and it is not an approach those favouring richer and stronger conceptions of modal notions are inclined to accept. So while someone such as Socrates is necessarily himself when described as his self, he – the same object – is not necessarily the teacher of Plato, even though there is no change in the objects involved. As another example, consider Hume's claim that causal relations do not exhibit necessity. Taking sufficient care in describing causal relations, we can express a necessary connection between cause and effect. While turning on the switch caused the light to go on exhibits no necessity, we can re-describe the same situation as follows:

> Necessarily, the cause of the light going on caused the light to go on.

The second way of understanding 'x is necessarily greater than 7' consists of invoking the essential property versus accidental property distinction. So while 9 possesses the property of being greater than 7 necessarily, the number of the planets does not necessarily possess that property. The explanation offered is that being greater than 7 is an essential property of 9 while being greater than 7 is only an accidental property of the number of the planets. Quine finds this distinction of properties into essential and accidental difficult to accept. It seems arbitrary which properties are essential and which not.

In *Word and Object* he presents the following problem.[6] Consider John, who is both a mathematician and a cyclist. As a mathematician he is necessarily rational but accidentally two-legged. As a cyclist he is necessarily two-legged but only accidentally rational. What is the essential and what is the accidental property of one and the same object John?

Quine has been challenged on this example by Ruth Marcus.[7] She indicates that the English sentences are ambiguous between *de dicto* and *de re* readings.

If we maintain *de dicto* readings throughout we have:

(1) Nec(x)(x is a mathematician $\rightarrow$ x is rational) and
not Nec(x)(x is a mathematician $\rightarrow$ x is two-legged)

(2) Nec(x)(x is a cyclist $\rightarrow$ x is two-legged) and
not Nec(x)(x is a mathematician $\rightarrow$ x is rational)

(3) John is a mathematician and he is a cyclist

and nothing strange follows. If we maintain the *de re* readings we have:

(4) $(x)(x$ is a mathematician $\rightarrow$ Nec x is rational$)$ and
$(x)(x$ is a mathematician $\rightarrow$ not Nec$(x$ is two-legged$))$.

(5) $(x)(x$ is a cyclist $\rightarrow$ Nec x is two-legged$)$ and
$(x)(x$ is a mathematician $\rightarrow$ not Nec x is rational$)$.

(6) John is a mathematician and he is a cyclist.

Marcus points out that on the *de re* reading the three sentences are inconsistent. Thus from 4 and 6 it follows that Nec John is rational, and from 5 and 6 that not Nec John is rational. On the *de dicto* reading nothing strange follows.

Given Marcus's reply, and possibly on other grounds, Quine does not repeat this mathematician–cyclist argument after *Word and Object*. It is important though to recognize that Marcus's reply does not provide a positive case for essentialism. Essentialist claims are not explicated in her reply. So Quine's other criticisms remain in force and he retains his scepticism of talk of essences and notions that rely on them.

Challenging Quine: possible world semantics and the new theory of reference

Significant developments concerning modal logic and its role in philosophy occurred with the birth of what has come to be known as "possible world semantics" and "the new theory of reference". In this section I will try to explain some of the challenges they posed for Quine and to explore his responses to them. The issues are rather complex and my summary will only outline some strands of Quine's thoughts: that the new truth conditions don't explicate necessity, and that these new developments still rely on questionable essentialist assumptions.

In "Two Dogmas", Quine laid down the challenge of breaking out of the circle of intensional notions (see Chapter 5). While one might define one such notion in terms of another, this does not help matters, since Quine is sceptical of each. His challenge is to explicate one of these in non-intensional/extensional terms. With respect to necessity, this challenge may be put in terms of giving a truth condition for when a statement of necessity of the form 'Nec*S*', for example, Nec(water is H_2O), is true. The traditional account is

> 'It is necessary that water is H_2O' is true if and only if it is true in all possible worlds that water is H_2O.

But if no account is given of 'possible', then since possibility is an intensional notion, we have not broken out of the circle.

At the time "Two Dogmas" appeared a popular explication of Nec*S* was in terms of analyticity.

> 'It is necessary that water is H_2O' is true if and only if 'Water is H_2O' is analytic.

This account does not meet Quine's challenge, since it relies on the notion of analyticity.

Quine's criticisms of modal notions served to spur others to give a better account of necessity. Modal logicians were also interested in providing precise truth conditions for reasons of their own. They wanted to give more exact explanations of the differences between modal assumptions such as in S4, S5 and to explore controversies surrounding claims such as the Barcan Formula. Exact truth conditions are needed to provide the statement of proofs of metalogical theorems such as the completeness of modal systems. To meet these needs, several authors (Kanger, Kripke, Hintikka and Montague) working independently of each other came up with a style of truth condition for 'Nec*S*' which, on the surface, meets Quine's constraint of breaking out of the intensional circle. The result was a metalinguistic extensional account of ''Nec*S*' is true'. The truth condition provides an extensional account that makes as precise as set theoretical notions can some key notions of modal logic. A world is just the domain of objects our variables range over along with an assignment of extensions to the predicates of the language; and domains and assignments after all are just sets. Sets are extensional items which Quine himself appeals to. The truth condition can be put somewhat informally as follows.

> A sentence is necessarily true when it is true
>
> a. as evaluated in a given world (for a specific domain/set such as the real world. The real world is the set containing whatever does exist with all their actual features)

b. and it remains true when it is in a given relation (that can be explicated extensionally) to all other worlds (domains/sets) with the same or different objects with the same or different features.

Looked at from a Quinian perspective this truth condition for 'Nec*S*' involves only sets (i.e. worlds), quantification over them (e.g. all worlds/sets) and extensional relations between worlds/sets. It would look somewhat like the following:

> 'Nec(Water is H_2O)' is true if and only if 'Water is H_2O' is true in a given world/set and in every world/set having a given relation to that given world.

Stated for the general case we have

> 'Nec *S*' is true if and only if '*S*' is true in the actual world *W* and true in every world *W′* which is related R to W (the actual world).

This approach has come to be called "possible world semantics". It is not quite the same as, and should not be confused with, earlier attempts to explain necessity in terms of simple appeals to the undefined notion of possibility.

Quine's importance consists not only in his positive views but also in his role as a critic, "a gadfly".[8] Viewing the development of possible world semantics as in part a response to Quine's criticisms is a case in point. To a certain extent these extensional conditions transform the nature of the debate about intensional notions. If we were to use modal notions as given extensionally to define the other intensional notions, we would have taken steps to establishing their legitimacy for extensionalists. However, by and large this is not the direction taken by those who appeal to modal notions. Neither analyticity nor synonymy has been explained in terms of necessary truth, and meanings have not been reformulated in terms of possible worlds. Philosophers such as Kripke at times appeal to analyticity without basing it on modal insights. Instead, for Kripke and others, modal distinctions can be based on logical, linguistic or metaphysical insights. Thus the synonymy and analyticity connected with bachelors being unmarried men is used to account for the necessity involved here and not the other way around. In addition to such linguistically based necessities Kripke introduces necessities that are metaphysically or scientifically based. It is taken as necessary that water is H_2O. This necessity is not simply based on matters of language, since it is not taken as analytic that water is H_2O. For Kripke, it is of the nature of water that it is two parts hydrogen and one part oxygen. Far from it being solely a matter of the language used, the necessity of water being H_2O is said to be scientifically and empirically discovered.

These developments in possible world semantics have not resulted in Quine endorsing modal logic. Although a number of his earlier criticisms, for example, his number of the planets example and his mathematical cyclist example, as well as his demand for a precise, extensional treatment of quantified modal logic, have been challenged, he still holds the view that modal notions are not desirable. To a large extent, as we are about to see, this is based on the charge of essentialism.

Quine has replied to the new possible world semantics as follows:

> The notion of a possible world did indeed contribute to the semantics of modal logic, and it behooves us to recognize the nature of its contribution: it led to Kripke's precocious and significant theory of models of modal logic. Models afford consistency proofs; also they have heuristic value; but they do not constitute explication. Models, however clear they be in themselves, may leave us still at a loss for the primary, intended interpretation. When modal logic has been paraphrased in terms of such notions as possible world or rigid designator, where the displaced fog settles is on the question when to identify objects between worlds, or when to treat a designator as rigid, or where to attribute metaphysical necessity.[9]

I will interpret Quine's remarks here to highlight two criticisms of these developments: (1) that there is only a surface sense in which the intensional circle is broached, and that implicit in these developments is the use of fully fledged modal notions such as possibility and necessity; and (2) richer more substantive modal claims presuppose essentialism.

(1) When the above truth conditions for the truth of 'Nec *S*' are stated as they were above (four paragraphs back), the notions involved are extensional and do allow for clarifying issues such as the consistency and completeness of systems of modal logic.

However, when the *R* relation is taken as though one world or domain is genuinely possible relative to another, the intensional notion of possibility is assumed. For Quine, the *R* relation (as given when the truth conditions are construed extensionally), does not justify equating *R* and possibility.

(2) A new theory of reference originated in connection with "possible world semantics". One of its prominent themes is that a name (and an individual constant – the correlate of a name in the logic of quantification) stands for the same object in every possible world. One way in which Kripke employed this theme was with his notion of a rigid designator. Names are an important type of rigid designator. A rigid designator is an expression that stands for an object in the actual world and for the same object in every possible world. So 'Aristotle' stands for an object that existed in the actual world and as a rigid designator it stands for that identical object in every possible world. It is at this point that Quine calls our attention to the problem of identifying the same individual from one world to the next. One of the places where the problem appears is with the notion of a rigid designator. How are we to identify the same object in different possible worlds? Quine holds that if such identification is a matter of the object having an essence or essential property which allows us to identify the object from world to world, then transworld identity relies on an untenable distinction. He is unable to accept the essential versus accidental property distinction.

So, while the general outlines of quantified modal logic are clarified by possible world semantics for the purposes of what we might call pure modal formulas and modal systems (questions of which formulas are truths of modal logic or which systems are consistent or complete), we are at a loss to genuinely explicate richer substantive modal claims such as those about Aristotle's or water's essential properties.[10]

The situation for modal claims may be compared and contrasted with that of non-modal claims. While Quine holds that the philosophically useful notion of existence is explicated by the logic of quantification, he denies that the notions of possibility, necessity and essence are explicated by the logic of quantified modal logic. What is the difference? For quantification and first order predicate logic we have a deductive system and model theoretic truth conditions. The same is true for a modal system such as the quantified modal form of

Lewis's S5 system. The truth conditions for the first order non-modal case will allow us to prove the consistency and completeness of that system as well as that some formulas are not logical truths. The conditions for quantified S5 will do the same for the purely logical claims of quantified S5. A significant difference between the modal and the non-modal cases arises with regard to substantive claims (not purely formal claims), made in the language of the respective systems. That Aristotle was a man and that water is H_2O require an account of the identity over the histories of Aristotle and of water. In the actual world such cases of identity over time are matters of spatial and temporal continuity. There are no gaps and no lack of continuity in spatial and temporal history of such actual objects from the time they come into existence to the time they cease to exist. The modal claims that Aristotle necessarily has some characteristic or that water necessarily is H_2O also require an account of identity, that is, that we can give an acceptable account of what it is to have the same individual such as Aristotle or an item of water in different possible worlds. However, for these modal cases, there are no notions comparable to spatio-temporal continuity to account for transworld identity, for example, of Aristotle or water from possible world to possible world.[11] It is at this juncture that the appeal to the notion of essence, which Quine rejects, can make an appearance. Transworld identity relies on an object having an essence that allows the object to be identified from world to world, and Quine remains sceptical of attempts to explain substantive modal claims that rely on the interrelated notions of quantifying into modal contexts, rigid designation and identity through possible worlds.

Quine, though, does accord a more limited non-modal role to the suspect notions:

> It [*de re* belief] and the notion of essence are on a par. Both make sense in context. Relative to a particular inquiry, some predicates may play a more basic role than others, . . . and these may be treated as essential. . . . The same is true of the whole quantified modal logic of necessity; for it collapses if essence is withdrawn. For that matter, the very notion of necessity makes sense to me only relative to context. Typically it is applied to what is assumed in an inquiry, as against what has yet to transpire.[12]

What Quine is indicating here by context is that in a particular setting, for example, a laboratory, one might infer enthymematically from that *x* contains water, that it contains H_2O. The background assumption is the non-modal suppressed premise that water is H_2O. The predicate 'is H_2O' plays a more basic role here in that the claim that water is H_2O is more central to our belief system and we are less likely to give it up than other, less central, claims. In this way typical cases of strong modal claims can be accommodated in a more innocuous form as non-modal background assumptions that one takes for granted while pursuing the subject at hand. In a similar way one takes for granted that Aristotle is a man in reasoning to more questionable or more interesting conclusions.

Early in this chapter I acknowledged that my survey of Quine's views on modal logic risks oversimplifying matters. The subject matter is technical and at times rather complex. My goal was to convey as accurately as possible an introduction to some of the key issues. To have pursued more details would have obscured the larger perspective on Quine's influence I wished to present. A fuller discussion would cover such topics as: Quine's responses to proposals to let intensional objects serve as the referents of expressions occurring in modal contexts; an extended discussion of varieties of essentialist views; and non-Kripkean versions of the new theory of reference. For surveys of these matters I recommend Dagfinn Follesdal's paper "Quine on Modality" and its sequel "Essentialism and Reference".

Propositional attitudes

The treatment of propositional attitudes runs parallel to that of modal notions, with at least one very important difference. While Quine is quite willing, indeed encourages us, to do without modal notions, he finds propositional attitudes to be indispensable. In a late work, *Pursuit of Truth*, Quine assigns to ascriptions of belief such as

Ralph believes that Ortcutt is a spy

the logical form

a R that *S*.

The *a* position is that of the believer (the attitudinist), in this case Ralph. The *R* position is that of the verb for the attitude, believing.

The *S* position is for the content sentence and the expression 'that' is a conjunction marking off the real world which contains the believer and his mental state from the believed world described by the content sentence. For Quine this marking off is best thought of in terms of semantic ascent and the quotation model. Also important is the ascriber of the belief to the believer, the one who holds the belief ascription, for example, Willard.

On Quine's account the ascriber/Willard empathizes with the believer/Ralph. The ascriber/Willard in his own language then constructs the content sentence. Belief ascriptions on this account describe a relation between a believer and a sentence framed in the ascriber's own terms as per the ascriber empathizing with the believer.

As in modal contexts, distinguishing occurrences of terms inside and outside the scope of opacity producing operators/functors is crucial. Besides accounting for clear-cut cases of allowable substitution, it facilitates making needed distinctions. A famous example of such a distinction occurs in "Quantifiers and Propositional Attitudes". Quine distinguishes an ambiguity connected with the sentence

'Ralph wants a sloop.'[13]

Does Ralph want a particular sloop, that is, the *de re*

$(\exists x)(x$ is a sloop & Ralph wants $x)$

or does he merely want "relief from slooplessness", that is, the *de dicto*

Ralph wants that $(\exists x)(x$ is a sloop$)$?

In *Word and Object* Quine initially develops a notation for intensions which serve as the objects of propositional attitudes and is thereby able to specify when a term occurs within or without the scope of the propositional attitude operator/functor. In a later section entitled "Other Objects for the Attitudes" he proceeds along the lines of the quotation model where linguistic items do the job of intensional objects for explaining opacity. As in the modal logic case, *de dicto* beliefs are benign when thought of along the lines of the quotation model. *De re* beliefs are the troublesome case.

In "Quantifiers and Propositional Attitudes", later in *Pursuit of Truth* and in *From Stimulus to Science* the sloop-type case also occurs with regard to the sentence

> There are some whom Ralph believes to be spies.

This is considered not merely as the innocuous counterpart of the *de dicto* desire that sloops exist:

> Ralph believes that there are spies.

In this innocuous case the ascriber is merely making an assertion about Ralph and his believed world. It is the *de dicto*:

> Ralph believes that $(\exists x)(x$ is a spy$)$

which quotationally can be put along the following lines:

> Ralph believes true 'There are spies'.

The difficult case for understanding

> There are some whom Ralph believes to be spies.

is where the ascriber is claiming something else: a relation between the real world of existing spies and Ralph's belief world. Problems arise if we try to put this as a *de re* belief, that is, as quantifying in

> $(\exists x)$ Ralph believes that x is a spy.

On the quotation model the result is an incoherent use–mention confusion

> $(\exists x)$ Ralph believes 'x is a spy'.

The occurrence of x in the initial quantifier '$(\exists x)$' is being used. It takes as its values objects in the real world. The occurrence of 'x' in the quoted portion is not a variable but just a letter (the twenty-fourth letter of our alphabet) that is part of the name of the quoted expression 'x is a spy'. The sentence

$(\exists x)$ Ralph believes '*x* is a spy'.

is a case of vacuous quantification of the same vacuous sort as

$(\exists x)$(Socrates is human).

Such strings are either not allowed as syntactically meaningful in some statements of rules of well-formedness or tolerated in the interest of relaxing such purely syntactical rules but then have no natural semantical interpretation. In summary, *de dicto* beliefs are construed as innocuous case of quotation and *de re* beliefs remain, like *de re* modalities, rather problematic.

> Propositional attitudes de re presuppose a relation of intention between thoughts and things intended, for which I conceive of no adequate guidelines. To garner empirical content for [*de re* belief] we would have to interrogate Ralph and compile some of his persistent beliefs de dicto.
>
> I conclude that propositional attitudes de re resist annexation to scientific language as propositional attitudes de dicto do not. At best the ascriptions de re are signals pointing a direction in which to look for informative ascriptions de dicto.[14]

Propositional attitudes (at least the *de dicto* ones) are indispensable for science.[15] They play a significant role in the social sciences and history. For example, part of the explanation of Hitler's invasion of Russia in 1941 was his belief that England could not be invaded. Modal claims, though, are dispensable; at best they are signs that certain assumptions are being taken for granted or that certain sentences follow.

Furthermore, it is with propositional attitudes that for Quine the mental is seen as in a sense irreducible to the physical.[16] The irreducibility is not the claim that we have an ontology of physical items and non-physical ones, with the latter ontologically irreducible to the former. The dualism is one of predicates, of predicates reducible to physical terms and those mental predicates not so reducible. The underlying ontology is that of physical objects described both physicalistically as well as mentalistically. Quine is here adopting the position known as anomalous monism that was developed by his former student, Donald Davidson.

Challenging Quine: attitudes without objects

In *Philosophy of Logic*, Quine introduces the notion of attitudinatives as an alternative way of providing the logical form of belief sentences[17] and then later he favours a more commonly held view.[18] In this "Challenging Quine" section a case will be made for attitudinatives understood along Lesniewskian lines.

The more common logical form assigned to sentences like 'Ralph believes that Ortcutt is a spy' focuses on the unit 'believes', taking it to be a predicate (a relational expression) standing for a relation between at least two objects, John and the proposition that Ortcutt is a spy. Quine avoids positing propositions and favours sentences as the object of the attitudes. This was the logical form he assigned in *Pursuit of Truth*, which was presented earlier where the believer/attitudinist is related to the quoted/mentioned sentence. The attitudinative account relies on 'believes that' (which is not a predicate) instead of 'believes' (a predicate) in assigning the correct logical form. Although Quine does not put it in just such terms, 'believes that' is best described as being a functor.

> A functor is a sign that attaches to one or more expressions of given grammatical kind or kinds to produce an expression of a given grammatical kind. The negation sign is a functor that attaches to a statement to produce a statement and to a term to produce a term.[19]

The 'believes that' functor attaches to a name (of the believer) and a sentence (the content sentence) to form a sentence (a basic belief ascription).

> *A* (believes that) *S*, i.e. Ralph (believes that) Ortcutt is a spy.

The notion of a functor originated in the tradition stemming from the Polish logician Stanislaus Lesniewski. A Lesniewskian functor is a generalization on the notion of a predicate and an operator/connective. A functor in this sense should not be confused with that of simply being a predicate or simply being an operator; it is a generalization on both notions. 'Believes that' as a functor is not simply a predicate nor is it simply an operator/connective. It is both. Arthur Prior seems to have had this conception in mind. In his words, "it is a predicate at one end and a connective at the other": a "connecticate".[20]

The "believes that" functor does the same work as the quotation paradigm in disallowing substitution into the scope of beliefs. On the quotation model this is explained in terms of the use–mention difference. On the belief functor model the explanation is simply that beliefs are not necessarily tied to objective real world referents; hence what applies to the referent need not apply to the belief. If we use the image of a belief box, then this point can be expressed by saying that it is a contingent empirical question of what actually is in a person's belief box. The belief functor is not a logical functor but a psychological one. So Julius might very well have in his belief box that the morning star is the morning star, but not that the morning star is the evening star, even though as a matter of fact in the real world outside Julius they are one and the same object.

An important difference between the relational and the functor approach is that the functor approach does not ontologically commit us to objects for propositional attitudes. For instance 'and' is a functor, a logical functor. Its conjuncts might require ontological commitment, but 'and' itself only requires that there be suitable sentences to serve as conjuncts. Similarly, all that 'believes that' requires is that there be a suitable noun (the name of a believer) and a sentence (the content sentence). The belief functor allows for propositional attitudes without objects. Instead of Quine's tactic of "other objects for the attitudes", of putting sentences for propositions, no objects at all are required. The predicate/relational approach has the believer in relation to an object. When 'believes' in '*a* believes that *S*' is construed as a relational expression, 'that *S*' is a singular term, a vehicle of ontologial commitment. On the relational predicate approach

'Ralph believes that Ortcutt is a spy.'

has the logical form

a R that *S* i.e. Ralph believes the sentence 'Ortcutt is a spy'.

Lesniewski took a serious interest in quantifiers for sentence and predicate positions. By contrast, Quine's view is that quantification is exclusively a matter of quantifiers for singular term positions (quantifiers in standard first order logic). This becomes an issue in giving accounts of reasoning concerning beliefs. Propositionalists use cases such as the following valid argument as evidence for their view. Given the premise

> Both John and Barbara believe that Ortcutt is a spy

which propositionalists assign the form

> John believes *p* and Barbara believes *p*

It follows that

> There is something that both John and Barbara believe

which is assigned the propositionalist form

> $(\exists p)$(John believes *p* & Barbara believes *p*).

With '*p*' as a propositional variable these logical forms are cited as evidence for our ontological commitment to propositions. The conclusion is an existential generalization asserting the existence of at least one proposition.

With attitudinatives as Lesniewskian functors we can account for this inference, providing it with a logical form and yet avoiding committing ourselves to propositions.

> John (believes that) Ortcutt is a spy and Barbara (believes that) Ortcutt is a spy.
>
> So, $(\exists S)$(John (believes that) *S* and Barbara (believes that) *S*)

Unlike Quine, in following Lesniewski we take quantification in sentence, predicate and other positions seriously and without incurring further ontological commitments. (See Challenging Quine, Chapter 5 and Hugly and Sayward (1996) for reasons for taking such quantification seriously.)

Chapter 8

Nature, know thyself

Epistemology naturalized

The opening paragraph of this book outlined Quine's position as one of the foremost representatives of naturalism of his time. As stated there, his naturalism insists upon a close connection (an alliance) between philosophical views and those of the natural sciences. This has been amply documented in the preceding chapters, starting in Chapter 1 with expressing an ontology in terms of the science of logic, and then in Chapter 2 determining which ontology to accept by abiding by the same broad theoretical constraints that are invoked in connection with scientific theories. Chapter 3 explored how Quine's holistic empiricism resulted in viewing purportedly non-empirical a priori subjects such as mathematics and logic as holistically empirical in the same spirit as the more theoretical reaches of science. In later chapters his naturalist and empiricist views of language yielded criticisms of less naturalistic accounts of language and of philosophical practice, and yielded as consequences the two separate indeterminacies of reference (inscrutability) and of meaning.

While earlier naturalists would agree with Quine that our ontology is naturalistic, with Quine this took the form that our ontological commitments are derived from the sciences by appealing to themes concerning values of variables and holistic empiricism. Another aspect of Quine's naturalism is his approach to questions in epistemology – the theory of knowledge. Arguing that there is no standpoint outside of nature, philosophy, and in particular, epistemology, is no exception.

Consider the traditional epistemologist on the problem of our knowledge of the external world. As traditionally stated it is one of how a Cartesian self with its private mental states can come to have knowledge of the external world. Quine's restatement is strikingly more naturalistic.

> I am a physical object sitting in a physical world. Some of the forces of this physical world impinge on my surface. Light rays strike my retinas; molecules bombard my eardrums and fingertips. I strike back, emanating concentric air waves. These waves take the form of a torrent of discourse about tables, people, molecules, light rays, retinas, air waves, prime numbers, infinite classes, joy and sorrow, good and evil.[1]

As formulated historically by empiricists like Berkeley and Hume, this problem concerns the justification of our knowledge of objects such as tables, chairs and so on. That is to say, starting with "experience" in the form of immediately given impressions or sense data, how do we ever justify our claims to know such objects? Proceeding on the assumption that "experience" constitutes certain and incorrigible knowledge, and that it ought to be the foundation for all other cognitive claims, traditional philosophers attempted to show how all our knowledge is linked to and thereby justified by "experience". In so doing they were attempting to justify everyday and scientific claims to knowledge by assuming a special and privileged vantage point. This vantage point was that of a first philosophy from which they sought to provide a foundation of certainty for the sciences by standing outside them and legitimizing their accomplishments by tracing the connections to the "experience" of the philosopher.

Quine, however, rejects this traditional way of pursuing epistemology. He rephrases the problem of our knowledge of the external world as one of how we learn to talk about, to refer to, objects. Put somewhat differently, what are the conditions that lead to talking scientifically? How is scientific discourse possible? Quine's reasons for taking this approach of substituting the study of the psychogenesis of reference for first philosophy consists of (1) pointing out that it is the only viable option for an epistemologist to take and (2) revealing the defects of the more traditional approaches to epistemology. We will begin by examining the latter reasons.

The traditional empiricists' accounts of the linkage between "experience" and our knowledge claims vary from mentalistic conceptions, like that of Hume, to the effect that all our ideas are copies of sense impressions, to more neutrally linguistic formulations, such as that all knowledge claims are translatable into observation sentences. If Quine's Duhemian empiricism is correct, then one cannot deal with the empirical content of sentences (much less of terms – the linguistic correlates of ideas) one by one, either via definition, translation or some other sort of linkage. Quine's own procedure for studying the relation of knowledge and science to observation sentences is to trace the psychological and linguistic development of the knower, that is, the potential user of scientific language. He is, in effect, taking the position of a natural historian of certain language skills as they develop in the individual and the species, in particular of those skills that are involved in speaking about and knowing the world. Observation sentences serve as both the genetic starting point in human language learning and the empirical grounds for science. The problem of knowledge for the empiricists is how, starting with observation sentences, we can proceed to talk of tables, chairs, molecules, neutrinos, sets and numbers. One of Quine's arguments for pursuing empiricist epistemology by studying the roots of reference is simply the failure on holistic/Duhemian grounds of the traditional empiricists' programme mentioned above. However, even without accepting Quine's Duhemian views, most empiricists now agree that the attempt to justify knowledge by defining, translating, or somehow reducing it to observation, has failed.

Yet another way in which Quine modifies traditional empiricist epistemology is his treatment of notions such as "experience" or "observation". Avoiding mentalistic idioms, he relies instead on two distinct components which are already part of his empiricist ontology and which are surrogates for "experience" and "observation". On the one hand, there is the physical happening at the nerve endings, the neural input or stimulus. On the other, there is the linguistic entity, the observation sentence. A behavioural criterion for being an observation sentence is that it can be learned independently of other language acquisition. By Quine's definition, observation sentences are those that can be learned purely ostensively and as such are causally most proximate to the stimulus:

> Linguistically, and hence conceptually, the things in sharpest focus are the things that are public enough to be talked of publicly, common and conspicuous enough to be talked of often,

> and near enough to sense to be quickly identified and learned by name. It is to these that words apply first and foremost.[2]

The traditional empiricist's account of his epistemological basis fares badly by comparison. Ontologically it commits the empiricist to the existence of private, non-scientific (i.e. non-testable), difficult to identify and possibly mentalistic objects such as the above mentioned impressions and ideas. The ontology required by Quine's account, on the other hand, consists of physical events, that is, nerve hits, and linguistic entities, that is, observation sentences. Furthermore, for those recent empiricists who rely on the notion of an observation sentence and who thus may avoid some of the ontological problems associated with the mentalistic approach, Quine's particular account of such sentences has great virtue. His account is not vulnerable to recent attacks on the notion of observation as relative to and dependent on the theories one holds, since Quine's observation sentences are precisely those sentences that are learnable without any background knowledge. Yet another point of difference with other empiricists concerns the alleged certainty or incorrigibility of observation. Although Quine's observation sentences are assented to with a minimum amount of background information and are thus included among those sentences least likely to be revised, they are not in principle immune from revision. As remarked on in Chapter 4, Quine's fallibilism incorporates the view that observation sentences may at times be edited, that is, that they are on a par with all other sentences in being potential candidates for revision as a result of some test.

A last argument for approaching epistemology in terms of the sciences of psychology and linguistics is, according to Quine, that there simply is no first philosophy – no special vantage point outside science from which one can link up science and knowledge to neural input and observation sentences:

> Epistemology, or something like it, simply falls into place as a chapter of psychology and hence of natural science. It studies a natural phenomenon, a physical human subject. This human subject is accorded a certain experimentally controlled input – certain patterns of irradiation in assorted frequencies, for instance – and in the fullness of time, the subject delivers as output a description of the three-dimensional external world and its history. The relation between the meager input and the

> torrential output is a relation that we are prompted to study for somewhat the same reasons that always prompted epistemology; namely, in order to see how evidence relates to theory, and in what ways one's theory of nature transcends any available evidence. . . .
>
> The old epistemology aspired to contain, in a sense, natural science; it would construct it somehow from sense data. Epistemology in its new setting, conversely, is contained in natural science, as a chapter of psychology, but the old containment remains valid too, in its way. We are studying how the human subject of our study posits bodies and projects his physics from his data, and we appreciate that our position in the world is just like his. Our very epistemological enterprises, therefore, and the psychology wherein it is a component chapter, and the whole of natural science wherein psychology is a component book – all this is our own construction or projection from stimulations like those we were meting out to our epistemological subject. There is thus reciprocal containment, though containment in different senses: epistemology in natural science and natural science in epistemology.[3]

This argument for why epistemology must be naturalized as the psychogenesis of reference involves one of the most integral of themes in Quine's philosophy – that we cannot stand apart from our scientific world view and make philosophical judgements. The philosopher's view is inevitably an extension of the scientist's. There is continuity, if not an actual unity, of science and philosophy. To bring this point home Quine has on a number of occasions made use of an image of Otto Neurath's: "We are like sailors who must rebuild their ship out on the open sea, never able to dismantle it in a dry-dock and to reconstruct it there out of the best materials".[4]

Indeed, this theme of the continuity of science and philosophy permeates all of Quine's work. We may review the terrain we have covered from that perspective. In Chapters 2 and 3, we examined Quine the philosopher as ontologist concerned with the concept of existence and the criteria for ontological commitment. Existence claims are clarified within the science or theory of quantification, and we are committed to precisely the ontology which results from choosing between ontological hypotheses in the same way as one does between those more readily construed as scientific, that is, by appeal to the explanatory power, simplicity, precision and so on, of the hypotheses in question. In Chapter 4, the problem of a priori knowledge was dealt with from within the framework of a Duhemian empiricism, which is itself a product of reflection on the role of testing in the physical sciences. Such an empiricism views the sciences of logic and mathematics as a gradual extension of the others and subject to the same general constraints. Philosophical analysis itself is an endeavour within the framework of our scientific scheme of things. It is not a new version of a first philosophy and there are no distinctively philosophical methods. So in Chapters 5 and 6 we contrasted Quine's explication of logical truth with the absence of any equally precise hypothesis/analysis of such concepts as analyticity, meaning, synonymy and so forth. In the earlier sections of Chapter 6, philosophical theories of meaning and reference were subjected to empiricist and behaviourist scrutiny, and finally, a psycholinguistic theory of empiricism was expounded.

Quine is in the tradition of those philosophers who have had the closest of ties with science. Examples come readily to mind: Aristotle's biological models; the appeals by Descartes and Spinoza to the methods of geometry; Hobbes's modelling the body politic on physical bodies; Hume's endeavour to apply Newtonian methods to problems in epistemology and moral philosophy; and the attempts by Bentham and Dewey to reconcile judgements of value with those of the sciences. Whatever the particular faults of such philosophers, the programme in general remains an eminently defensible one. Quine may well prove to be the twentieth century's most important exemplar of the position that the philosopher's perspective is of a piece with that of the scientist. His own sentiments provide an excellent summary of that position:

> As naturalistic philosophers we begin our reasoning within the inherited world theory as a going concern. We tentatively believe all of it, but believe also that some unidentified portions are wrong. We try to improve, clarify, and understand the system from within. We are the busy sailors adrift on Neurath's boat.[5]

A natural history of reference

How does an individual come to respond linguistically and eventually to refer to things as diverse as concrete physical objects and abstract entities like sets and properties? Since this is the distinctive feature of scientific language, Quine is also asking how we learn to talk scientifically. The investigation of learning to talk of cabbages, kings, electrons and sets demands a reconstruction of the psychology of learning applied to reference. Quine has called this 'the psychogenesis of reference', and its objective is to give an empirical description of "the roots of reference". Since, for Quine, empiricism in the philosophy of language constitutes adopting the stance of a behaviourist, the question is one of gaining a behaviourist reconstruction of language acquisition. How, given a child's stimulation, can we account for his acquiring referential skills?

Quine has taken up this topic in a number of places: in "Speaking of Objects", in the third chapter of *Word and Object*, entitled the "Ontogenesis of Reference", and in his books *The Roots of Reference*, *Pursuit of Truth* and *From Stimulus to Science*. In this section we shall sketch an outline of the stages involved in the psychogenesis of reference, concluding with a brief comparison with a different theory of language acquisition, that of the linguist Noam Chomsky.

The study of how we learn to refer presupposes work in learning theory in general and in more primitive phases of language learning than those involving reference. We can isolate three stages, which prepare us for acquiring referential skills:

(1) prelinguistic learning;
(2) prereferential language learning; and
(3) learning to refer.

Animals as well as children are capable of learning. Various episodes occur with respect to their sense organs, and perception is a matter of responding to these episodes. A key factor in a subject's responding is the ability to perceive similarities, declares Quine:

> A response to a red circle, if it is rewarded, will be elicited again by a pink ellipse more readily than by a blue triangle; the red circle resembles the pink ellipse more than the blue triangle. Without some such prior spacing of qualities, we could never acquire a habit; all stimuli would be equally alike and equally different. These spacings of qualities, on the part of men and other animals, can be explored and mapped in the laboratory by experiments in conditioning and extinction. Needed as they are for all learning, these distinctive spacings cannot themselves all be learned; some must be innate.

> If then I say that there is an innate standard of similarity, I am making a condensed statement that can be interpreted, and truly interpreted, in behavioral terms. Moreover, in this behavioral sense it can be said equally of other animals that they have an innate standard of similarity too. It is part of our animal birthright. And, interestingly enough, it is characteristically animal in its lack of intellectual status.[6]

This spotting of similarities occurs also at more sophisticated stages of learning such as when learning a colour word. The child learns to respond to the same red-stimulations and to the same verbal stimulation, that is, to recognize the same word 'red' in different occurrences.

The disposition (dispositions are ultimately explainable as physical mechanisms) to recognize similarities is sometimes learned and sometimes innate. The innate, that is, gene-determined, dispositions are necessary, Quine maintains, for recognizing similarities and hence for learning in general, and not merely for language learning.

> If an individual learns at all, differences in degree of similarity must be implicit in his learning pattern. Otherwise any response, if reinforced, would be conditioned equally and indiscriminately to any and every future episode, all these being equally similar. Some implicit standard, however provisional, for ordering our episodes as more or less similar must therefore antedate all learning, and be innate.[7]

Thus learning is partly a matter of gene-determined dispositions and partly a matter of episodes leaving traces in a child's neurological system. Stimulus and reinforcement of selected responses are the crucial elements in the process. According to Quine, pleasant and unpleasant episodes play especially important roles.

> Thus consider the learning of the word 'red'. Suppose the child happens to utter the word in the course of the random babbling that is standard procedure in small children, and suppose a red ball happens to be conspicuously present at the time. The parent rewards the child, perhaps only by somehow manifesting approval. Thus in a certain brief minute in the history of overall impingements on the child's sensory surfaces there were these

features among others: there were light rays in the red frequencies, there were sound waves in the air and in the child's headbones caused by the child's own utterance of the word 'red', there were the impacts on the proprioceptors of the child's tongue and larynx occasioned by that utterance, and there were the impacts, whatever they were, that made the episode pleasant. On a later occasion a red shawl is conspicuously present. Its colour makes for a degree of perceptual similarity between the pleasant earlier episode and the present, thus enlivening the trace of that episode. The child contorts his speech muscles so as to add what more he can to the similarity: he again says 'red', and we may hope that the similarity is yet further enhanced by a recurrence of the reward.

Or take again the animal. He had been through a pleasant episode whose salient features included the circular stripe, the pressing of the lever, and the emergence of food. His present episode is perceptually similar to that one to the extent of the circular stripe, or, what is fairly similar for him, the seven spots. He adds what more he can to the similarity by again pressing the lever.[8]

The first stage in language acquisition that leads eventually to the mastery of the full referential apparatus is the learning of a primitive type of observation sentence. These sentences play an important role by serving as a basis in three ways: (1) as a pedagogical basis for breaking into language learning; (2) as the basis for a theory of translation (as discussed in Chapter 6); and (3) as the empirical basis of all science. Recall the role of observation sentences in translation. They are those which can be understood (or translated) solely in terms of the stimulus conditions present, that is, their meaning was exhausted by the concept of stimulus meaning. The infant, like the linguist and the scientist, generally learns its first bit of language by being conditioned to recognize a connection between the sound 'Mama' and a physical presence. 'Mama' is learned as a one-word observation sentence, the meaning of which is exhausted in the presence of the mother. The child's appropriate babbling on recognition of Mama is rewarded and a speech pattern is inculcated. But while this is a stage of language learning, it is prereferential. To the extent that the expression 'Mama' is learned here, it is learned not as a term but as an appropriate sentential response to a stimulation. In fairness, the infant's use of 'Mama' evidences recognition of something, but not strictly speaking reference. Furthermore, to the extent that 'Mama' at this stage is likened to a term, it is what is called a mass term. The initial learning of 'Mama' or 'water' associates these expressions with a discriminable observational situation but not with an individuated physical object, Quine asserts:

> We in our maturity have come to look upon the child's mother as an integral body who, in an irregular closed orbit, revisits the child from time to time; and to look upon red in a radically different way, viz., as scattered about. Water, for us, is rather like red, but not quite; things can be red, but only stuff is water. But the mother, red, and water are for the infant all of a type: each is just a history of sporadic encounter, a scattered portion of what goes on. His first learning of the three words is uniformly a matter of learning how much of what goes on about him counts as the mother, or as red, or as water. It is not for the child to say in the first case 'Hello! mama again,' in the second case 'Hello! another red thing,' and in the third case 'Hello! more water.' They are all on a par: Hello! more mama, more red, more water. Even this last formula, which treats all three terms on the model of our provincial adult bulk term 'water,' is imperfect; for it unwarrantedly imputes an objectification of matter, even if only as stuff and not as bits.[9]

The child uttering 'Mama' from one occasion to another is not at the level of language for indicating on a later occasion 'Mama again' but only 'More Mama'; 'Mama' is learned initially as 'water' is. 'Water' is a paradigm mass term as opposed to a count noun like 'man'. We can, for instance, count with respect to count nouns, for example, 'one man', 'two men', but not with respect to mass terms 'one water', 'two water'. With mass terms we can only say 'water' or 'more water'. In this sense the word 'water' is used at best to refer cumulatively to all water or to scattered parts of water. Similarly, the child first learns 'Mama' as a mass-term sentence for a temporally scattered observable presence.

The stage of genuine reference first takes place with the mastery of general terms, for example, count nouns and demonstrative singular terms. Here for the first time, as in words like 'apple', 'dog', 'man', 'Fido' and so on, and with the apparatus of predication, we distinguish one individual dog from another. The general term 'dog' has "divided reference", in that it can be used to refer to this dog and that dog, and so forth, as opposed to mass nouns like 'water'. We count and individuate dogs and form the notion of a physical object over and above mere physical presences. We can now also form demonstrative singular terms like 'this man'. At the next stage we learn to form compound general terms by joining one general term with another, thus attributing the one general term to the other, as in 'fat man'. Mastery of the mechanism of demonstrative singular terms and attributive general terms does not make for reference to any new kinds of objects. We are still limited to observable spatio-temporal entities. The next stage in mastering the tools of reference ushers in access to new types of objects. This stage consists of applying relative terms to singular ones, for example, 'smaller than that speck'. We can now make reference to non-observable but still spatio-temporal objects. The last stage brings in the possibility of referring to abstract objects. This is accomplished by abstract singular terms, for example, 'redness' and 'mankind'.

Quine's purpose was to exhibit an empirical/behavioural reconstruction of how we acquire the full referential apparatus. The preceding sketch is intended merely to suggest his programme for reconstruction; his actual work contains too many subtle points and details to do justice to them in a short outline.

This empirical/behavioural account of language acquisition has not been without its critics. The most well-known challenge is from the work of the linguist Noam Chomsky. Chomsky, as a critic of other behaviourists such as the psychologist B. F. Skinner and the linguist Leonard Bloomfield (both of whom Quine refers to approvingly), naturally turns his attack to Quine.[10] One of Chomsky's main points is intended to be antibehaviourist and antiempiricist. He argues that in order to account for the infinite capacity involved in language learning we must posit an innate basis for learning language. This innate structure consists of rules for generating sentences of the languages learned. According to Chomsky, although particular languages differ on the surface, the underlying rules for all languages are the same and are not acquired but part of the makeup of human beings. In other words, Chomsky hypothesizes that these innate rules are linguistic universals and species specific, that is, distinctive of human beings. Chomsky argues that only on this hypothesis can one explain how children learn languages so rapidly. His point is intended to be antibehaviourist in that he explains language acquisition utilizing principles that are not reducible to stimulus–response theory. Indeed, Chomsky is saying that stimulus–response theory cannot in itself account for the facts of language learning. Furthermore, he intends his point to be a rationalist's one (antiempiricist) in the sense that he regards the positing of an innate structure as continuous with Descartes's positing of innate ideas. Chomsky sees himself as a modern-day champion of this aspect of Cartesian thought.

On the surface, then, there seems to be a rather blatant clash between Chomsky and Quine. However, the issues between them are not clear if left at the level of appealing to labels and saying Chomsky as a rationalist and antibehaviourist proponent of innate structures is opposed to Quine, who is an empiricist and well entrenched in the behaviourist tradition. To begin with, Quine and Chomsky have somewhat different overall goals. The part of Quine's programme relevant here is concerned with the problem of how we master the referential function of language. As a linguist at the outset, Chomsky has a broader goal: the study of language as such. In good part, this is an attempt to discover the grammars which will generate the sentences of a given language.

One conflict occurs when we contrast their views of how language is acquired, that is, Chomsky's theses in psycholinguistics and Quine's thesis of the psychogenesis of reference. Some of Quine's views as to how we learn to refer clash with Chomsky's principles as to how we acquire language. One of the issues is the innateness hypothesis. To begin with, it is not simply that Chomsky posits an innate structure and Quine does not. Quine posits an innate mechanism for spotting similarities which functions at both the prelinguistic and linguistic stages of learning. Labels such as behaviourist, empiricist or rationalist can be misleading here. Quine no less than Chomsky is antiempiricist where empiricism is unfairly construed so narrowly as to prohibit positing theoretical structures. The positing of innate mechanisms by either Quine or Chomsky is on the order of the positing of non-observable entities, for example, molecules or electrons, to explain physical phenomena. Both would hold that innate structures are needed to explain how learning takes place, and there is nothing unempirical in this practice. As to the behaviourism/antibehaviourism labels, there is no reason why a behaviourist must not posit internal mechanisms in the behaving being in order to account for its behaviour. Of course, those internal structures in keeping with behaviourism have no peculiarly dualistic mental status but are either explicitly or implicitly connected with the nervous system of the organism. Thus, for Quine, innateness is a matter of gene-determined dispositions, and dispositions are to be dealt with in terms of the body's physical mechanism.

There is, though, a genuine conflict as to what is innate. Quine's mechanism for spotting the similarities operates at prelinguistic as well as linguistic levels of learning. It is posited for animals as well as humans. Chomsky, on the other hand, posits innate rules that operate primarily at the stage of language learning. They are intended to be species specific for human beings and constitute the basis of a belief that there are certain linguistic universals, that is, features of the structure of language that are common to all languages because they are innately contributed. Chomsky and his followers claim that these innate linguistic structures are needed because they alone account for a language user's capacity to recognize an infinite amount of grammatical sentences and for such facts as the rapidity with which children acquire a language. Quine and others argue that these rules can be acquired and that the apparently rapid mastery of a language by a child can be explained by crediting him with a richer fund of pre- and non-linguistic learning techniques, for example, an ability to spot similarities.

Quine is also suspicious of giving a set of rules for generating sentences the special status for guiding linguistic behaviour which Chomsky accords it.[11] For one thing, he doubts that the idea can be empirically justified. In addition, he is sceptical of the thesis of linguistic universals. The problem with such universals is similar to that of making claims about translating languages. The thesis for such universals is that certain grammatical constructions occur in all languages. But Quine finds that here, as in the 'Gavagai' case, the empirical data of translation do not furnish evidence for such an ambitious thesis.

Challenging Quine on epistemology

A prominent topic in non-naturalists' criticisms of Quine's naturalized epistemology is the issue of normativity. One of the best known is that of Jaegwon Kim. He argues that traditional epistemology essentially involves normative notions such as justified belief, good reasons and rationality.[12] Kim is inaccurate, though, when he depicts Quine's naturalized epistemology as reducing such notions to non-normative ones. Quine's programme is not one of reduction. It is one of replacing those parts of traditional epistemology that Quine maintains should be saved with naturalistic accounts. We must separate two questions: whether a Quinian can have traditional normative notions and whether the notions he does employ save enough of traditional epistemology to still warrant being called epistemology.

Can Quinians find a place for normativity? On Quine's version of anomalous monism, *de dicto* belief talk is not reducible to physicalist talk, but the underlying realities – the values of the variables – are purely physical objects. There is a dualism here of predicates, not of ontology. There is no reason why normative language cannot be treated in a fashion suggested by anomalous monism. One can argue that there is a further linguistc dualism (beyond the mentalistic/psychological and non-mentalistic/physicalist predicates of anomalous monism) between the non-normative psychological language, (e.g. belief) and the normative language (e.g. justified, rational belief). This further dualism is well recognized in the fact–value distinction, suitably reconstrued via semantic ascent as a linguistic dualism without change in underlying ontology. If one imports a notion of supervenience here, then just as an anomalous monist might be able to say that the mental supervenes on the physical (no difference in the mental without a difference in the physical), one might be able to say that the normative supervenes on the non-normative.

Quine's conception of the norms associated with epistemology is that they are technical norms. They involve a technical sense of 'ought': if one aims at or wants certain goals, then one ought to do certain things. To oversimplify, if one wants to get at the truth, then one ought to follow the scientific method. Getting at the truth requires fitting theory to observation and abiding by constraints for choosing between theories, for example, simplicity and conservatism.

> Naturalization of epistemology does not jettison the normative and settle for the indiscriminate description of ongoing procedures. For me normative epistemology is a branch of engineering. It is the technology of truth seeking, or, in a more cautiously epistemological term, prediction.
>
> . . . normative epistemology gets naturalized into a chapter of engineering: the technology of anticipating sensory stimulation.[13]

So it looks as though a Quinian can allow for normative notions. The question then is whether the notions he chooses to save are sufficient to entitle him to say that he is doing epistemology and not just changing the subject. Let us look at concepts such as those of knowledge, justification and evidence, which some say are missing from Quine's account and then let us close by commenting on the problem of induction.

Among the criticisms of Quine's views on epistemology some come from other naturalists and others from non-naturalists. To begin with one alternative within naturalism is not so much a criticism as a suggested emendation. It is the reliabilist approach to knowledge.

Quine himself avoids the notion of knowledge. He neither appeals to it for serious purposes nor offers an explication of it. The reason, as best one can tell, is found in the entry on knowledge in his philosophical dictionary, *Quiddities*. He seems to despair of having a precise account of that notion. Given the many counter-examples to proffered accounts of knowledge (the most famous of which is the Gettier problem) and the patchwork of attempted repairs, knowledge seems to have suffered a death by a thousand qualifications. Nonetheless, reliabilist accounts have engaged the interests of many sympathetic to Quine's naturalism. The central theme is that knowledge can be explicated as reliably caused true beliefs wherein the explicans can be formulated in naturalistic terms. So, although Quine himself has not adopted this reliabilist approach it is quite compatible with his views on naturalizing epistemology.

Anthony Grayling, Keith Lehrer and Laurence BonJour are among those who question whether "naturalized epistemology is truly epistemology".[14] They focus on concepts such as those of evidence and justification. Quine has certainly not proposed conceptual analyses of them. He has not even offered more modest explications. Perhaps he has not done this for the same sort of reason that he has foregone doing so for the concept of knowledge. However, he has discussed exemplary cases of evidence and justification. Some of these cases are bound up with the role of observation in science.

> Where I do find justification of science and evidence of truth is rather of successful prediction of observations.[15]

Another variety of evidence is appealing to simplicity and logical links to other parts of theories when arriving at hypothesis.

> In both these domains I see no departure from the old epistemology.[16]

While Quine is saving these notions of the old epistemology, he is denying that they yield certainty or that they have some sort of transcendent role to play. His fallibilism is similar to Peirce's and Dewey's in denying that there is certainty. Of course, Quine's argument for it differs from Peirce's and Dewey's. It stems from his holistic empiricism. On denying that epistemology can be done from a specially privileged vantage point, Quine is restating Neurath's argument that there is no transcendent position to adopt. We cannot get off the boat and on to some dock to repair it. We cannot step out of our cognitive skins and adopt some transcendent vantage point. There is no alternative to being the natural knowing subjects that we actually are. In us, a part of nature knows itself.

The problem of induction is frequently stated as scepticism about knowing whether the future will resemble the past. If this scepticism is stated as requiring a justification of induction, in the sense that we provide a deductive or an inductive argument for the future (in relevant respects) resembling the past, then we should refuse to accede to that request. It is well known that such arguments are either question-begging or require a standpoint beyond our natural cognitive abilities which there is little reason for thinking we can attain to. "The Humean predicament is the human predicament."[17] Since justification in the above sense is out of the question, what should and what can we do? Quine deals with this problem by adopting the stance of a scientist examining scientific practice. The psychogenesis of reference consists of hypotheses as to how we talk about objects. This involves hypothesizing an innate ability to spot similarities. Induction in its most primitive forms is of a piece with recognizing similarities. We have a built-in mechanism to expect similarities. However, it does not guarantee that we will find them.

> Perceptual similarity is the basis of all expectations, all learning, all habit formation. It operates through our propensity to expect perceptually similar stimulations to have sequels perceptually similar to each other. This is primitive induction.
>
> Since learning hinges thus on perceptual similarity, perceptual similarity cannot itself have been learned – not all of it. Some of it is innate.

> The survival value of primitive induction is anticipation of something edible, or of some creature by which one might be eaten. Thus it is that natural selection has endowed us with standards of perceptual similarity that mesh pretty well with natural trends .... The future is as may be, but we persist hopefully.[18]

Observation categoricals (a primitive sort of scientific law such as 'When it is an apple, it can be eaten', and 'When it has claws, it can harm you') are records of spotted similarities. These categoricals are linked with the problem of induction when it is stated as the justification of laws of nature. The sceptic would have us justify our belief in the regularities described in natural laws. What Quine offers us instead is that

> The survival value of the apes' cries, and of our ordinary observation sentences, lay in vicarious observation [such as "It has claws"] ... Observation categoricals bring us much more . ... they bring us vicarious induction. One gets the benefits of generalized expectations ....[19]

Such is Quine's treatment of Hume's problem of why we believe that similar causes have similar effects. He deals with the problem in the setting of evolutionary psychology where Hume dealt with it in terms of the associationist psychology of his times. Quine, like Hume, is not attempting to justify induction in the sense of providing an argument for something like the uniformity of nature. As did Hume (arguably a traditional empiricist epistemologist), Quine offers an empirical account: a theory within empiricism of why we believe the future will resemble the past. Both hold that the source of this belief is "subjective", that is, found in the human subject. They differ in that Hume holds that the subject acquires this belief as a result of "experience" and association whereas Quine says its source is a gene-determined disposition to spot similarities, which Quine supplements with an account from evolutionary psychology.

Other comparisons with traditional epistemology come to mind. Quine's perspective on scepticism and induction is from within naturalized epistemology. He questions the validity of the sceptic's request for a certain type of justification that he thinks it is impossible to achieve. Quine is here sharing in the tradition of other twentieth-century epistemologists who have also undermined the sceptic's request. What Quine offers is an explanation of our belief in induction. Is this a "justification"? If one answers negatively, as Quine's critics do, then they must make clear what is missing and convince us that it is attainable.

The normative element appears as a matter of adopting techniques that have been found to be successful in pursuing science.

> Normative epistemology is the art or technology not only of science, in the austere sense of the word, but of rational belief generally. . . . Normative epistemology [is in essence] correcting and refining . . . our innate propensities to expectation by induction.[20]

Notes

Chapter 1: Introduction

1. The material in this biographical introduction is derived mainly from Quine's intellectual autobiography in the Library of Living Philosophers series, L. E. Hahn and P. A. Schilpp (eds), *The Philosophy of W. V. Quine* (La Salle, IL: Open Court, 1986), and to a lesser extent from his autobiography *The Time of My Life* (Cambridge, MA: MIT Press, 1985).
2. Hahn and Schilpp (eds), *The Philosophy of W. V. Quine*, p. 18.
3. *Ibid.*, p. 19.
4. *Ibid.*
5. The papers and books by Quine mentioned in this chapter are included in the bibliography of works by Quine (p. 201) by book title or in one of the collections of his papers.
6. *Ibid.*, p. 32. See also P. A. Schilpp (ed.), *The Philosophy of Rudolf Carnap* (La Salle, IL: Open Court, 1963), pp. 35–6.
7. *Time of My Life*, pp. 478–9.

Chapter 2: Expressing an ontology

1. See the translated selections from Brentano's *Psychologie vom Empirischen Standpunkt*, in *Realism and the Background of Phenomenology*, R. Chisholm (ed.) (Glencoe, IL: The Free Press, 1960). Brentano's views on these questions were made known to English readers in an article in J. P. N. Land, "Brentano's Logical Innovations", *Mind* **1** (1876), p. 289.
2. G. Ryle, "Systematically Misleading Expressions", in *Logic and Language*, A. Flew (ed.) (Garden City, NY: Anchor Books, 1965), pp. 19–20.
3. I. Kant, *Critique of Pure Reason* (1781), N. K. Smith (trans.) (London: Macmillan, 1953), pp. 239–52, 500–507.
4. See M. Thompson, "On Aristotle's Square of Opposition", in *Aristotle: A Collection of Critical Essays*, J. M. E. Moravcsik (ed.) (Garden City, NY: Anchor Books, 1967), pp. 60–62 and B. Mates, "Leibniz on Possible Worlds", in *Leibniz*, H. G. Frankfurt (ed.) (New York: Anchor Books, 1972), pp. 342–7. See Orenstein 1999.
5. G. Frege, "Begriffsschrift", in *From Frege to Gödel, A Source Book in Mathematical Logic 1879–1931*, S. Bauer-Mengelberg (trans.), J. van Heijenoort (ed.) (Cambridge, MA: Harvard University Press, 1967), pp. 6–7.

6. C. S. Peirce, *Collected Papers*, C. Hartshorne and P. Weiss (eds) (Cambridge, MA: Harvard University Press, 1960), pp. 111, 213–14.
7. L. J. F. Wittgenstein, *Tractatus Logico-Philosophicus*, D. F. Pears and B. F. McGuinness (trans.) (London: Routledge and Kegan Paul, 1961), and B. Russell, "The Philosophy of Logical Atomism", in *Logic and Knowledge* (New York: Macmillan, 1956).
8. W. V. Quine, *Word and Object* (Cambridge, MA: MIT Press, 1960), p. 228. See also p. 161.
9. Quine, "Existence", in *Physics, Logic and History*, W. Yourgrau (ed.) (New York: Plenum Press, 1970), p. 92.
10. *Ibid.*, p. 89.
11. Quine, "A Logistical Approach to the Ontological Problem" (1939), in *The Ways of Paradox and Other Essays* (New York: Random House, 1966), pp. 64–70. This paper appeared in a different form as "Designation and Existence", in *Readings in Philosophical Analysis*, H. Feigl and W. Sellars (eds) (New York: Appleton-Century-Crofts, 1949), pp. 44–52.
12. Quine, "Designation and Existence", pp. 49–50.
13. Quine, "Existence and Quantification" (1966), in *Ontological Relativity and Other Essays* (New York: Columbia University Press, 1969), pp. 95–6.
14. Quine, "On What There Is" (1948), in *From a Logical Point of View*, rev. edn (Cambridge, MA: Harvard University Press, 1961). Compare the above treatment of definite descriptions with the one offered by Quine in *Mathematical Logic*, rev. edn (New York: Harper Torchbooks, 1951), pp. 146–52.
15. Quine, "Existence", p. 92.
16. A. Tarski, "The Semantic Conception of Truth", *Philosophy and Phenomenological Research* **4** (1944), pp. 341–75; reprinted in *Semantics and the Philosophy of Language*, L. Linsky (ed.) (Urbana, IL: University of Illinois Press, 1952). Tarski, "The Concept of Truth in Formalized Languages", in *Logic, Semantics, Metamathematics: Papers from 1923–1938*, J. H. Woodger (trans.) (Oxford: Oxford University Press, 1956).
17. Quine, "Notes on the Theory of Reference", in *From a Logical Point of View*, pp. 137–8.
18. Lejewski is one of the best expositors of Lesniewski's view. See C. Lejewski, "Logic and Existence", *British Journal for the Philosophy of Science* **5** (1954), pp. 104–19 and "On Lesniewski's Ontology", *Ratio* **1** (1958), pp. 150–76. See also K. Ajdukiewicz, "On the Notion of Existence, Some Remarks Connected with the Problem of Idealism", in *The Scientific World-Perspective and other Essays, 1931–1963*, J. Giedymin (ed.), pp. 209–21 (Boston, MA: D. Reidel). I have made a case for presenting the Lesniewskian and an Aristotelian view of existence as a feature of first order predicate logic, and in doing so have offered a more extensive version of this challenge to Quine, in A. Orenstein, "Plato's Beard, Quine's Stubble and Ockham's Razor", in *Knowledge, Language and Logic: Questions for Quine*, A. Orenstein and P. Kotatko (eds) (Dordrecht: Kluwer, 2000), and see Quine's reply. See also my paper for a conference on analytic metaphysics held at the University of Bergamo in June 2000, "Existence and an Aristotelian Tradition", in *Individuals, Essence and Identity: Themes of Analytical Metaphysics*, A. Bottani, M. Carrara and P. Giaretta (eds) (Dordrecht: Kluwer, forthcoming).

Chapter 3: Deciding on an ontology

1. Quine, "On What There Is", pp. 14–17.
2. *Ibid.*, pp. 16–19.
3. Quine, "Designation and Existence", pp. 50–51.
4. A. Church, "The Need for Abstract Entities in Semantics", in *Contemporary*

Readings in Logical Theory, I. M. Copi and A. Gould (eds) (New York: Macmillan, 1967), pp. 194–203.

5. Quine with J. S. Ullian, *The Web of Belief* (New York: Random House, 1970), Chs 5, 7.
6. *Ibid.*, p. 44. See also Quine, "Posits and Reality" and "On Mental Entities", in *The Ways of Paradox*.
7. Russell, "The Relation of Sense-data to Physics", in *Mysticism and Logic* (New York: Barnes and Noble, 1971), p. 115.
8. Quine with Ullian, *The Web of Belief*, pp. 65–6.
9. Quine, "The Scope and Language of Science", in *The Ways of Paradox*, pp. 229–31.
10. Quine, "On What There Is", pp. 17–18.
11. Quine, "Posits and Reality" and "On Mental Entities", in *The Ways of Paradox,* pp. 238–40; Quine, *Word and Object*, pp. 234–8; Quine, "Epistemology Naturalized", in *Ontological Relativity and Other Essays*, pp. 69–90; Quine, "Grades of Theoreticity", in *Experience and Theory*, L. Foster and J. W. Swanson (eds) (Amherst, MA: University of Massachusetts Press, 1970), pp. 1–17.
12. Quine, "Epistemology Naturalized" and Quine, *The Roots of Reference* (La Salle, IL: Open Court, 1973), pp. 1–4, 33–41.
13. Quine, "The Scope and Language of Science", p. 215.
14. Quine, *Methods of Logic*, 3rd edn (New York: Holt, Rinehart and Winston, 1972), pp. 165–6 and *Word and Object*, p. 171.
15. From Hahn and Schilpp (eds), *The Philosophy of W. V. Quine*.
16. Quine and N. Goodman, "Steps Toward a Constructive Nominalism", *Journal of Symbolic Logic* **12** (1947), pp. 105–6.
17. *Ibid.* p. 122.
18. Quine, "Existence", pp. 95–6 and Quine, *Methods of Logic*, pp. 237–8, 240.
19. Intellectual autobiography in Hahn and Schilpp (eds), *The Philosophy of W. V. Quine*.
20. Quine, "New Foundations for Mathematical Logic", in *From a Logical Point of View*, pp. 91–2.
21. Intellectual autobiography in Hahn and Schilpp (eds), *The Philosophy of W. V. Quine*.
22. For an excellent account of some of the philosophically relevant features of these systems see G. Berry, "Logic with Platonism", in *Words and Objections: Essays on the Work of W. V. Quine*, Donald Davidson and Jaakko Hintikka (eds) (Dordrecht: Reidel, 1968), pp. 243–77.
23. Quine, "On Carnap's Views on Ontology", in *The Ways of Paradox*, p. 126.
24. R. Carnap, *Meaning and Necessity*, 2nd edn (Chicago, IL: University of Chicago Press, 1956), p. 43 (originally published 1947).
25. Wittgenstein, *Tractatus Logico-Philosophicus*, p. 57. and Carnap, *The Logical Syntax of Language* (Paterson, NJ: Littlefield, Adams and Co., 1959), sections 76 and 77.
26. Carnap, *The Logical Syntax of Language*, p. 295.
27. Carnap, *Meaning and Necessity*, appendix, pp. 205–21.
28. *Ibid.*, p. 208.
29. Quine, "On Carnap's Views on Ontology", pp. 130–33.
30. Quine, "Existence", p. 94. See also Quine, *Word and Object*, pp. 270–76.
31. *Quine with His Replies, Revue Internationale de Philosophie* **51**, no. 202, December 1997, P. Gochet (ed.), p. 573.
32. Quine, *Ontological Relativity and Other Essays*, p. 32.
33. H. Leblanc, "Alternatives to Standard First-Order Semantics", *Handbook of Philosophical Logic*, Vol. 1, D. Gabbay and F. Guenther (eds) (Dordrecht: Reidel, 1983), p. 260, n. 43.
34. G. Harman, *Change in View* (Cambridge, MA: Bradford-MIT Press, 1986) pp. 67–75; P. Lipton, *Inference to the Best Explanation* (London: Routledge, 1989).

35. H. Field, *Realism, Mathematics and Modality* (New York: Basil Blackwell, 1989), pp.16–17. For another fictionalist account see J. Azzouni, "On 'On What There Is'", *Pacific Philosophical Quarterly* **3** (1998), pp. 1–18.
36. Field, *Realism, Mathematics and Modality*, p. 19.
37 *Ibid*., p. 5.
38. E. Sober, "Mathematics and Indispensability", *Philosophical Review* **102** (1993), pp. 35–7 and "Contrastive Empiricism", in *From a Biological Point of View* (Cambridge: Cambridge University Press, 1994). See also M. Resnick, "Scientific vs. Mathematical Realism, in *The Indispensability Argument*", *Philosophia Mathematica* **3** (1999), pp. 166–74.
39. Quine, in *Knowledge, Language and Logic*, p. 411. Also see Quine's entry on himself in T. Mautner (ed.), *The Penguin Dictionary of Philosophy* (Harmondsworth: Penguin Books, 1996), pp. 466–7.
40. P. Maddy, "Indispensability and Practice", *Journal of Philosophy* **89** (1992), pp. 275–89.
41. B. Van Fraassen, *The Scientific Image* (Oxford: Oxford University Press, 1980).
42. Quine, *Pursuit of Truth* (Cambridge, MA: Harvard University Press, 1992), p. 95; for a survey and further references see J. Burgess and G. Rosen, *A Subject With No Object: Strategies for Nominalistic Interpretations of Mathematics* (Oxford: Oxford University Press, 1997), Pt III.
43. Quine, *The Roots of Reference*, pp. 112–13.
44. See the entries on "Impredicativity" and "Real Numbers" in Quine, *Quiddities* (Cambridge, MA: Harvard University Press, 1987).

Chapter 4: The spectre of a priori knowledge

1. Quine, "Two Dogmas of Empiricism", in *From a Logical Point of View*, pp. 20–46. Quine's misgivings on this subject can be traced back to lectures he gave on Carnap in 1934. Some of this material is incorporated in papers dating from this period in *The Ways of Paradox*. Carnap's remarks on his 1940–41 year at Harvard and his conversations with Quine and Tarski can be found in *The Philosophy of Rudolf Carnap*, pp. 63–5.
2. Quine, "Two Dogmas of Empiricism", pp. 40–41 and see also Quine, "Mr Strawson on Logical Theory", in *The Ways of Paradox*, pp. 135–40.
3. This example is adopted from one found in I. Copi, *Introduction to Logic*, 4th edn (New York: Macmillan, 1972), pp. 449–52. My use of the example is quite different, though.
4. P. Duhem, *The Aim and Structure of Physical Theory*, P. Wiener (trans.) (New York: Atheneum, 1962), particularly Ch. 4, "Experiment in Physics", pp. 144–64, Ch. 6, "Physical Theory and Experiment", pp. 180–218 and Ch. 7, "The Choice of Hypotheses", pp. 219–72.
5. Quine with Ullian, *The Web of Belief*, pp. 43–4. See also Quine, *Philosophy of Logic* (Englewood Cliffs, NJ: Prentice Hall, 1970), p. 100.
6. Quine with Ullian, *The Web of Belief*, pp. 12–20.
7. This example is from R. Feynman, *The Character of Physical Law* (Cambridge, MA: MIT Press, 1965), pp. 24–5.
8. Quine with Ullian, *The Web of Belief*, pp. 21–32. See also Quine, *Methods of Logic*, pp. 1–5.
9. Quine, "Two Dogmas of Empiricism", pp. 42–3.
10. A. J. Ayer, *Language, Truth and Logic*, 2nd edn (New York: Dover Publications, 1952), pp. 74–7.
11. G. Rey, "A Naturalistic A Priori", *Philosophical Studies* **92** (1998), pp. 25–43; see also M. Devitt, "Naturalism and The A Priori", *Philosophical Studies* **92** (1998), pp. 45–65.

12. L. BonJour, *In Defense of Pure Reason: A Rationalist Account of A Priori Justification* (Cambridge: Cambridge University Press, 1998), p. 76.
13. *Ibid.*, pp. 77, 89.
14. Field, "Epistemological Non-Factualism and the A Prioricity of Logic", *Philosophical Studies* **92** (1998), pp. 1–24 and "The A Prioricity of Logic", *Proceedings of the Aristotelian Society* (1996), pp. 359–79.
15. Field, "Epistemological Non-Factualism and the A Prioricity of Logic", p. 12.
16. *Ibid.*, pp. 17–18.

Chapter 5: The nature of logic

1. Quine, *Mathematical Logic*, pp. 1–2. Quine's first statement of this definition of logical truth was in "Truth by Convention" (1935), which is reprinted in *The Ways of Paradox*, pp. 70–99. It is presented along with four other definitions in Chapter 4 of *Philosophy of Logic*, pp. 47–60.
2. Quine, "Reference and Modality", in *From a Logical Point of View* and "Three Grades of Modal Involvement", in *The Ways of Paradox*, contain some specimen criticisms. For a fine summary of these criticisms see D. Føllesdal, "Quine on Modality", in *Words and Objections*, pp. 175–85.
3. Quine, "On the Limits of Decision", *Akten des XIV. Internationalen Kongresse für Philosophie* (1969), pp. 57–62.
4. Quine, *Philosophy of Logic*, pp. 61–4.
5. *Ibid.*, pp. 64–74.
6. Contrast the scope of logic in Quine, "New Foundations for Mathematical Logic" (1937), in *From a Logical Point of View*, pp. 80–81 with Quine, "Carnap and Logical Truth", in *The Ways of Paradox*, pp. 103–4.
7. Church, "Mathematics and Logic", in *Logic, Methodology and Philosophy of Science*, E. Nagel, P. Suppes and A. Tarski (eds) (Stanford, CA: Stanford University Press, 1962), pp. 181–6 and Church, "The Need for Abstract Entities in Semantics", reprinted in *Contemporary Readings in Logical Theory*, I. Copi and J. A. Gould (eds) (New York: Macmillan, 1967), pp. 194–203.
8. Quine, "On Universals", *Journal of Symbolic Logic* **12** (1947), pp. 74–84. (This appeared in amended form as "Logic and the Reification of Universals", in *From a Logical Point of View*, pp. 107–17, and in *Philosophy of Logic*, pp. 66–70.) See also the much earlier Quine, "Ontological Remarks on the Propositional Calculus", reprinted in *The Ways of Paradox*, pp. 57–63.
9. Quine, "Logic and the Reification of Universals", in *From a Logical Point of View*, pp. 118–19.
10. Quine, *Mathematical Logic*, pp. 34–5.
11. R. B. Marcus, "Interpreting Quantification", *Inquiry* **5** (1962), pp. 252–9; H. S. Leonard, "Essences, Attributes and Predicates", *Proceedings of the American Philosophical Association* **37** (April–May, 1964), pp. 25–51; M. Dunn and N. D. Belnap, Jr, "The Substitution Interpretation of the Quantifiers", *Nous* **2** (1968), pp. 177–85; and Orenstein, "On Explicating Existence in Terms of Quantification", in *Logic and Ontology*, M. K. Munitz (ed.) (New York: New York University Press, 1973), pp. 59–84.
12. Quine, "Ontological Relativity", in *Ontological Relativity and Other Essays*, pp. 62–7; Quine, *The Roots of Reference*, pp. 98–141; and "Substitutional Quantification", the Marrett Lecture given in the autumn of 1974 at Oxford University. See Orenstein, "Referential and Non-Referential Quantification", *Synthese*, Summer (1984), 145–58.
13. Quine, *The Roots of Reference*, pp. 135–41.
14. Orenstein, "Referential and Non-Referential Quantification".
15. Quine, *The Roots of Reference*, pp. 110–15.

16. Quine, *Philosophy of Logic*, p. 66.
17. Quine, "Quantifiers and Propositional Attitudes", in *The Ways of Paradox*, pp. 186–94 and Quine, *Word and Object*, pp. 168–9.
18. Quine, "Carnap on Logical Truth", in *The Ways of Paradox*, p. 112.
19. *Ibid.*, p. 109.
20. Quine, "Truth by Convention", in *The Ways of Paradox*, p. 81.
21. Quine, "Carnap on Logical Truth", pp. 112–13.
22. W. James, *Pragmatism*, selection reprinted in *The Writings of William James*, J. J. McDermott (ed.) (New York: Random House, 1968), pp. 376–7.
23. Quine, "Carnap on Logical Truth", p. 106.
24. Quine, *The Philosophy of Logic*, pp. 82–3, 96–7 and Quine's reply to B. Stroud in *Words and Objections*, pp. 316–19.
25. Quine, *The Philosophy of Logic*, p. 97.
26. G. Boolos, "To Be is to Be the Value of a Variable (or to be Some Values of Some Variables)", *Journal of Philosophy* **81** (1984), pp. 430–48; J. Higginbotham, "On Higher Order Logic and Natural Language", *Philosophical Logic, Proceedings of the British Academy*, T. Smiley (ed.) (Oxford: Oxford University Press, 1999); Orenstein, "On Explicating Existence in terms of Quantification", pp. 75–80.
27. Orenstein, "Plato's Beard, Quine's Stubble and Ockham's Razor", in *Knowledge, Language and Logic*, pp. 208–9.
28. B. Mates, *Elementary Logic* (New York: Oxford University Press, 1972).
29. Church, "Mathematics and Logic", pp. 181–2; Orenstein, *Existence and the Particular Quantifier* (Philadelphia: Temple University Press, 1978), pp. 144–9; S. Lavine, "Review of Ruth Marcus' *Modalities*", *British Journal for the Philosophy of Science* **46** (1995), p. 271.
30. P. Hugly and C. Sayward, *Intensionality and Truth: An Essay on the Philosophy of A. N. Prior* (Dordrecht: Kluwer, 1996).

Chapter 6: Analyticity and indeterminacy

1. Quine, "Two Dogmas of Empiricism" and "The Problem of Meaning in Linguistics", both in *From a Logical Point of View*, pp. 20–64.
2. Quine, "Notes on the Theory of Reference", pp. 130–38.
3. Quine, "Philosophical Progress in Language Theory", in *Metaphilosophy* **1** (1970), pp. 4–5, and in *Contemporary Philosophical Thought*, H. Kiefer (ed.) (Albany: State University Press, 1969). See also Quine, "Ontological Relativity", pp. 26–9 and *The Roots of Reference*, pp. 32–7.
4. Church, "The Need for Abstract Entities in Semantics", pp. 194–203.
5. Quine, "The Problem of Meaning in Linguistics", in *From a Logical Point of View*, pp. 47–64.
6. Quine, *Word and Object*, p. 206.
7. *Ibid.*, pp. 257–62.
8. *Ibid.*, pp. 193–5, and Quine, "Propositional Objects", in *Ontological Relativity and Other Essays*, pp. 139–44.
9. Quine, "Propositional Objects", pp. 139–60.
10. Quine, *Word and Object*, pp. 258–9.
11. Quine, "Two Dogmas of Empiricism", p. 37.
12. *Ibid.*, pp. 40–41. See also Quine, "Mr Strawson on Logical Theory", in *The Ways of Paradox*, pp. 136–8.
13. Quine with Ullian, *The Web of Belief*, pp. 30–31.
14. Quine, "Intensions Revisited", in *Theories and Things* (Cambridge, MA: Harvard University Press, 1981), pp. 113–24.
15. D. Davidson, "Truth and Meaning", *Synthese* **7** (1967), pp. 304–23.
16. Reprinted in Carnap, *Meaning and Necessity*, Appendix D, pp. 233–47.

17. D. Føllesdal, "In What Sense is Language Public?", in *On Quine*, P. Leonardi and M. Santambogia (eds) (Cambridge: Cambridge University Press, 1995).
18. Quine, *Pursuit of Truth*, pp. 47–8.
19. Quine, *Ontological Relativity and Other Essays*, p. 27.
20. Quine, *Pursuit of Truth*, p. 48.
21. Quine, *From Stimulus to Science* (Cambridge, MA: Harvard University Press, 1995), p. 22.
22. See R. Gibson, *Enlightened Empiricism: An Examination of W. V. Quine's Theory of Knowledge* (Tampa, FL: University of South Florida, 1982), Ch. 5, for an excellent discussion of the issues surrounding this topic.
23. See N. Chomsky in *Words and Objections*.
24. Quine, "Facts of the Matter", *The Southwestern Journal of Philosophy* **IX**(2) (1979), p. 167.
25. Quine, "On the Reasons for Indeterminacy of Translation", *The Journal of Philosophy* **67** (1970), p. 179.
26. Quine, *Theories and Things*, p. 23.
27. Quine, "Reply to Horwich", in *Knowledge, Language and Logic*, p. 420. In *Wittgenstein On Rules And Private Language* (Cambridge, MA: Harvard University Press, 1982), pp. 55–7, Saul Kripke has offered a comparison of Quine's indeterminacy conjecture and Wittgenstein's private language argument. In the course of doing this he offers some thoughts on the difference between indeterminacy and inscrutability.
28. Quine, *Ontological Relativity*, p. 33.
29. Quine, "Reply to Anthony", in *Knowledge, Language and Logic*, p. 419. In 1995 I was asked by Paul Gochet to do a paper for an issue on Quine (see Orenstein, "Arguing From Inscrutability to Indeterminacy" in *Quine with his Replies,* pp. 507–20. I was in contact with Quine, who initially was not pleased with the paper. On reconsideration he thought it had a virtue:

    > There is a deeper point and Orenstein has done well to expose it. The indeterminacy of translation that I long since conjectured, and the indeterminacy of reference that I proved, are indeterminacies in different senses. My earlier use of different words, "indeterminacy" for the one and "inscrutability" for the other, may have been wiser.

    As a result Quine appears to have adopted the "conjecture" versus "proof" terminology I used in that paper to discuss the conflation of indeterminacy and inscrutability in his replies to Anthony cited here, in the body of the paper, and to Horwich, cited earlier.
30. Quine, *Pursuit of Truth*, p. 50.
31. Quine, "Reply to Orenstein", in *Quine with His Replies*, pp. 573–4.
32. *Ibid.*, p. 573.
33. Quine, *Pursuit of Truth*, p. 50. Quine refers here to some possible examples of holophrastic indeterminacy.
34. Quine himself has tried to temper the impression that essay has made. See Quine, "Two Dogmas in Retrospect", *The Canadian Journal of Philosophy* **21** (1991), pp. 265–74.
35. J. Katz, "Some Remarks on Quine on Analyticity", *The Journal of Philosophy* **64** (1967), pp. 40–51, and see Quine's reply in the same journal that year.
36. P. Grice and P. Strawson, "In Defense of a Dogma", *Philosophical Review* **65** (1956), pp. 145–58.
37. Harman, *Reasoning, Meaning, and Mind* (Oxford: Clarendon Press, 1999), pp. 126–7.
38. This classification is from Roger Gibson's entry "Radical Interpretation and Radical Translation", in *Encylopedia of Philosophy*, E. Craig (ed.) (London:

Routledge, 1998). Also see the Kirk essay in Gibson's forthcoming *Companion to Quine* (Oxford: Blackwell).

Chapter 7: Intensional contexts

1. Quine, *From Stimulus to Science*, pp. 90–91.
2. Quine, "Reply to Marcus", *Synthese* **13** (1961), p. 323. Also see Marcus, "Quine's Animadversions to Modal Logic", in *Perspectives on Quine*, R. B. Barrett and R. Gibson (eds) (Oxford: Blackwell, 1990), p. 230, and reprinted and updated in Marcus, *Modalities* (New York: Oxford University Press, 1993).
3. Quine, "Reference and Modality", p. 143. See Marcus, "Quine's Animadversions to Modal Logic", p. 236, for a discussion of the evolution of Quine's views.
4. A. Smullyan, "Modality and Description", reprinted in *Reference and Modality*, L. Linsky (ed.) (Oxford: Oxford University Press, 1971).
5. Using Russell's notation for distinguishing the scope of definite descriptions we can represent the occurrence of the definite description inside the scope of the necessity functor as:

   Nec (ιx (x = the number of the planets) > 7)

   and when the theory of definite descriptions is applied, the English sentence appears in canonical form as

   Nec (ιx)(x is the number of the planets and (y)(y is the number of the planets $\rightarrow y = x$) and $x > 7$)

   The *de re* occurrence appears as follows:

   $\exists x$ (x = the number of the planets) Nec($x > 7$)

   and in primitive notation as

   ($\exists x$)(x is the number of the planets and
   (y)(y is the number of the planets $\rightarrow y = x$) and Nec $x > 7$)
6. Quine, *Word and Object*, p. 199.
7. Marcus, "Quine's Animadversions to Modal Logic", pp. 237–8 and M. Sainsbury, *Logical Forms* (Oxford: Blackwell, 1991), pp. 242–3.
8. Marcus, "Quine's Animadversions to Modal Logic", p. 241.
9. Quine, "Responding to Kripke", in *Theories and Things*, pp. 173–4.
10. Quine, "Reply to Føllesdal", in *The Philosophy of W. V. Quine*, pp. 114–15:

    > Ruth Marcus and Terence Parsons pointed out that the formalism of modal logic does not require us to reckon any trait as essential unless it is universally shared – thus existence, or self-identity. See my reply to Kaplan. This is not surprising, since they and their complements are the only traits that can be singled out in purely logical terms. A richer store of essential traits would be wanted for modal logic in use. But need it ever be so rich as to yield essential traits that are peculiar to single objects, shared by none? It was only in making sense of rigid designation and identity across possible worlds, as Føllesdal remarks, that I found need of wholly unshared essential traits.
11. Quine, "Reply to Hintikka", in *The Philosophy of W. V. Quine*, p. 228.
12. Quine, "Intensions Revisited", p. 121. See also *From Stimulus to Science*, p. 99.
13. Quine, "Quantifiers and Propositional Attitudes", p. 189.
14. Quine, *Pursuit of Truth*, pp. 70–71.
15. *Ibid.*, pp. 72–3.
16. Quine, *From Stimulus to Science*, pp. 85–6, 98 and *Pursuit of Truth*, pp. 71–3.
17. Quine, *Philosophy of Logic*, pp. 32, 78–9.

18. See Quine's comments on the reactions to his attitudinatives as part of Quine's replies in P. Leonardi and M. Santambrogia (eds) *On Quine* (Cambridge: Cambridge University Press, 1995), pp. 355–9.
19. Quine, *Methods of Logic*, p. 129.
20. A. Prior, *Objects of Thought* (Oxford: Oxford University Press, 1971), p. 135. P. Hugly and R. Sayward, *Intensionality and Truth: An Essay on the Philosophy of A. N. Prior*, (Dordrecht: Kluwer, 1996); reviewed by Orenstein in *Review of Metaphysics*, March (1999), pp. 688–9.

Chapter 8: Nature, know thyself

1. Quine, "The Scope and Language of Science", p. 215.
2. Quine, *Word and Object*, p. 1.
3. Quine, "Epistemology Naturalized", pp. 82–3.
4. O. Neurath, "Protocol Sentences", in *Logical Positivism*, A. J. Ayer (ed.) (Glencoe, IL: The Free Press, 1960), p. 201. The quotation appears at the beginning of *Word and Object* and is referred to in, among other places, "Epistemology Naturalized", p. 85.
5. This is a paraphrase of Quine's own rephrasing of Neurath's point. It occurs in a mimeographed copy of a paper by Quine, "The Pragmatist's Place in Empiricism", p. 9.
6. Quine, "Natural Kinds", in *Ontological Relativity and Other Essays*, p. 123.
7. Quine, *The Roots of Reference*, p. 19. See also "Linguistics and Philosophy", in *Language and Philosophy*, S. Hook (ed.) (New York: New York University Press, 1969), pp. 95–8 and "Reply to Chomsky", in *Words and Objections*, pp. 305–7.
8. Quine, *The Roots of Reference*, p. 29.
9. Quine, "Speaking of Objects", in *Ontological Relativity and Other Essays*, p. 7.
10. Chomsky, "A Review of B. F. Skinner's *Verbal Behavior*" (1957), *Language* **35** (1959), pp. 26–58; Chomsky, "Quine's Empirical Assumptions", *Words and Objections*, pp. 53–68.
11. Quine, "Methodological Reflections on Current Linguistic Theory", *The Semantics of Natural Languages*, G. Harman and D. Davidson (eds) (Dordrecht: Reidel, 1972), pp. 386–98.
12. J. Kim, "What is Naturalized Epistemology?", *Philosophical Perspectives 2*, J. Tomberlin (ed.) (Asascadero, CA: Ridgeview Publishing, 1998). This essay has been reprinted with other essays on Quine on naturalized epistemology in J. S. Crumley (ed.), *Readings in Epistemology* (Mountain View, CA: Mayfield, 1999) and L. J. Pojman (ed.), *The Theory of Knowledge*, 2nd edn (Belmont, CA: Wadsworth, 1999).
13. Quine's reply to Morton White in *The Philosophy of W. V. Quine*, pp. 664–5.
14. Orenstein and Kotatko (eds), *Knowledge, Language and Logic*, p. 411 and BonJour, *In Defense of Pure Reason: A Rationalist Account of A Priori Justification* (Cambridge: Cambridge University Press, 1998) pp. 83–5.
15. Orenstein and Kotatko (eds), *Knowledge, Language and Logic*, p. 412.
16. *Ibid.*, p. 411.
17. Quine, "Epistemology Naturalized", p. 72.
18. Quine, *From Stimulus to Science*, p. 19.
19. *Ibid.*, p. 25.
20. *Ibid.*, pp. 49–50.

Bibliography

Works by Quine

For more complete bibliographies see L. E. Hahn and P. A. Schilpp (eds), *The Philosophy of W. V. Quine* (La Salle, IL: Open Court, 1986), A. Orenstein, *Willard Van Orman Quine* (Boston: K. G. Hall, 1977) or the Quine web pages on the internet.

Books

1934. *A System of Logistic*. Cambridge, MA: Harvard. Reissued, New York: Garland Press.

1940. *Mathematical Logic*. New York: Norton. Emended 2nd printing (1947), Harvard University Press. Revised edition (1951). Paperback (1962), New York: Harper Torchbooks.

1941. *Elementary Logic*. Boston: Ginn. Revised edition, Cambridge MA: Harvard University Press, 1966. Paperback, New York: Harper Torchbooks, 1965.

1944. *O Sentido da Nova Ldgica*. São Paulo: Mirtins. Excerpts translated (1943) in "Notes on Existence and Necessity", pp. 140–44, 146–58, 179–83.

1950. *Methods of Logic*. New York: Holt. Revised edition (1959 and London: Routledge, 1962). Fourth edition, revised and enlarged (1963), Cambridge, MA: Harvard University Press. Paperback (1982), London: Routledge.

1953. *From a Logical Point of View*. Cambridge, MA: Harvard University Press. Revised edition (1961). Paperback (1994), Cambridge, MA: Harvard University Press.

1960. *Word and Object*. New York: John Wiley & Sons and Cambridge, MA: MIT Press. Paperback (1964).

1963. *Set Theory and Its Logic*. Cambridge, MA: Harvard University Press. Revised edition (1969). Paperback (1971), Cambridge, MA: Harvard University Press.

1966. *The Ways of Paradox and Other Essays*. New York: Random House. Paperback, revised and enlarged (1976), Cambridge, MA: Harvard University Press.

1966. *Selected Logic Papers*. New York: Random House. Enlarged paperback edition (1995), Cambridge, MA: Harvard University Press.

1969. *Ontological Relativity and Other Essays*. New York: Columbia University Press.

1970. *The Web of Belief* with J. S. Ullian. New York: Random House.
1970. *Philosophy of Logic*. Englewood Cliffs, NJ: Prentice Hall. Paperback (1970).
1974. *The Roots of Reference*. La Salle, IL: Open Court.
1981. *Theories and Things*. Cambridge, MA: Harvard University Press.
1985. *The Time of My Life*. Cambridge, MA: MIT Press.
1987. *Quiddities: An Intermittently Philosophical Dictionary*. Cambridge, MA: Harvard University Press.
1990. *Dear Carnap, Dear Quine*, the Quine–Carnap correspondence with related work, edited and with an introduction by R. Creath. Berkeley, CA: University of of California Press.
1992. *Pursuit of Truth*. Cambridge, MA: Harvard University Press.
1995. *From Stimulus to Science*. Cambridge, MA: Harvard University Press.

Papers

(Referred to in this work but not included in Quine's books)

1939. "Designation and Existence", *Journal of Philosophy* **36**, pp. 701–9. Reprinted in H. Feigl and W. Sellars (eds) (1949), *Readings in Philosophical Analysis*. New York: Appleton. Reprinted in part in Quine, *From a Logical Point of View*.
1943. "Notes on existence and necessity", *Philosophy* **40**, pp. 179–83; translation of part of *O Sentido da Nova Logica*.
1947. "On Universals", *Journal of Symbolic Logic* **12**, pp. 74–84. This appeared in amended form as "Logic and the Reification of Universals", in Quine, *From a Logical Point of View*, and in Quine, *Philosophy of Logic*.
1947. Quine and N. Goodman, "Steps Towards a Constructive Nominalism", *Journal of Symbolic Logic* **12**, pp. 97–122.
1947. "On the Limits of Decision", *Akten des XIV. Internationalen Kongresse für Philosophie*.
1970. "Philosophical Progress in Language Theory", in *Metaphilosophy* **I**, pp. 2–19.
1969. "Existence", in *Physics, Logic and History*, W. Yourgrau (ed.). New York: Plenum Press.
1970. "Grades of Theoreticity", in *Experience and Theory*, L. Foster and J. W. Swanson (eds), pp. 1–17. Amherst, MA: University of Massachusetts Press.
1991. "Two Dogmas in Retrospect", *Canadian Journal of Philosophy* September, **21**(3), pp. 1–17.
1992. "Structure and Nature", *Journal of Philosophy* January, **89**(1), pp. 6–9.
1996. Quine's entry on himself in *The Penguin Dictionary of Philosophy*, T. Mautner (ed.). Harmondsworth: Penguin Books.

Further reading

Arrington, R. and Glock, H. (eds) 1996. *Wittgenstein and Quine*. London: Routledge.
Baldwin, T. 2001. *Contemporary Philosophy*. Oxford: Oxford University Press.
Barrett, R. B. and Gibson, R. (eds) 1990. *Perspectives on Quine*. Oxford: Blackwell. (Papers given at a conference for Quine's 80th birthday, followed by his replies.)
Davidson, D. and Hintikka, J. (eds) 1975. *Words and Objections*. Dordrecht: Reidel. (A collection of essays followed by Quine's comments.)
Føllesdal, D. (ed.) 1994. *Inquiry* December, **37**. (A journal issue with Quine's comments on the essays.)

Føllesdal, D. (ed.) 2000. *The Philosophy of Quine*. New York: Garland Press. (Five volumes of papers on Quine.)
Gochet, P. 1986. *Ascent to Truth*. Munich: Philosphia Verlag.
Gochet, P. (ed.) 1997. *Quine with His Replies, Revue Internationale de Philosophie* **51**, no. 202, December. (A journal issue with essays on Quine and including his replies.)
Haack, S. 1993. *Evidence and Inquiry*. Oxford: Blackwell.
Hahn, L. E. and Schilpp, P. A (eds) 1986. *The Philosophy of W. V. Quine*. La Salle, IL: Open Court; enlarged edition, 1998. (The Quine volume in a distinguished series, containing an intellectual autobiography by Quine, essays on his work, and his replies.)
Hankinson Nelson, L. and Nelson, J. 2000. *On Quine*. Belmont, CA: Wadsworth.
Hugly, P. and Sayward, C. 1996. *Intensionality and Truth: An Essay on the Philosophy of A. N. Prior*. Dordrecht: Kluwer.
Hylton, P. forthcoming. *Quine: The Arguments of the Philosophers*. London: Routledge.
Leonardi, P. and Santambrogia, M. (eds) 1995. *On Quine*. Cambridge: Cambridge University Press. (A conference volume on Quine with his comments.)
Orenstein, A. and Kotatko, P. (eds) 2000. *Knowledge, Language and Logic: Questions for Quine*. Dordrecht: Kluwer.

Five Quine Scholars

Burton Dreben

1990. "Quine", in *Perspectives on Quine*, R. B. Barrett and R. F. Gibson (eds). Oxford: Basil Blackwell.
1992. "Putnam, Quine – and the Facts", *Philosophical Topics* Spring **20**(1), pp. 293–315.
1994. "*In Mediis Rebus*", *Inquiry* December **37**(4), pp. 441–7.
1996. "Quine and Wittgenstein: The Odd Couple", in *Wittgenstein & Quine*, R. Arrington and H. Glock (eds), pp. 39–62. London: Routledge.

Gilbert Harman

1999. *Reasoning, Meaning, and Mind*. Oxford: Clarendon Press.
1967. "Quine on Meaning and Existence, I", *Review of Metaphysics* **21**, September, pp. 124–51.
1967. "Quine on Meaning and Existence, II", *Review of Metaphysics* **21**, December, pp. 343–67.

Roger Gibson

1982. *The Philosophy of W. V. Quine: An Expository Essay*, with a foreword by W. V. Quine. Tampa, FL: University of South Florida.
1982. *Enlightened Empiricism: An Examination of W. V. Quine's Theory of Knowledge*, with a foreword by Dagfinn Føllesdal. Tampa, FL: University of South Florida.
1986. "Translation, Physics, and Facts of the Matter", in *The Philosophy of W. V. Quine*, L. E. Hahn and P. A. Schilpp (eds), pp. 139–54. La Salle, IL: Open Court.

1987. "Quine on Naturalism and Epistemology", *Erkenntnis* **27**, pp. 52–78.
1990. *Perspectives on Quine*, co-editor R. B. Barrett. Oxford: Blackwell.
1994. "Quine and Davidson: Two Naturalized Epistemologists", in *Language, Mind, and Epistemology: On Donald Davidson's Philosophy*, G. Preyer, F. Siebelt, A. Ulfig (eds), pp. 79–95. Dordrecht: Kluwer.
1995. "Quine on the Naturalizing of Epistemology", in *On Quine: New Essays*, P. Leonardi and M. Santambrogia (eds), pp. 89–103. Cambridge: Cambridge University Press.
1996. "Quine's Behaviorism", in *The Philosophy of Psychology*, W. O'Donohue and R. E. Kitchener (eds), 96–107. London: Sage.
1998. "Quine's Philosophy: A Brief Sketch", in *The Philosophy of W. V. Quine*, enlarged edition, L. E. Hahn and P. A. Schilpp (eds), pp. 667–83. La Salle, IL: Open Court.
1998. "Radical Translation and Radical Interpretation", *The Routledge Encyclopedia of Philosophy*, vol. 8. London: Routledge.
Forthcoming. *The Cambridge Companion to Quine*, editor. Cambridge: Cambridge University Press.

Dagfinn Føllesdal

1966. *Referential Opacity and Modal Logic*. Oslo: University of Oslo. (This is a reprint of his doctoral dissertation and is forthcoming in a series of reissued Harvard doctoral dissertations, New York: Garland Press.)
1966. "A Model Theoretic Approach to Causal Logic", in *Det Kgl Norske Videnskabrs Selskabs Skrifter Nr 2*. Trondheim: I Kommisjon Hos F. Bruns Bokhandel.
1968. "Interpretation of Quantifiers", in *Logic, Methodology and the Philosophy of Science*, B. Van Rootselaar and J. F. Staal (eds), pp. 271–81. Amsterdam: North Holland.
1968. "Quine on Modality", in *Words and Objections: Essays on the Work of W. V. Quine*, D. Davidson and J. Hintikka (eds), pp. 175–85. Dordrecht: Reidel.
1973. "Indeterminacy of Translation and Under-Determination of the Theory of Nature", *Dialectica* **27**(3–4), pp. 289–301.
1975. "Meaning and Experience", in *Mind and Language*, S. Guttenplan (ed.), pp. 25–44. Oxford: Clarendon Press.
1980. "Comments on Quine", in *Philosophy and Grammar*, S. Kanger and S. Ohman (eds), pp. 29–35. Dordrecht: Reidel.
1982. "Intentionality and Behaviorism", in *Proceedings of the 6th International Congress of Logic, Methodology and Philosophy of Science, Hannover, August 22–29, 1979*, L. J. Cohen, J. Los, H. Pfeiffer and K.-P. Podewski (eds). Amsterdam: North Holland.
1982. "The Status of Rationality Assumptions in Interpretation and in the Explanation of Action", *Dialectica* **36**(4), pp. 301–17.
1990. "Indeterminacy and Mental States", in *Perspectives on Quine*, R. B. Barrett and R. F. Gibson (eds), pp. 98–109. Oxford: Basil Blackwell.
1994. *Inquiry* **37**, December, editor. (A journal issue devoted to Quine edited by Føllesdal and containing a foreword by him.)
1995. "In What Sense is Language Public?", in *On Quine: New Essays*, P. Leonardi and M. Santambrogia (eds), pp. 53–67. Cambridge: Cambridge University Press.
1998. "Essentialism and Reference", in *The Philosophy of W. V. Quine*, L. E. Hahn and P. A. Schilpp (eds), pp. 97–113. La Salle, IL: Open Court.
1999. "Triangulation", in *The Philosophy of Donald Davidson*, L. E. Hahn and P. A. Schilpp (eds), pp. 718–20. La Salle, IL: Open Court.
2000. *The Philosophy of Quine*, editor. New York: Garland Press. (Five edited volumes of papers on Quine.)

Daniel Isaacson

1992. "Carnap, Quine and Logical Truth", in *Science and Subjectivity: The Vienna Circle and Twentieth Century Philosophy*, D. Bell and W. Vossenkuhl (eds), pp. 100–30. Berlin: Akademie Verlag.

Forthcoming. "Quine and Logical Positivism", in *The Cambridge Companion to Quine*, R. Gibson (ed.). Cambridge: Cambridge University Press.

Alex Orenstein

1973. "On Explicating Existence in Terms of Quantification", in *Logic and Ontology*, M. K. Munitz (ed.), pp. 59–84. New York: University Press.

1977. *Willard Van Orman Quine*. Boston: G. K. Hall. (An earlier version of the present work.)

1977. "The Limited Force of Moore-Like Arguments", in *Science and Psychotherapy*, J. Lynes, L. Horowitz and R. Stern (eds), pp. 133–44. New York: Haven Publishing.

1979. *Existence and the Particular Quantifier*. Philadelphia, PA: Temple University Press.

1979. "Universal Words: Pseudo-Concepts or Ultimate Predicates?", in *Wittgenstein, The Vienna Circle and Critical Rationalism*, H. Berghel, A. Hubner, and E. Kohler (eds), pp. 272–4. Dordrecht: Reidel.

1980. "What Makes Substitutional Quantification Different?", in *Proceedings of the IVth International Wittgenstein Symposium*, R. Haller and W. Grassl (eds), pp. 346–49. Dordrecht: Reidel.

1983. *Developments in Semantics*, co-editor R. Stern. New York: Haven Publishing.

1983. "Towards a Philosophical Classification of Quantifiers", in *Developments in Semantics*, A. Orenstein and R. Stern (eds), pp. 88–113. New York: Haven Publishing.

1984. *Foundations: Logic, Language and Mathematics*, co-editors H. Leblanc and E. Mendelson. Dordrecht: Kluwer. (Also appeared as two issues of *Synthese* **60** in 1984.)

1984. "Referential and Non-Referential Substitutional Quantification", in *Foundations: Logic, Language and Mathematics*, H. Leblanc, E. Mendelson and A. Orenstein (eds), *Synthese* Summer, pp. 145–58.

1990. "Is Existence What Existential Quantification Expresses?", in *Perspectives on Quine*, R. B. Barrett and R. F. Gibson (eds), pp. 245–70. Oxford: Basil Blackwell.

1990. "Review of Quine's *Quiddities, A Philosophical Dictionary*", *Canadian Philosophical Reviews*.

1995. "Existence Sentences", in *The Heritage of Kazimierz Ajdukiewicz,* J. Wolinski and V. Sinisi (eds), pp. 227–35. Amsterdam: Nijoff.

1995. "How To Get Something From Nothing", in *Proceedings of the Aristotelian Society,* pp. 93–112. Oxford: Blackwell.

1997. "Arguing From Inscrutability of Reference to Indeterminacy of Meaning", *Revue International de Philosophie* **51** (1997), pp. 507–20.

1998. Quine entry in *Encyclopedia of Philosophy*, E. Craig (ed.). London: Routledge.

1999. "Reconciling Aristotle and Frege", *Notre Dame Journal of Formal Logic* **40**, Summer, pp. 375–90.

2000. *Knowledge, Language and Logic: Questions for Quine*, co-editor P. Kotatko. Dordrecht: Kluwer.

2000. "Plato's Beard, Quine's Stubble and Ockham's Razor", in *Knowledge, Language and Logic*, Orenstein and Kotatko (eds).

2000. "The Logical Form of Categorical Sentences", *Australasian Journal of Philosophy* December, pp. 517–33.
2000. "Quality, Not Quantity, Determines Existential Import", in *Logique en Perspective: Mélange offert à Paul Gochet,* F. Beets and E. Gillett (eds), pp. 465–78. Brussels: Editions Ousia.
Forthcoming. "Existence, Identity and an Aristotelian Tradition", in *Individuals, Essence and Identity: Themes of Analytical Metaphysics*, A. Bottani, M. Carrara and P. Giaretta (eds) (Dordrecht: Kluwer, forthcoming).

Index